Apple Box Boy

Slices of Life

James Heintz

iUniverse, Inc.
New York Bloomington

Apple Box Boy
Slices of Life

iUniverse books may be ordered through booksellers or by contacting:

iUniverse
1663 Liberty Drive
Bloomington, IN 47403
www.iuniverse.com
1-800-Authors (1-800-288-4677)

ISBN: 978-1-4502-5353-6 (sc)
ISBN: 978-1-4502-5352-9 (ebk)

Printed in the United States of America

iUniverse rev. date: 9/13/2010

FORWARD

My life's different than my son's, and very different than my grandsons'. Telling my oldest grandchild stories about my childhood most often wins a response like, "Tell me the truth, Grandpa. You didn't really do that…did you?"

The vignettes I have filled this book with will be reminders of another time for readers my age and maybe spark moments of envy, laughter, or tears for those younger than myself.

My Mother described me as "creative." She would smile, raise her brows, and cock her head a little to the side when she used the word. No one would deny that she loved and appreciated me. No one would say it was easy for her to watch me live my life.

I was a chatty and innovative little boy who was blessed with building skills, a sweet disposition and a love of life and people.

The first fourteen years of my life were spent in the same neighborhood with twelve kids that never moved away. Everyone was proud to live in the Yakima Valley, which was known as the "Fruit Bowl of the Nation."

Mom and Dad started out with little, like most young couples in the 1940's. Little back then was very different than little today. They worked hard and bought everything with cash, except their home. Dad got up early six days a week and worked ten-hour days. Mom took care of us. She was always there to feed, hug, support, protect, clean, educate, and patch us up. She tucked us in every night and was by our sides after every nightmare.

Dad worked hard and was tired when he got home. Despite the demands to support his family, Dad was there to drive nails, repair broken strollers, rebuild bicycles, maintain the house, and play a little with us. He was also there to spank us when he was told to do so by Mom, and he spent too many nights on the wrong side of a vodka bottle.

In my day the kids on Fourteenth Avenue had freedoms and adventures few children today will experience. Many of them are recorded in the ditties on the following pages.

For years I have processed my memories and experiences by writing. It's my hope that you will enjoy the moments I have captured as I grew up, dated, married, discovered my spiritual path, became a Dad, worked, divorced, celebrated the joys in my life, and suffered under my tests, in years very different than the ones we are living today.

MOM & DAD 1940

My Mama was a good-looking woman. She wasn't the bouncy cheerleader type, although she was one. She was taller than most and wore glasses that gave her the appearance of an academic... something she never claimed to be. Her blue gray eyes were guarded and evaluating at first glance, then relaxed into playful glances when she felt secure and welcomed. Most of the girls in her school wore short hair and she kept hers a bit longer, liking the look of her natural waves and the glow that reflected off her thick chestnut brown locks. Her arms and legs were slim. She always said her figure would have been better proportioned if some of what was on top had been on her backside.

Her mother noticed Mom's musical talent when she was young and saved money from her seasonal job packing fruit to purchase a piano. Mom appreciated the sacrifice and quickly developed her musical skill. By the time she was in high school, she was teaching little ones and buying many of her own clothes. Not only was she a skilful pianist, she was blessed with a beautiful voice that mixed nicely with the sounds of the piano, pleasing her and her friends.

Pictures of Mom during her school years fill the front pages of an old photo album. She might remind you of a slim and young Bea Arthur. It wasn't so much that Bea and Mom looked alike...it was more the holding of the head and the attitude. I could find only one picture of Mom with her head thrown back in full laughter. She was, in that photograph, a young married woman and was sitting on top of an upright piano with a drink in one hand and a cigarette in the other. Most often she had the look of a woman who knows the joke and is waiting to watch your reaction as it plays out.

When talking about her courting years, she told stories of young men and high school adventures in the upper end of the Yakima Valley. I don't know how involved she was with her boyfriends before Dad, but I do remember her talking fondly about several of them. I'm sure she considered herself a catch and wasn't willing to take up with just any boy, and certainly wasn't interested in being unmarried and pregnant.

Mom was the oldest of three, with Uncle Don in the middle and Aunt Kathryn, the baby. Although Don and Kathryn had their own lives, Mom seemed to be in charge when the family gathered together. For sure, my mother was in charge in our home, and had no problems telling all of us how it was going to be. Sometimes how it wasn't going to be.

Pictures of Dad are mixed in with the ones of Mom, although there aren't as many. He wasn't a local boy and she hadn't attended school with him. He had been raised on a farm outside of Yakima and when his brother, Joe, opened a bakery in Naches, Dad went to work for him. Checking out the bakery with several of her girlfriends, Mom spotted my father working in the back. After that she seemed to find excuses to visit the Bakery and was successful tossing him one of her Bea Author smiles.

There were a handful of pictures of Mom and Dad as a young couple. She was a fashion plate, with her strapped heels and dresses with lots of buttons and bows, and her hair up and crafted in roll after roll. When she dressed more casually she was fond of her quilt-patterned skirt, bright open-collared blouse, and a cardigan sweater with pearls around her neck.

Dad liked baggy pants, white undershirts with a Hawaiian cover shirt, when he wasn't in his army uniform. I have few pictures of them smoking…they always were. If I looked hard enough I could probably spot a cigarette or two burning tracks into furniture in the photo's background.

Dad was tall, close to six feet one, and lean. Like Mom he wore glasses and unlike her he wasn't quiet and reserved. His hair had already begun its migration up his forehead and his nose was large and straight. What won Mom's heart was his smile and laugh. As she was Bea, he was Kevin Costner, and a couple of years older than her. I think she considered him a good catch. Following her graduation from school and a summer of getting to know each other, they married and began the business of making a living and raising a family in the early 1940's.

HOME 1944

The house wasn't large. Mom and Dad had purchased it when my sister was little and I, a baby. They needed a secure place for us to live while Dad went off to war. It was only a few blocks from his parents' home, and Dad found comfort knowing that his father could keep a protective watch over Mom and the kids. She, in later years, would talk of Grandpa's difficulty keeping his hands to himself and her wishing that he would busy himself with tasks other than watching over her.

Our house was the smallest on the block, probably less than eight hundred square feet. During the war everyone was making-the-best-of-things and it was several years before Dad and Grandpa added Mom's long-awaited front room with the big picture window. Mom would talk of how modern it looked and how much she liked the light.

The house was placed in the center of a long narrow lot between Fourteenth Avenue and the dirt alley behind. The original front room was small and the freestanding stove, which always smelled of oil, took up more than its fair share of the room and provided most of the heat. A teapot was kept on the stove during the winter months and Mom's backing up to the stove's warmth was a fond memory she talked about years later when Alzheimer's was robbing her mind and old memories were all she could remember.

The old Maytag wringer washing machine was on the back porch during the warm months. When it started to freeze, Dad would roll it into the bathroom and drain the water into the tub. During the warm months, Dad extended the drain with a long rubber hose that watered the gardens. The soap suds didn't seem to bother Mom's gladiolas, and she told her sister that she was pretty sure they liked the soapy mixture.

In the early fifties she moved all her washing indoors and used a Bendix front loader that Dad had to bolt to the floor. Left to it's own, it would travel across the room restricted only by the length of its water hoses. The clothes lines in the backyard were used until the late-fifties when we moved up to Thirty-First Avenue. After Dad returned from the war he replaced the old wooden posts with steel. There must have been thirty feet between the posts, and when the five lines were filled with sheets I would love running up and down the drying rows, smearing my dirty hands across the clean bleached surfaces. The smell of wind-dried sheets is lost to most modern folks, and a big part of my memory of Mom. Even in the winter, when the sheets would freeze dry on the lines, they would have that incomparable smell.

The bedroom, there was only one, was on the front of the house and would in future years be shared by my brother and myself. The room wasn't fancy and the chenille spreads, that covered Mom's bed, were always white and bleached like the crochet doilies on her dresser top. Behind the bathroom and off of the kitchen was a small storage room, painted pink, which served as my sister's room for all the years we lived on Fourteenth Avenue.

The kitchen was long and skinny. Beside the back door the wood trash burner, with its two cast iron lids, stood cold and useless until winter. On occasion paper and wax box trash would be burned, but only in the early morning before the heat of the day warmed the house. The sides of the stove were white enamel and chipped on the edges where care wasn't used. The stovepipe, at the back of the heater, was small and oval. It rounded as it rose and bent into the mortared hole in the red brick chimney. If caution wasn't taken and timely cleaning completed, the flue would catch fire and clean itself. Mom was scared when these rare fires occurred, so Dad would busy himself with a thorough chimney cleaning and assure her it would be the last flue fire.

The icebox was on the far end of a short section of counter top. The iceman would come every few days to deliver, with his big steel tongs, one block of ice that sat on the bottom of the box below the food it was cooling.

The counter tops were kept clean and were covered with pieces of linoleum that had developed cracks and checks over the years of hard use and meat cutting without a cutting board. The edges of the counter were rounded, with metal edgings that were screwed into the wooden planks.

The only framed art on the walls were photographs of family or decorative mirrors that were etched with deco designs and flowers. Smaller photographs were pushed into the hinged frames that allowed quick access when visitors came by and asked about family.

During winter months the house was sealed with sheets of ice that covered the inside of the windows where the warmth of the home battled with the cold freezing weather. Most often the ice melted with warming weather and towels were rolled and placed on the sills to reduce the damage and avoid excess dry rot.

During the summer months, using ropes and buckets, Dad dug tunnels below the six-inch crawlspace. This allowed him easier access during the winter months when the pipes would freeze. Using a gasoline blowtorch, he would heat yards of pipe until the ice blockage would release and allow the water to flow.

Our summer days often found Mom and the neighborhood ladies sitting on blankets in the front yard smoking cigarettes and talking about their children. During the winter, snowmen were built on the same spot with carrot noses and Dad's old scarves around their necks.

THE STROLLER AND PLANE 1945

Taylor Company made the used baby stroller Mom and Dad bought for my big sister and myself. It was red and white with a wood seat carved like a pizza paddle. A handle was mounted on the front, so I could steer when my Mom pushed us down the street. The edges were sanded smooth and finished to protect my fat little thighs. Wrapped around the back of the seat was a metal support with a basket insert. It was very handsome. I could push it with my feet, or Mom could unfold the handles on the back and push me around. It had metal bumpers on both the back and front, and when I was tired I could put my feet on the stainless steel panel that was mounted under the seat. Mom made me wear a little knit cap with a bill when we went out, and sometimes she would let my big sister push.

Just about the time I got a handle on turning my stroller, my father bought me a Silver Pursuit Pedal plane. Wow! It was great. Its body looked a lot like a fat football with an opening just big enough for the round steering wheel and me. It was painted silver with red stripes on the tail and around the nose. The tail had two small wings and a fin, while the front wings were big with five pointed stars on top and one wheel mounted under each of them. The front wheels had chrome hubcaps and the nose of the plane had a big propeller that would spin if I peddled the wheels.

I looked great sitting in my new airplane and I didn't have to wear the silly little hat Mom kept on my head when I was in the stroller. The only problem I had with the airplane was my inability to move the pedals. The plane was steel and heavy and as hard as I pushed, all I could do was make it rock back for forth. Sometimes my Dad, who felt sorry for me, would push and then the propeller would spin and I could fly. Most of the time I had to be content just sitting in my Silver Pursuit Pedal plane looking good.

THE VALLEY 1949

The first twenty years of my life were spent in the Yakima valley. It was a spectacular place to grow-up and my mind is rich with remembrances. The valley's river bottom was green with manicured lawns, diverse trees and acres of fertile fruit farms. On both sides of the valley rolling sage-brushed hills reclined like curvaceous women basking in the sun. During spring months layers of new sage green would spread over the hips and shoulders like sheets of velvet. By June the hot summer sun would fade the velvet into dirt and rocks where rattlesnakes baked themselves, and kept strangers away.

Before the arrival of Europeans, the valley was home to several tribes of Native Americans, snakes, coyotes, and the trees that bordered the Yakima River and ran across the valley floor. The smaller Tieton River dropped down from White Pass and mixed mid-valley with the Yakima. The bottle green rivers wound themselves across the barren earth like a dancer's boa dropped on a stage.

Farmers who came to the valley knew irrigation and drew river waters from their beds and guided them across the land. Like little boxes of garden store sprouts, cultivation spread until the valley floor was rich and green. On the river's edge, the city that began with dirt streets and wooden walks rose to tall office buildings, many square miles of patterned residences, and acres of fruit storage and processing plants.

In the late 1940's, when I was growing up in Yakima, the railroad tracks ran the short distance across the length and width of the valley and did much more than transport boxcars. Racism and separatism were as much a part of the town as apple boxes and fruit warehouses.

You had a pretty good idea where folks lived by the color of their skin. The tracks separated the east from the west and the poor folks lived on the east side where the city was old and the residential areas were underprivileged.

As a child I was told that driving through the east section of town was dangerous, but from time to time my father would make that drive and we were never hurt. The Chinese and Mexican families lived in a small and less dangerous area that was northeast and boxed in by lumber mills and the river.

The Golden Wheel on First Street and Ding Ho's on south Sixteenth Avenue by the airport were Chinese owned restaurants and the only eating places Mom and Dad would patronize when our family ate out. It was also the only place I ever saw Chinese people.

Parallel to the railroad tracks was Front Street, also known as Skid Row. It was there that I first saw real Indians. The books I had at home showed them with feathers and horses. They looked powerful and I was a bit afraid of them. The Indians I saw from my Dad's car window were drunk and lying against old tavern walls. Dad said, "Indians and alcohol don't mix." I was disappointed that I could not see them riding their horses.

Many taverns and two old movie houses were in the block between First Street and Front. My Dad said that his father, who was a German immigrant with a very basic understanding of English, would walk from his house on south Thirteenth Avenue to the Roxie or Avenue Theaters on Skid Row and practice his English watching cowboy movies.

There was a gun and cigar shop downtown that had a sheet metal man standing on a platform attached to the front of the building and shooting a rifle into the sky. The sign was turning around and around as if the shooter was following a flock of pheasant with the sight of his rifle. It was trimmed in neon and is still spinning today.

It was common to see police walking the streets downtown. Often there were two of them and they walked slowly. They could be seen helping men who were drunk to their feet and talking to women who wore bright dresses and smoked cigarettes.

Driving through town required a pass through Skid Row and it was always a time that my face was pressed against the back seat window.

I did not want to miss a view of this world that was so different than mine.

I lived on the west side of the tracks where everyone was white. The further west you lived the higher was the value of your property. It seemed that those who had money wanted to be as far as possible from those who didn't.

I was raised on South Fourteenth Avenue just fourteen blocks west of the tracks. We were not rich, but did not feel poor. We even had a rarely seen Mexican family living a block away. They lived on South Thirteenth Avenue and had several girls who were great playmates.

My Father worked hard and called himself, like most of the fathers in my neighborhood, a blue-collar man. That meant that he worked with his hands. Some folks in our neighborhood were white collar, but Dad's collar color was the norm. I had no contact with people from the other side of the tracks until I attended high school at A.C. Davis, which was called Yakima High when my Dad attended the same school.

I attended Yakima Valley College for a couple of years and then I left Yakima for the first time and moved to Ellensburg to attend Central Washington State College. After college I returned home for a few years, then left, and only returned for visits or to heal myself. Yakima was a great place to grow up.

NACHES CHRISTMAS 1950

It was Christmas morning and Dad was proud to be driving his brand new 1950 four-door custom Ford to Naches. My brother and I couldn't break our pattern of fighting and separation seemed to be our parents' only solution. Being smaller and gathering more sympathy, Steve rode in front seat between Mom and Dad. My sister and I, who weren't strangers to our own battles, were consigned to the back seat. Even on Christmas day Dad would say, "If you kids don't straighten up you'll get a spanking when we get to Grandma's house." Mom would put out her cigarette in the ashtray and join Dad with her own, "Jimmy, can't you keep your hands to yourself?"

The narrow asphalt road from Yakima to Grandma's wandered beside the Naches River which, on this beautiful Christmas morning, wore a white winter cloak. Black shallow water rushed over rocks and branches, while it nipped at the snowdrifts hanging over its banks.

We parked beside Grandma's house to avoid jumping across the irrigation ditch that was frozen and dangerous. Mom, concerned about keeping our outfits clean, held Steve's hand and warned Judy and I with a, "you kids be careful on the ice." We safely negotiated our path across the fresh snow and entered Grandma's house through the back porch.

The dining room table was covered with ironed linen and all the settings were in place. Branches of holly were mixed with red candles and glass bulbs to form the centerpiece. Dad set the cardboard box with Mom's candied yams and fruit salad on the kitchen counter and took off his wide-brimmed hat. He took Mom's hat and fox-headed shoulder wrap and hung them over his arm with his long topcoat. The men all wore suits, but were quick to loosen their ties and lay their coats across Grandma's bed. The dark slacks and white shirts of the men served as plain backgrounds for the colorful dresses of the women. Mom's dress had dark burgundy flowers with leaves that were green and trimmed in black. Her hair was up and held with combs, which were rhinestone edged like her glasses. Dad greeted Grandpa with a, "Merry Christmas, Fred. How are you feeling today?" All the family's hats and coats were piled on Grandma's bed, making an impressive pile.

Grandma and Grandpa had their own bedrooms and we all knew that there wasn't much love left between them. Mom would often say, "My Dad, when he was twenty-three, pulled that little fifteen year old girl out of her safe Kentucky home and dragged her half way across the country to Oregon where she didn't know a soul. She worked hard all her life as a fruit sorter in a cold warehouse and never got to see her home again." Mom was almost as mad as Grandma when it came to Grandpa Fred.

The smell of the turkey flooded the kitchen and Grandma, in her red and white buffalo plaid apron, was quick to hug us. "You kids get yourselves over here so I can get a little sugar," was a greeting all her grandchildren recognized. She was old and gray and probably close to fifty.

Grandpa sat in the front room beside the oil stove. He smoked Camels and shook hands with us boys. His hand was hard, with tobacco-stained fingers. "How are you boys doing today? Ya think old

Santa is bringing ya something good?" He kept his cigarette between his lips while he talked and offered Dad a Tom and Jerry. Grandpa's voice always sounded like he had a cold and a difficult time talking.

My aunt and uncle arrived with their three children and we all ran outside to play in the backyard snow. "One, two, three, four, here I come, ready or not." The sounds of our merriment could be heard through the frosted glass windows on the sides of Grandma's dining room while shafts of winter sun filtered through the panes and brightened the Christmas table.

Unlike the Christmas tree in our house, which was green with multicolored lights and lots of homemade stuff, Grandma's trees were always flocked white and this year she had blue bulbs and long-tailed bows. She had spent her few extra dollars on the window painter who came every year to cover the two big windows in the front room corner with holiday scenes. All the women would congratulate Grandma with, "My, oh my… have you ever outdone yourself this year, Irene." Grandma didn't like being called Grandma, even by us kids, so we all called her Irene. She had class and would often dress herself in soft pink with fancy matching hats and gloves. She had a black ceramic panther with green eyes that was the focal point of her front room. Only during Christmas was he tucked away to make room for the baby Jesus and the manger. The salt and pepper carpet with white vinyl furniture brought accent and coordination to the flocked tree.

My mom's family was large with three uncles, three aunts and all their kids. Other families, like the Wollums, who were my Aunt Inga's people from Norway, would attach themselves to us for the celebration and the house would be filled with joy.

There wasn't a fireplace in Grandma's old house, but the oil stove had a fire, and if Grandpa had cleaned the isinglass, we could watch it burn. The stove was particularly enjoyed after we kids had half frozen our toes and fingers off packing snowballs and attempting to build apple box igloos.

All the men in our family smoked and my modern Mama often joined them. The house was packed with people and the cloud of blue gray smoke from the tobacco was never considered a problem. Grandpa was always offering the other men one of his Camels, but most of them preferred their filtered Marlboros or Winstons.

Both Uncle Keith and Dad were mechanics who scrubbed their hands extra hard for the holidays to remove most traces of grease and grime. Uncle Don's farming hands weren't blackened, but were cracked and hard from a season of harvesting and his recent pruning. Dad would ask Uncle Don, "Are you going to make any money this year with the farm?" He would always reply with, "Hell no, farming isn't about making money." Every one would laugh, even though the adults knew that Don was having a hard time keeping his beloved fruit farm.

The women, above the age of twelve, wrapped themselves in aprons and prepared dinner. The kids were kept outside playing with their new Christmas Eve gifts while the men gathered in the front room and discussed politics, farming and automobiles. My mama always brought the fruit salad that was a delectable mixture of sliced apples, cans of fruit cocktail mix, and whipping cream. She sprinkled the top with walnuts and cinnamon. Her candied yams were another contribution which she cooked just enough to set a golden shadow on the marshmallows. Usually she used the big round marshmallows, not those new little bitty ones.

Aunt Kathryn brought the ham and beans, while Aunt Inga did the pies and breads. The mashed potatoes, turkey, dressing, vegetable trays and cranberries, the ones that look like the can when you put them in a bowl, were all prepared as a group effort. Grandma would have stuffed and put the bird in the oven early in the morning. We could hear her proclaim as she removed the lid from the roasting pan. "My, isn't Henrietta a sight to see?" Our turkeys were always named Henrietta. I could never figure out the difference between a Henry and a Henrietta. Once we were all sat around the family table we would drop our heads and Uncle Don would ask God to bless all that had gathered on this, the birthday of Jesus. He would thank God for the good food, and say a little something about friends or family that had passed away during the year. Dad's, "Let's eat!" would bring laughter to all and the food would begin the first of several passes around our Christmas table.

With the main course done, the men would be slow to leave the table. With their stomachs full and their cigarettes smoking they would talk and argue until the women shooed them away. "You guys move your conversation to the front room. We have work to do in here."

The women were kissed and swatted on their bottoms as the men paraded into the front room. Soon they were laying on sofas and chairs reading newspapers or sleeping. The women seemed pleased to have the fellows out of their way while they cleaned up the dinner leftovers and prepared more coffee and the desserts.

After the naps and pie eating, the table was cleared and the poker game began. Kids could watch but had to be quiet and not tell others what cards were in their Dad's hands. Some of the women joined the game and were very welcome. The table was surrounded with smiles, laughter and loud whoops when hands were won. The stakes were high, penny antis with a maximum of three-nickel raises. The game would continue until the light outside the windows disappeared and folks grew tired. I remember falling asleep on the drive home with my favorite Christmas toy nearby and memories that could not be improved upon.

PICKET FENCE 1950

The pickets were white, just as they should be, and the arbor was simple with a gate. The entire yard was fenced, including the flowerbeds that were filled with amaryllis and dahlias. The grass was thick and green. When dandelions or other weeds attempted to take hold...Grandpa was on them. On his knees with his bucket at his side, the weeds were dug and burned before a single foul seed could grow and spread across his yard.

The rental house next to Grandma and Grandpa had one of those cheap roll out fences whose pickets were skinny and wound together with wire. Unlike Grandma's fence, this one was always leaning one way or the other. Most of the weeds that Grandpa battled came from this lot and it irritated him. The rust red fifty-gallon oil tank that was high on wooden stilts and leaned against the rental house was unattractive and also irritated Grandpa. He didn't like looking at it and wished they had placed it on the back of the house like he did his.

Their house was in Naches and across the street from the block-long warehouse where Grandma hated working. It was built with red brick and was the main processing plant in that end of the valley where fruit was cleaned and packed for market. Its flat roof and high prison-like windows were a daily reminder for our Grandma of the many backbreaking hours she had spent working over a sorting table.

Despite their location, Grandma's spirit and appreciation of beauty could not be squelched. She pushed and demanded that Grandpa keep the house and yard up. Every Sunday of my entire childhood was spent in Grandma's home or yard and I loved it. They had a big picnic table that Grandpa had built from one of the old houses he had remodeled. We had many lunches on it where we enjoyed each other's company.

There were four or five Adirondack chairs painted white like the fence. Grandpa liked to use enamel on the chairs, unlike the whitewash he used on the fences. I remember afternoons when the adults, leaning back in different positions in the chairs, would sit in a circle while others sat on the grass and held their knees as they visited. Most often the women wore housedresses and the men dark slacks with white shirts with long sleeves. It was the outfits they had all worn to church and hadn't taken the time to drive home and change.

We kids would play badminton, without the net, and other games we dreamt up while we tried to keep our Sunday dresses, slacks and sweaters clean.

I remember my favorite Uncle Don sitting in one of the Adirondacks as he visited with me. He had injured his back again and was walking with a cane. We always tried to steal his cane away, but he was too quick. Don was my mother's brother and like a father to me. When I was born, my father was in the service serving in Japan and my Uncle Don had completed his tour in the air force. He watched over me for the first year or so of my life and won my heart forever. He was a handsome man in his double-breasted gray suit with the broad lapels and the baggy slacks. His wife Inga was a stylish woman who looked great in the fitted dresses of the early fifties. Her short hair curled over her forehead and down the sides of her face.

Lots of quality living happened in Naches behind those white picket fences. It was there that our parents talked about us with the family and planned our futures. Our parents supported each other and worked hard to provide us all with the childhoods they wanted us to have.

LAKE WILDERNESS 1950

My heart wildly beat in my chest as my sister held my ankles and I squeezed the wooden sides of the forty-foot waterslide. Her smile left me unsure of her trustworthiness as I leaned back and felt the cold water running across the surface of the sheet metal. I clasped my hands behind by head like I had seen the older boys do and yelled, "OK, Judy." She let go and I rocketed down the slide faster than my body had ever moved before. Judy laughed and I squealed as the lapped edges of the metal passed under my back until it bent and I hit the water. Like Slo-mo-shun IV I shot across the surface of the water bouncing from one shoulder blade to the other like the pontoons on a hydroplane.

We were on our yearly vacation and had returned to Lake Wilderness and Gaffney's Grove Resort near Tacoma, Washington. It was 1950 and my life couldn't have been better. The Resort featured baseball fields, tennis courts, dance pavilions, a skating rink, and two swimming beaches with slides, trapezes, and diving towers. There were several beaches on the lake and the one our family frequented had several long sections of dock that were tied together to identify a large safe swimming area. On the outside of the dock, row boats were tied and rented to fishermen, who were old or didn't have the courage to swing on the trapezes or jump from the diving towers. They certainly wouldn't have taken the ride down the forty-foot wooden slide on their backs and headfirst.

The cabin we rented for the week was small with only one bedroom that Mom and Dad used. Judy slept on the sofa, and Steve and I on the floor. We had our new military surplus mummy sleeping bags so were ready to sleep outside if necessary. The cabin was tucked into the trees behind the road and only a hundred yards or so from the edge of the lake. Most of the distance between the cabin and water was filled with picnic tables and grass. On the weekends, when everyone came to play, the tables were full and many blankets were spread across the grass, giving the appearance of a patchwork quilt. The sandy beach was filled with small children who busied themselves with shovels, buckets and digging holes.

I am sure our parents kept an eye on us, but we were oblivious to anything but the water and fun. Mom and Dad had rules and our swimming in the safe area was one of them. The only time I saw anyone swim in the lake itself was our last day at Lake Wilderness. I was standing on top of the tower preparing to make my seventy-third cannonball splash. In the lake, far from the safe area, I saw the head of a man swimming away from the security of the dock. I thought that the guy was either crazy or a really good swimmer. When I looked closer, I saw that he was wearing red shorts and that he was my father. My chest swelled with pride as I understood why I was able to jump from the tower and ride the slide like the big boys.

Mom liked to swim but spent most of her time sitting on a blanket watching us. When we weren't in the water she liked to walk in the woods or cook. It seemed she had more fun cooking in our cabin than she did at home. I never understood why they didn't just buy the hotdogs at the concession stand. They were cheap and tasted really good.

It didn't take long to find playmates, and every day was full of adventure. Mom and Dad were always trying to talk us into checking out croquet or badminton games but we preferred the water from sunrise to sunset.

We visited Lake Wilderness twice in my childhood and my memories of those two weeks remain rich and valued in my mind.

SAINT PAULS CATHEDRAL SCHOOL 1950 – 1958

The full block belonged to the Catholic Church and my Dad resented the priests coming by his business and our home to collect pledge dollars most families couldn't afford. St Paul's Cathedral School was built in southwest Yakima where the lot was covered with asphalt and half a dozen buildings. The only flowers to be seen were around the rectory and in front of the school on Chestnut where the flagpole stood, and where we would make our morning pledge and sing "God Bless America."

In the northeast section the Cathedral, the most important structure, stood with its tall spire. The ornamented architecture gave the church a look like St. Nicholas in Prague, only smaller.

I remember climbing the steel ladder next to the choir loft and pushing open the ceiling panel to the bell tower. We weren't allowed up there, but that didn't stop us. Once inside the tower you could climb up several levels and get a good view of the city. The pigeon poop was thick, diminishing the pleasure of the adventure and occasionally discouraging us. Several years ago, when I attended my nephew's wedding in the Cathedral; I took a peek beside the choir loft and noticed the panel door was pad-locked shut.

Beside the church the old school served as classrooms for the seventh and eight grade students. It was there my big sister, Judy, attended school for her first three years. West of the church, the rectory stood on a high point of grassed land. It was there that the priests lived and it was the one building I never entered. Mom told me that she and Dad had to attend classes there before they got married. She wasn't a big fan of the Catholic Church but had made a promise to raise us Catholic and kept her word.

All of the structures were stucco with red tile roofs, with the new school being the only exception. It was built in 1949 and I began the first grade the next year. It stood five stories tall and was finished with smooth concrete and long wide vinyl floors. The basement, (I snuck down there a couple of times with Jim Ibach,) was off limits to students and was filled with the furnace and lots of pipes wrapped in paper or something that looked like cardboard. The next three floors were classrooms, gym, assembly room, cafeteria and the Sister Superior's office. I had the opportunity to visit the Sister Superior in her office several times, and so did my mother. The top floor was where the nuns lived. We didn't know anything about what went on up there. Lots of stories were told. Some of them might have been true.

After school and on our way home, we would use the large asphalt terrace beside Walnut Street as a rocket launching pad for our bikes and boast about the distance we were able to jump. There were several levels of asphalt playground that were used as parking lots on Sundays. We spent hours riding our bikes up and down the ramps that separated the levels and thrilled ourselves as our skills developed.

On the playground there was very little equipment. In the middle of the property there was a basketball court for the older kids and a

Tetherball pole for the little ones. We did play dodge ball, jump rope, hide and seek, and hopscotch while we teased the girls.

During the cold winter months Father Queen would have the school janitor flood the outside basketball court with water. It made a fabulous ice skating rink. After school and during the evenings the neighborhood parents would gather around the fifty-five gallon barrel frozen in the middle of the rink and build a fire from scrap wood. They would warm their hands and enjoy each other while we skated and tossed snowballs.

Everyone wore uniforms. The girls had maroon jumpers with white blouses while the boys had corduroy salt and pepper pants and gray shirts with maroon ties. Every fall we would get new shoes, which had to last the school year. Most often they were black oxfords with thick durable soles. Sometimes if the shoes didn't hold up well, we would take them to the shoe shop next to Jordan's Drug Store and have new heels or soles stitched on.

Attending Saint Paul's wasn't a good thing for me. The classes were large, the nuns were harsh, and my creative spirit wasn't appreciated. Being easy to control and quiet seemed to be the school's goals, and I wasn't very good at either one.

GENEVA 1950

By the age of six I had buried several pets and had found my county fair chameleon cooked on mom's table lamp bulb. I had some understanding of death, but hadn't attended a funeral or seen anyone I knew...dead. Geneva was my first and probably the first for most of my classmates at St. Paul Cathedral School. She had started the first grade with the rest of us and then stopped coming. We knew that she was sick and were asked by the nuns to pray for her.

We all walked into the little chapel together and sat on the edge of the pew. Our salt and pepper pants and gray shirts were extra clean and the girls wore white blouses and their maroon jumpers. Many of the adults were crying. I didn't understand. She was little in her coffin and dressed in a very pretty dress. Her hair was gold and curly. She looked the same as the last time I had seen her at school, but that day I noticed that she didn't move at all.

DAD'S STORY 1951

Time was well spent in my father's garage. He had lots of hand tools and power equipment he slowly taught me to use. I have an old scroll saw in my shop today that was Dad's and in his garage when I was a kid. It is a bright blue jig saw that had belonged to his father. On that very saw, I slice my thumb to the bone while creating a machine gun out of my broken BB gun. I was good at creating something out of nothing. Dad said he was the same way.

Around the age of twelve Dad and several of his buddies from nearby farms got together and created an experience that tops anything that I ever had. He said it all started with an idea from a Tom Swift book. The story told about divers that went far below the surface of the sea wearing big brass helmets. They had thick glass plates they could see through and a compressor attached to a hose that pumped air from the surface.

Dad decided that he could build a diving helmet and with two of his friends began to gather parts for the first Yakima Valley Diving Expedition. The basic helmet was the hog's slop bucket that was old and didn't leak. Dad's father had recently replaced the viewing plate in the oil stove with new isinglass and had a four-inch piece left over from the cutting. One of the guys came up with an old tire pump and the valve from a bike wheel. Hoses were easy to find when you lived on a farm where irrigation was a way of life.

Once all the parts where gathered they began the project by cutting a hole in the bucket for the glass. Black rubber glue was heavily applied and the glass was held in place with tape until it dried. The thick glue compensated for the curved side of the bucket and the flat plate of glass. They then cut the lip of the bucket and shaped it like a camel saddle. The sharp rim was edged with sliced garden hose and leather lacing was strung through small holes in the bucket and around the hose to protect the neck and shoulders. The tire valve was bolted through the bottom of the bucket and the tire pump was attached to ten feet of garden hose. The equipment was ready.

It was agreed that on the following Friday, after the glue had set up, all three would meet at the irrigation ditch where history would be made.

When Friday arrived it was a typical summer day. The temperature was in the mid nineties and the sky was blue with massive white clouds moving down the long narrow valley. Dad arrived first with the diving gear in a wagon tied behind his bicycle. He had hid it in an old potato bag to avoid any questions his mother might have had. It was best to be on the safe side when you were dealing with highly experimental things that moms don't understand.

Soon the threesome was together working hard to get the helmet properly placed on Dad's shoulders. The eyehooks they had bolted to the bottom of the helmet held ropes that went under Dad's armpits and kept the helmet from floating up. The section of ditch they were diving in was about six foot deep and eight feet wide. The current was swift and would normally wash a swimmer down stream. Recognizing this problem Dad had decided to jump into the ditch holding a twelve-pound rock. If a bigger rock was needed there were others stacked by the telephone pole.

Dad striped down to his shorts and with one friend on the pump and the other managing the hose he jumped in. The water was cold and the rock did its job. As he settled into the ten inches of ditch slime Dad opened his eyes. It worked. He could hear the air that was pumping into his bucket and could look up and see the surface of the water and his friends looking down at him. He said that there wasn't much to see but it was fun to sit on the bottom of the ditch breathing bike pump air and thinking about Tom Swift.

HALLOWEEN 1951

I'm pretty sure most five and dime stores like Woolworth sold Halloween costumes, but none of the families on my block could afford them so all of ours were homemade. Some kids bought masks that were thin plastic or pressed cardboard from Jordan's Drug Store. They all had holes pressed out for the eyes and mouth and were hot and hard to breathe through. Light stretchable strings with little metal tabs on the end were pushed through the holes on the sides of the masks and pulled over the head. There were pirates, bunny rabbits, hobos, pigs, cats and lots of other animal and cartoon characters. I don't remember seeing the terrible monster or scary guy masks that show up on my doorstep today but back then there were lots of vampires and hunchbacks. I didn't like masks and most often had my Mom or sister paint my face to match my Halloween outfits.

I remember being a cowboy with my Lone Ranger double holster set with the words, "The Lone Ranger" stamped where the two were joined together with a buckle. I also remember being a hobo, ghost, a robot with a cardboard box body that wasn't comfortable and my favorite...a vampire. That year, after my Mom had painted me up, I scared myself when I looked in the mirror. The ghost was the easiest costume requiring only an old sheet with holes for my eyes and a cord around my neck. The problem that year was the lower half of my face getting soaked from slobber and trying to shove candy into my mouth through my eyeholes. My other outfits were mostly composed of old clothes and lots of Mom's make-up.

I don't remember Mom and Dad going out with us. They stayed home and handed out candy to the sixty or so goblins and Bo-peeps that "trick or treated" our house. When I was little Judy watched over my little brother and myself, but I don't remember being restrained in any way. Most of my memories were with Butch, John and our little brothers running like wild ones from one door to the next. We used grocery bags and buckets to capture our sweet loot, and were always afraid when we started out that they weren't big enough.

One rule we disliked but never broke was waiting until dark to start our rounds. What we thought was dark and what our Mothers thought wasn't the same. Once we were released we were on the run for hours and wouldn't return home unless something horrible happened like a torn candy bag.

Yakima was cold around Halloween so we were bundled up under our costumes. When we were first big enough to "trick or treat" we were allowed to visit all the homes on our block and as the years passed and our bags and buckets got bigger we ventured further away from home and stayed out longer. The only fears our parents had was our being tripped up by our costumes, or our not looking both ways when we crossed Fourteenth Avenue. The real Bogeyman, which kids fear today, wasn't a part of our lives.

Butch's big brother Dean told us about putting a paper bag filled with dog poop on a porch and setting fire to the bag. He said that when the home owner opened the door and saw the fire he would stomp it out and got poop all over his foot. We thought it was a great idea and late one Halloween evening we tried his trick, but were disappointed. After we got the bag lit, knocked on the door and ran to hide behind the shrubs the old man who opened the door just laughed and swept the stinky bag off his porch with a broom. Maybe he was the same guy Dean tricked ten years before.

For weeks after Halloween my brother and I gobbled up the candy we kept in separate hiding places. Judy had hers for months, despite Steve and me hunting for it in every corner of her room. We never found her stash and never understood how she could make it last for so long.

BARN 1951

The barn was filled with mystery and upon entering had the feel of an old Indian longhouse. Uncle Don owned twenty acres on a hillside above Selah, Washington. Most of his land was devoted to apple trees with a handful of cherry trees up by the house. The best times of my childhood were on Uncle Don's farm. His house wasn't much, just an old building that had little rooms tacked on all sides to accommodate the growing needs of his family.

Inga, Uncle Don's wife, was shorter than most and quick to hug. She tole painted everything and had decided, upon their purchase of the farm in the early fifties, that its exterior would be red. Not that toned down burgundy red, but the red of late summer tomatoes. It also had to be trimmed in white. The sight of that farm, as Dad drove our Ford sedan up McDonagal road, offered me all the feelings of adventure a young boy could handle.

Don kept the grass between the house and barn mowed. The old ash trees on the far side of the yard provided the summer shade needed to escape the mid-day heat. The cistern, just outside the back door, was filled with cool water, and the bright red-handled pump was off limits unless an adult was there to help with the priming.

The south end of the yard, under the cherry trees, was where the river rock fireplace was located. My brother, sister, and the rest of my cousins, roasted hundreds of hotdogs there and lost as many in its hot ashes. The taste of roasted frankfurters is a memory branded in my mind and probably the minds of all the other kids who stood around that fireplace on those hot summer days. If you turned your back to the flames, to dry your sprinkler soaked shorts, you would see the barn. It was also red and must have taken gallons and gallons of paint to fill all the cracks in the boards that had split and dried with the years.

The shop was on the south side of the building. It was here that the trucks, tractors and other equipment were kept in order. The big field sprayers and trailers were left out in the weather and parked beside the chicken coop. The shop's ramp was wooden and ground round with the work of supporting heavy equipment headed for repairs. The paned windows were low, running the shop's full length. Below them were workbenches that were hand milled in gone by years to hold weights greater than most farmers could lift. The drawers below were filled with tools that kids didn't know about and would, in their adult years, examine in efforts to guess their purpose. Playing in the shop was not ok. A quick, "don't mess around on the way through," was allowed.

There were several storage areas along the east side of the building that were accessible from the outside. One was a tack room that had once been a chicken coop. It was where Uncle Don, shortly after he purchased the farm, found the oak table set he gave my folks. The layers of enamel paint had protected the wood from the thick and aged chicken droppings. Mom and Dad raised us on that set and I raised my children on it also. It sits today in my dining room and knows many family secrets and secrets of others that knew it before Dad and Uncle Don ambitiously rescued it.

The heart of the barn could be entered through the north side where there was a pair of large swinging doors. They were centered just below the hayloft opening. These doors were locked and opened only when my Uncle was unloading firewood or moving equipment in or out.

When we entered the barn through the shop our eyes were greeted by a darkness that was punctured with beams of bright light peeking through the dry cedar shingles. We would hear the sounds of startled birds disliking our visit. Most of them were sparrows flying through the high and dusty rafters. There were the occasional hens, who, having tasted freedom, had decided that they preferred barn nesting rather than the coop. They were willing to take their chances with the weasels and other critters that preyed upon them or their eggs.

The Catholic Cathedral in Yakima matched the feeling of openness and reverence of the barn. I would always stop for a moment on the shop's threshold. If a bowl of holy water had sat there, I would have felt good about blessing myself before entering.

The barn was filled with bales of sweet summer hay stacked like windowless buildings. We spent hours climbing, sliding, hiding and finding all we could. Living creatures were trapped and boxed and if they were dead they were examined in detail. The cowboy saddles stored on their sawhorse were pulled close together for posse rides across the prairies of our imaginations. Unused wooden planks were stretched across and covered by hay bales to create hiding places from adults who would visit from time to time. Ropes were tossed over rafters and with Tarzan like screams we would swing from one side of the barn to the other dropping in the softest of broken hay bales.

Time lost all meaning in the barn. The smells of kid sweat, dirt and hay have found their own space in my soul and mind beside the hotdogs, Grandma's pies and the kisses of our parents. It was always hard to leave the barn when it was time for dinner or the drive back home even though we all knew another day would come when we would bless ourselves and re-enter the Cathedral that stood on my Uncle Don's farm.

ROAD TRIPS 1951

"Jimmy don't drop that candy wrapper on the floor…toss it out the window. If we keep all your trash in the car there won't be room for us," were Mom's words as we rolled, with all of our windows open, down the trash-strewn highway.

It was a ten-year-old Lincoln Continental with V12 motor and bad brakes. Dad had bought it from its owner for free maintenance for a year on one of his other cars and two hundred dollars. It turned out to be a good deal for the old owner and a loss for Dad.

Several months after we got it we were driving down Spruce Street beside Yakima High when the woman in front of us slammed on her brakes to avoid some students and Dad couldn't stop his big heavy car. He grabbed the steering wheel with one hand and tried to hold me in place with the other and failed. I slid past his large, protective hand and smashed my face against the windshield. It cracked and Dad talked for months about my hard head and the loss of his Continental.

Before the car was hauled off to the junkyard we had taken a trip to British Columbia to visit Dad's big brother Lawrence who lived near Josephstall. In addition to bad brakes the Continental was inclined to overheat so Dad hung a two-gallon water bag over the hood ornament in front of the grill. The water that evaporated in the bag helped keep the motor cool and if the hills were high he would stop for a while, let the motor cool off, and then pour the water into the radiator. It was a good system and we only had to stop a couple of times.

On hot days we would all roll down our windows and us kids would stick our heads outside to cool off. Mom would yell at us," Get your heads back in the car." We would be content for a while moving flying our hands through the wind until we would again find our heads outside the window.

The little wing windows on the front doors could be turned to direct wind into the car and across our sweaty bodies. This worked very well except when the bugs were thick.

As long as we behaved we were allowed to climb around the back seat of the Lincoln where we played many games and fought some battles. If the battles got out of hand we were forced to sit side by side with our hands in our laps like the bad kids on the bench outside Mother Superior's office.

If we were taking short trips and were close to town we could listen to the radio but when we drove through the mountains we would lose the signal and the sound of static was often louder than the music. Both Mom and Dad liked listening to country crooner Eddy Arnold and big band music.

I remember Dad having a flat tire outside of Cle Elum and our sitting on the side of the road as he wrestled to remove the big skirts on the rear fenders before he jacked up and replaced the tire with the spare. Dad was a good mechanic and we all trusted him to fix everything.

The highways were mostly two lane and they were covered with trash. Tossing stuff out the window was the norm and cleaning up the roadside was something I never saw any one do. It was years later and after auto air conditioning became common that the debris disappeared and tossing trash became unacceptable.

STICK IN THE EYE 1951

"It wasn't my fault. We didn't see him looking." Johnny was screaming and I didn't know what to do. It was a few weeks before Christmas and we were playing in a foot of fresh snow that had fallen the night before. We had plans of making a monster snowman and had spent most of the morning rolling gigantic snowballs and getting them on top of each other. It had been hard work and had taken the combined strength of Butch, Johnny, our little brothers, both of the Immely girls and myself. We packed the snowman's waist with extra snow to avoid its rolling off and possibly killing one of us. Once the head was in place we dug up some gravel from the alley and packed his face with rocks until we had created the perfect face. Judy Immely found an old red hat in her garage that sat well on his head and wouldn't be missed by her mother.

Johnny's mother had stood on her covered front porch several times to watch our progress while holding her coffee cup with both hands. "Now you kids be careful," she would croon as she closed the door behind her and returned to her household tasks. Butch and I were concerned about the kids on the next block sneaking over and knocking down our snowman. We couldn't let that happen and decided to strengthen our snowman with a broom handle through his middle. We both climbed on the snowman's back and began pounding the stick into the top of his head. Johnny had told us that we couldn't push anything all the way through three balls of hard packed snow. He didn't even think his Dad could do it. I decided I needed to wipe my nose on my snot-crusted scarf and jumped to the ground. Butch kept working on the stick and squealed in delight when it poked through the side of the base. He pulled the stick out and peeked down the iced shaft and saw Johnny's black rubber boot. It hadn't been our intention to poke the stick out in that spot but we couldn't hold the broom handle strait up and down and push as hard as we needed to. Johnny didn't see the stick go through, couldn't find the hole at the base of the snowman and didn't believe Butch.

"OK! I'll show you again," were Butch's words as he reinserted the wooden handle and jammed it back through the snowman one more time. Johnny, convinced that we had tricked him, was lying on the snow and was looking up through a hole he had just found. To his surprise and ours the end of the broom handle and Johnny's eye collided.

I was sure that he was blind as he rolled in the snow and screamed for his mother. The door flew open and Johnny's mother shrieked in distress, "I told you kids to be careful. Now look what you have done."

We stood to the side as she attended to her boy and when it became apparent that he would be OK I slipped out of their yard and went home without a word to my Mother. The next day we were back at play and all was well except Johnny's eye was black and blue and under a black pirates patch. It was kind of cool.

RABBITS 1952

Blackie and Cinnamon were the names of my rabbits and their lives were altered by my creative and time saving idea. I had owned Blackie for some time and during the summer Butch had sold me Cinnamon for one dollar and fifty cents. He wanted to buy a model airplane and was selling lots of his good stuff to get enough money.

Often when we were playing in our backyard Butch and I would let the rabbits out of their cage and let them enjoy eating lawn. We were easily distracted and would forget about the rabbits and run off to play. We never knew why but the rabbits would always slip under our fence, hop across the alley and end up in the Hidgon's garden. It was our guess that the rabbits loved flowers as much as Mrs. Higdon did and that got me in lots of trouble.

My Mom would call me home and with her very disappointed look remind me of my pet ownership responsibilities and send me across the alley to catch them. It usually didn't take long to find them particularly if Butch or Johnny would help. I hated looking up at the big window on the back of the Hidgon house and see her standing there with her arms folded across her chest and that angry look on her face.

Another pet ownership responsibility I had was cleaning the cage. The bottom of the cage I had built was wooden where the rabbits were fed and the rest of it was screened. The screened part was where the rabbits should have deposited their pellets and didn't. Their choice to use the wrong side of the cage as their bathroom disappointed me and undermined my cage cleaning design.

I would use an old metal fireplace scooper when I cleaned the cage and shovel the pellets over the screen where they would fall to the ground. In order to do this I had to open the cage and take out the food bowls and the wooden rabbit house I had also built. It all took too much time.

One bright and sunny day I decided that I would use the garden hose and flush the wooden corner clean. It was a grand idea and only took a few minutes. The cage looked great and the rabbits got a good bath in the process. They didn't look dirty but they had never had a bath and I was sure that they would enjoy their clean fur. When I refilled their food bowl and walked away, they were busy licking themselves and exploring the fresh corners of their hutch.

The next morning I approached their cage expecting to see their extra fluffy fir and bright eyes but discovered that both rabbits were laying flat on the screen floor frozen into thick slabs of ice. It was mid-December and below thirty degrees.

Some times the best ideas of young boys are poor. I'm guessing that if Mrs. Higdon had known about my mistake she would have been delighted.

NEPHRITIS 1952

School was out, I was eight and a half years old, we were on vacation and I was sick. Mom was concerned enough about my symptoms that she cut the family vacation short and returned to Yakima. When we left Moclips and the beaches we were all disappointed and after my appointment with Dr Kennedy, Mom and Dad were very concerned.

I was told that I had Nephritis, that I would have to go to bed, take medicine and put up with my Aunt Kathryn, who was the charge nurse at St Josephs Hospital, drawing blood from my arm on a regular basis.

I watched the summer pass through my parents' bedroom window. At night I slept in my bunk bed above my brother and in the mornings Mom would come to the side of my bed and have me climb on her back. She would then pack me to the toilet and wouldn't let my feet touch the floor. When I was done I would climb on her back again and she would pack me to her bedroom where I would spend my day with occasional back trips to the bathroom.

I lived on seven-up pop and grew three inches during that summer. Mom was always pushing me to drink this and drink that. I wasn't happy being sick.

I watched my friends set off fireworks on the 4th of July. They put on a special show for me and Mom let me stay up later than normal so I could watch the sparklers in the dark. Day after day the neighborhood kids skated up and down the sidewalks and played hide-n-go-seek in front of my window. At night I would watch parents play baseball with their kids and when they spotted me they would wave. I would wave back and cheer them on.

The kids wanted to visit during the day but my Mom and the sun-filled sky demanded that they play outside and only visit for short periods of time...except for Judy Immely. She was happy to sit on the bed and read stories to me while I slipped in and out of sleep.

I hated it when Aunt Kathryn visited. I remember it being every day and am sure that it couldn't have been. She was a big, powerful and bony person like my Dad and far from gentle. When I heard her car pull up to the curb I would pull the covers over my head. When she spotted the lump in the bed she would say in her loud voice, "Well how is my little man? Do you have any blood left for me today?" My Mom said that it was very kind of her to come by our home and draw the blood that was needed to keep track of my Nephritis. She hurt me often and when she died I wouldn't go to her funeral.

There were lots of kindnesses that summer. Dr. Kennedy did a trade with my Dad and would come buy our home once a week to check on me. Dad fixed up an old car for him and he kept me out of the hospital which kept the costs of my care at a minimum.

After a summer in bed my feet touched the ground for the first time one week before school started. They hated being walked on, but it only took a few days before I was back to normal, other than my looking like an escapee from one of the German concentration camps.

Dr. Kennedy said that if I made it to twenty-one without the Nephritis returning I would be OK. I guess he was right.

FRIENDS 1952

My best friends growing up were John Crimin and Butch Yeager. The three of us were together almost every day and were partners in many adventures. Butch and I spent a small part of most days rolling around on the grass or in the snow fighting. He wanted to be the boss of our pack and so did I. Butch would usually ended up sitting on top of me and he was pretty sure that made him boss. I didn't agree, but we would always make amends in time for our next escapade.

There were girls in the neighborhood. Judy and Patty Immely lived four houses down and across the street next to Butch. They had a little brother named Bobby and their mom was tough. She was a tall woman who would look a lot like the ladies in history books standing beside covered wagons.

Her husband was a really big man who scared us and never had anything to say. We spotted him from time to time picking up his morning paper in a white nightgown and a funny bed hat. Our dad slept in underwear or nothing. My Mom hated it when Mr. Immely would, in his bed cloths, walk into the middle of our street and fire his pistol on New Years Eve. She always said, "What is he thinking? Those bullets have to come down somewhere."

Mr. Immely was a route driver for Grandma's Cookies. His son, Bobby, liked to trade the factory cookies his dad delivered for the tasty homemade ones Butch's mom made most everyday. Butch always thought he was getting a good deal...I didn't think so.

Mrs. Immely would stand on her porch and challenge us guys by saying,"Come up and squeeze my arm. You guys think you are so strong. I bet I can beat ya with one hand behind my back." I think she liked us, but we were never sure. She also made it clear that she would kill us if she caught us cutting through her back yard or tromping on her flowers. This posed us a serious problem because her back yard was next to Butch's and when we played war we needed to jump over her fence so we could hide behind her begonias. We had no other choice.

The Immely's also had sawhorses in their back yard stacked beside their garage. Those sawhorses, with a few blankets on them, were as close to a horse us city boys were going to get. We would take turns riding them and always had a new adventure and people to save as we rode them across the plains of our imaginations.

Our greatest adventure in the Immely backyard was building the tree house no adult knew about. We were sly and found our building materials in the neighborhood's unlocked garages. We dragged our lumber, one board at a time, high into the tree and nailed it together with the bent and rusty nails we found in a coffee can in one of the garages. Behind the leaf-crowded branches, it was almost invisible, and we used it often until autumn came and the falling leaves exposed our creation. Mr. Immely was furious and we were again banned from his yard forever.

Butch had a real name. It was Truman. We never called him that, but when we started high school, he wanted to go by Truman. We didn't understand why a guy would change his name, but he wanted it that way...so we did it.

Butch's house was a two-story unlike the houses the rest of us lived in. It was really old and his bedroom was in one of the rooms upstairs. We would make model airplanes there and the smell of glue, which we amply used, was so strong that our heads would spin. When our models were complete with decals and paint, we would set them on fire and toss them out his window. We were sure that the neighbors, who were always watching, would think they were real.

On the way to Butch's room we had to cut through his sister space. Her room was at the top of the steep steps and unavoidable. We loved it when we, as quiet as mice, would creep up the steps and catch her getting dressed. She would scream, "Damn it Butch, don't bring the whole God damn neighborhood up here." She liked to talk tough. If she wasn't there we would glance over all the girl stuff we weren't allowed to touch and some we were too young know about.

Besides his mother and father, Butch had other sisters and several big brothers who we didn't know. Butch was the baby of his family and his older brothers and sisters had grown up and moved away except for Janet and a brother named Dean who we all idolized. Dean had long black hair which was slicked back into a duck tail and best of all he owned a car. It was a two-door Ford and had a pair of burned out mufflers that could be heard blocks away. We didn't know a lot about cars but we did know that Butch's brother was cool.

Mrs. Yeager was old. She was a lot older than my Mom and Dad and had long white hair. She was tall like Mrs. Immely and liked us kids and would feed us. Her husband, Butch's Dad, was named Silas. He was older than Mrs. Yeager and never talked at the dinner table. He just banged his silverware. I could never figure out what he wanted from his banging but they all seemed to know and would pass him things. Two bangs with the spoon got salt. One fork bang got more milk. Some times he would bang and look right at me. I didn't like that because I didn't understand his banging and didn't want to tick him off. Butch told me that his family, before moving to Yakima, had lived at Priests Rapids out in the desert. They had to move to Yakima when Grand Coolie Dam was built and their town went under the backwaters.

"Jimmy, would you go out on the back porch and bring me a little dill for the pickles?" Mrs. Yeager's called from her dinning room. Her back porch was off the kitchen, screened in and served as her pantry. She kept lots of things hanging out there like dill and chamomile. There were also big baskets of potatoes and onions.

Mrs. Yeager liked to tell a story about me. She would say, "I warned that Jimmy to not eat any of our pears off the tree while we were away on our vacation. Last year when we left he ate them all. He even ate the ones high in the tree. We never could figure how such a little guy could get so high in that old pear tree, but when we got home there wasn't a pear to be had. Jimmy said that he didn't eat them but we knew he had and was afraid that he would get a spanking if he 'fessed up. So the next year I took special effort to warn him. I wanted to have the fruit and didn't want him to get in trouble. I held his face in my hand and said,

'Jimmy, don't you pick a single pear off my tree.' He said OK. When we returned all the pears were still hanging on the tree and every one had a big bite out of it. Jimmy, Jimmy, Jimmy."

Across the Yeager backyard was a garage and a tired old shed. We were pretty sure that if we could get on top of one of the buildings we would be able to jump from roof to roof and maybe even make it across to the Carrol's garage. We looked all over the neighborhood and couldn't find a ladder tall enough so I decided to cut a hole in Mr. Yeager's garage roof. My Dad had a great saw that was pointed on the end and with it I cut a square hole big enough for a kid to climb through. I made a little holder that held the roof panel when we weren't using it. Butch's dad never noticed. Like my dad, he worked hard, and was often too tired to notice the minor changes we were continually making.

Once on the roof we were able, just as we thought to jump from roof to roof to roof. Butch said later that the skills he learned on the garage tops in our neighborhood helped keep him alive in Viet Nam.

The tired old shed leaned in the direction of Tieton Drive. It became our neighborhood clubhouse and held many of our secrets until it was demolished or fell in during the mid 1980's. I heard roomers that it was burned to the ground by some of the neighborhood kids. It was a miracle that it survived our tenancy.

The building had two sections, one with a dirt floor and the other wood. The entrance door swung open over the dirt and was not more than eight foot by ten. The alley bordered the back of the building that had a shuttered opening and the wooden floor. It was in this section, with the shutter open to vent toxic fumes, that we conducted most of our experiments. Johnny and I had gotten chemistry sets with microscopes for Christmas and we quickly converted the clubhouse into the neighborhood laboratory.

Butch's dad had a pile of old lumber he salvaged when he dismantled the front of his garage where we had cut the access panel in the roof. The garage was in poor repair like the wood shed and had to be partially demolished due to Dean backing his car into the southwest corner making the building a hazard.

The lumber was excellent for the shelving that held our experiments. I had discovered my mother had an excessive number of canning jars, or at least I thought so, which served as containers for our chemicals.

There was a booklet of chemical instruction with both our kits and much of what we used was common in our mother's kitchens. There was baking soda and powder, sugar, salt, vinegar, flour and catsup. Catsup always added to the drama of chemical development. We had hopes of developing something dangerous and were only successful in mixing bad smells. "Be careful Jimmy!!! You mix those two together with that vinegar and…and…it might explode."

Truman and John still live in Yakima. I wonder if they remember and value our childhoods as I do.

STEEL ROLLERS 1952

The sound of steel rollers on the sidewalk was common in our neighborhood. It seemed that when birthdays came around skates were a popular gift during the early 1950's. I had a great pair that had red leather straps that buckled and held the skate to my shoe. The front clamps needed a key that I kept on a shoelace around my neck. The best shoes to buckle skates to were the ones with thick leather soles. I don't remember having tennis shoes for the street back then but I do remember that the girls had shoes that were thin soled and didn't work very well.

There were days when we would all be on the sidewalks racing up one side, quickly skating across the street, and then down the other side. Our jubilant voices were hard to hear over the noise of our skates. It must have been nice for our parents to watch and listen to us delight in our play.

It seemed that having hunks of skin ground off knees, palms, elbows and occasional chins was normal for boys and girls alike. One of our favorite skating games was the caterpillar. We would get our parents OK to skate in the street and then we would hang on to each other as if we were dancing the bunny hop. With a little speed and a few quick swerves the kids on the end would have an exciting ride and occasionally…add to their collection of knee scars.

There were times when skates broke and were deemed useless by our dads. That was when we began to build apple box scooters. They were each "one of a kind" and required skill in the making. In my neighborhood there were only a few homemade scooters and I was proud to have made one. The design was a simple one. You would take the skate apart and nail the wheels to the front and back of a two or three foot long board. You would then nail an old wooden apple box, which we always had plenty of, on top of the board leaving a space behind for your foot to ride. If you want handles on the top of the box you could get some nice round wood from your mom's broom or maybe an old mop. Brooms were usually too long anyway and cutting them down a little was good. Some kids nail cans on the side of their boxes to get a headlight look like their dad's cars. I didn't do that because I thought it would slow me down and I wanted to be fast.

Scooters were good for shopping and made the trip to the grocery fun. Loading the apple box up with a couple of grocery bags was easy and the handful of penny candy we earned made the trip extra sweet.

We didn't have much to do with the kids from the other neighborhoods but I do remember one day when we had a race down St. Paul's hill. There were several scooters in our neighborhood and a few more in the blocks around us. The word spread through the neighborhoods that there was going to be an apple box race and we decided to participate.

I was young and it was my first race down the hill. The fastest I had ever gone before was the day Johnny Crimin tied a rope between his bike and my scooter and pulled me around the block. After that pull I knew my scooter was safe. I had driven extra big nails into the board when I attached the skates and was confident that they would hold.

On race day I wanted to save my energy and asked Johnny to tow me behind his bike to the hill. He was able to pull me several blocks but found the hill too hard to peddle up.

We laid his bike in a driveway and pushed my scooter to the top of the hill. By the time we got to there and looked over the other scooters I lost some of my confidence. They were from a neighborhood two blocks away and I could tell by looking that their dads had built most of their scooters. The skates were bolted to the bottom boards...not nailed. They also had bicycle handle bar attached to the apple boxes rather than broom or mop sticks.

Once we had all the scooters pointing down the hill one of the kids yelled GO and that was the last I saw of the other racers. I gave my scooter four hard pushes and then jumped on behind my box. From the front all you could see of me was my crew cut and eyes. I wished that I had thought of my goggles. My Uncle Don, who was in the Air Force, gave me a pair. They didn't have the glass in them anymore, but they made me look like a real racer.

There's a sound that steel wheels make when they roll really fast. It was a great sound and I heard it when I first started my decent. That sound passed at the halfway point and was replaced with a sound more like my Mom's Bendix washing machine when her load wasn't in balance. I was afraid that I was loosing a bearing and if I did…I would be in big trouble. The sound changed from a grinding to a squeal and then as if God really did want me to win, it sounded normal.

When the other guys caught up with me I was laying on my back on the grass of the parking strip. They told me that I had a great scooter and I told them that I knew it.

TELEVISION 1952

It was a beautiful fall day and Butch, Johnny and I were watching the neighborhood like the finely tuned security team we were when we spotted a delivery truck pulling up in front of our neighbor's house. We were all, before the driver was out of the cab, parked at the head of their sidewalk. We dropped our bikes and watched as the men hefted a big blonde television set out of the back of the truck. We couldn't believe it. We had presumed they were getting a chair or maybe a sofa but when we saw the 17" Zenith in the beautiful blonde cabinet we were amazed. My Dad had told me that they were so expensive it would be years before we would get one. He also said that television would never be as good as radio.

Although the only contact I had with the owners of this unbelievable television was waving as I peddled my bike past their home I was able to procure an invitation, that night, not just for myself, but also for my whole family to watch their TV.

When we arrived they had placed folding chairs in rows in front of the set. Our host was putting the final touches on the rabbit ears antenna system and adjusting the volume as we settled into the chairs. His wife offered us some orange Kool Aid over ice cubes without straws.

They didn't have any children. Steve and I were happy to sit on the floor with our heads as close to the screen as they could be without blocking the view for everyone else.

The show we watched was "I Love Lucy." We all laughed as we watched Ricky, Lucy, Fred, and Ethel play out their silly story about the show biz redhead, her Cuban bandleader husband, and their landlords and best friends.

When the show was over the set was turned off and we thanked and said good night to our hosts. Steve and I danced around Dad like puppies begging for a snack as we walked down the street to our house. "Daddy, Daddy…lets get a TV." Money was scarce during those years and television wasn't high on the what-the-family-needs-list.

Several years later the truck pulled up in front of our house and we began watching Lucy and Ricky in our front room. Dad spent hours yelling down from the roof as he happily adjusted our antenna for the best reception.

Eight years later in the home of my buddy, Larry Keeler, I watched Bonanza and couldn't believe it when the porch light changed from bright white to a warm and golden glow just like the real light on the front of Larry's house.

My love affair with television, like so many others, continues today. From time to time, with my remote in hand, I will surf across "I Love Lucy" and remember the Kool Aid introduction I had to TV.

MY ALLEY 1952

Butch lived on the odd side of the street and my house was on the even side. We both had alleys behind our homes and I thought that mine was better than his. My alley was graveled with packed ruts where the garbage trucks and cars drove and pushed the rocks to the side. Butch's alley was dirt and in the summer months dust would kick up when folks drove too quickly. Sometimes the city would spread oil across the surface to control the dust and mess up our play area for weeks.

Butch's alley had a fairly steep slope where it connected with Tieton Drive and was the best place to build a wooden ramp for bicycle jumping. With practice you could soar off the ramp and upon landing spin your bike around on the gravel, slide across the concrete sidewalk and stop before moving into the traffic on the street. To do this without losing an elbow or knee required skill. We never were concerned with the possibility of being struck by a car.

His alley was where we played the big games that required lots of kids like "kick the can" and "baseball." Because his alley was mostly dirt and not gravel like mine it was easy to slide into base like professional ball players. There were lots of special rules we had for our alley games such as it being an automatic game loss if you hit the ball into the Immely yard. We knew that Mr. Immely was a day sleeper and if we woke him up he would sit in his kitchen window and watch us play. If a ball flew into his yard he would open his back screen door, keep us at bay and then grab up the ball that we would never see again.

Fouls were called when the ball went anywhere else other than straight down the alley. There were lots of fouls in our games and after three of them you were called out. The Davis girls would join us for our games, as did Jane LeVere. We liked the five Davis girls who were beautiful and often babysat us. They lived on Thirteenth just behind Butch and were delighted when their mom had a baby boy after all the girls. Jane LeVere was a different story. She also lived on Thirteenth about eight houses north of the Davis family. She always wore an untucked white t-shirt and was the toughest girl we knew. We were pretty sure that, when Jane needed to beat someone up, she would come hunting for us. When Jane's family left the neighborhood and the Torres family moved in, we were very happy and the Torres girls were very cute.

The alley behind my house was flat from one end to the other and wasn't good for bicycle ramping but had lots of unlocked garages. The garages all had two wooden doors that would open like barn doors and were kept shut with latches and sometimes a lock. Most of the garages on Butch's alley were owned by old people without kids and were locked except for the Ceamers who lived on the end of the alley and Spruce Street. Burt Ceamer's doctor had told him that he had a heart condition that could be improved with a little alcohol. Burt took his doctor's advice. As a result his garage was always being filled up with very valuable five-cent mixer bottles. When his empty bottles became a problem he would let one of our parents know and we would empty his garage. We would fill paper grocery bags with four or five bottles and then bike to Highland market and cash them in. We all had a fond feeling in our hearts for Mr. Ceamer and were thankful his heart didn't work very well.

We had no idea what was in all the other locked garages on Butch's alley and we always watched for a door ajar. For some unknown reason most of the garages on my alley were always open. Maybe it was because we had more kids who kept their bikes in them.

It was in these open garages that we found most of the three-cent beer and pop bottles. Bottles translated into candy when they were traded in at Gordon's Highland Market or the Bungalow Market on Sixteenth Avenue. Most of the bottles we found were the small three cent ones with Mr. Ceamer being the exception.

Every few days we would check the garages and most always scored. The best garage belonged to Johnny's dad. Johnny was my friend and his dad, like mine, drank beer. Entering a garage with stealing on the mind was very exciting. One of us would stand guard in the alley where he could see in both directions while the others would quickly dash in, grab all the pop and beer bottles they could carry and run down the alley where we had parked our bikes and bags. The other great garage we ripped off was mine. When I think about it, we only raided bottles from two garages, Johnny's and mine. We didn't have the guts and knew it was wrong to steal from our neighbors but stealing from our parents seemed OK in some strange way.

My alley had lots of kids while Butch and the Immely girls were the only children on his side of the street. When it came time to build forts, have secret meetings, and spy on folks my side of the street was by far the best. Trouble was the final proof that the even side was best. Everyone knew that if you were having fun you were probably getting into trouble. We were always grounded while Butch and the girls weren't.

CHRISTMAS 1953

As a child Christmas was bigger than life. It was more than I could have hoped for and continues to be my richest memories of family togetherness. I was lucky to have a praiseworthy and loving family that taught me and all the other children in our family how to be quality adults.

Naches was a little town of four hundred people at the foot of White Pass that often had more snow than Yakima and that always pleased the children. The adults also liked the snow but would complain about the cold and poor road conditions.

The town center was composed of a half a dozen single-story commercial buildings surrounded by several neighborhoods of modest residential homes. A few blocks up the little Main Street you would see a large brick warehouse with my grandma and grandpa's little white house across the street. At Christmas Grandpa would always trim the eves of his home with the big, green, red and white lights that were popular in the fifties. He was a grumpy man and yet, every year, he hung the lights and they were a beautiful sight to see from the frosted windows of our Ford as we turned the corner and drove towards their home.

On Christmas Eve all the families arrived within an hour or so of each other and the number of gifts grew until Grandma's gray carpet disappeared. There were big and little packages all colorfully wrapped and bowed. We would stack them around the white, flocked tree spending our time inspecting tags until it was time for one of the adults to be Santa. The adults worked hard and made us take turns and only open one gift at a time. It took us hours to unwrap all the bundles and boxes and we were all delighted with our gifts and seeing what the brothers, sisters and cousins got from Santa. The moms would keep busy stuffing used gift-wrap into boxes while the men stood back and proudly watched. Some time during the process the assigned Santa would toss up their hands and let mass gift opening take place.

Late in the evening after desserts and coffee the adults would pack-up their cars with gifts and kids and drive back down Main Street towards the highway and our homes in Yakima, Selah and Terrace Heights. On the way home my sister and I would fall asleep in the back seat and my little brother would snooze in his spot between Mom and Dad.

For the first twelve years of my life I experienced Christmas Eve in the home of my grandparents and for that I am thankful.

Christmas mornings were even greater than Christmas Eves and what happened in our home between the two celebrations was something that Mom, Dad and Santa knew about and I didn't.

My little brother rarely out did me. On the Christmas morning of my tenth year he did. He was the first to see the greatest gift we ever received. "Jimmy...Jimmy...it's a train," he squealed. I sat up in my top bunk, opened my eyes, and with the early morning light filtering through our rodeo curtains saw the light of a small train station beside a long set of tracks. Our Hop-a-long Cassidy wallpaper was the perfect backdrop for our new Lionel double loop train. The track was mounted on a gloss, gray sheet of plywood that was edged with 2x2's and rounded corners. There were two oval tracks, one inside the other. Every section of track was screwed tightly to the deck and a de-coupler was tacked down on the far side of the small oval beside the double switching tracks. The lit station house was in front of the transformer and the switching buttons. A round black whistle button was on the left of the transformer and little lights were mounted on the two crossing signals. There was a tunnel on the outside track and trees and other train things that brought the station to life were perfectly mounted.

"We got a train!!! Mom, Dad...Santa brought us a train," I yelled as Dad came into our room and turned on our lights. He was in his robe and Mom was behind him with her arms folded and shoulder against the doors frame. Judy slid by Mom and sat on Steve's bed while Dad introduced us to our new train.

The engine was big, heavy and black. Behind it was the coal car followed by the flat bed, boxcar and the red caboose. The engine had a light on its front and when you dropped a little white pellet into its stack it would smoke. Dad showed us how to use the transformer, increase speed, reverse, decouple and switch the tracks. Both Steve and I were quick with mechanical things and within a few minutes Dad had joined Judy and Mom on the lower bunk. Within hours we had toy trucks, plastic army men, cowboy guys and small spools of Mom's thread for passengers and cargo.

This toy was the ultimate gift. The smell of the engine smoke, hot transformer and the lubricating oil coupled with the sound of the whistle and the sight of that loaded train rounding the corner with its stack of smoke and piercing light was magic, pure Christmas magic.

THE GUTTER 1954

When the Valley was traveled only by native Americans you could have stood on one of the parched mountain ridges that cradled it and watch the Yakima River snake itself across the desert floor keeping green only the trees that existed on its sides. Summer rainfall is rare and when it comes it makes up for all the dry days of summer.

Irrigation brought water to the valley floor and our rich green yards were a testimonial to how successful it was. Most families had little red or green sprinklers manufactured by Hubbard or Rain King attached to rubber hoses that would be dragged around the yard all summer long. We had rain birds that would cast a long stream across the yard with a spring-loaded brass piece that interrupted the waters flow and made a unique swishing sound I loved.

On hot summer days when all the sprinklers were running and the water was flowing down to the drain we would build gutter boats. These small hand crafted wooden boats were created on the bright blue scroll saw my father had in his garage. He told me that it had belonged to my grandfather and it was the first piece of power equipment to rip through the flesh on my thumb.

The boats were simple and made of small six to seven inch long sections of 1x2s. I would cut away a section on the back of the board in the shape of a U and tack small blocks on top to look like cabins. I would then whittle two small pieces of wood with slots that would fit together and make a paddle system that looked like a Mississippi river boat. The paddles were placed between rubber bands that were stretched over the ends of the U, wound up, and then placed in the water for a quick trip up the gutter. We loved them.

Gutter boating became exceptionally fun when we had the occasional down pour. On these days we would, soaked to the bone, pile dirt or any debris we could find on the down water side and create dams. These dams would flood the street and create lakes of impressive size. It didn't take long to make the boats and by the time we had the water backed up we had half a dozen little paddle boats being attended to by five or six boys who wouldn't have been anywhere else but in the gutter.

Our mothers would discourage this behavior and try to coax us away from the water with concerned words like Polio. They were never successful. We were probably protected by the gallons of DDT that was sprayed, several times every summer, on the big maple trees above our water playground.

MOVIES 1954

After we parked the car on the street in front of the Crother's store and walked past the Commercial Hotel to the theater, we bought our tickets from a girl wearing a black hat and vest. She was in a little booth that had a glass front with a talking hole cut just above another slot for purchased tickets. Above us a big red and gold neon sign was hung on the front of the building above the marquee that extended out over the sidewalk and advertised today's Jules Verne movie.

I loved "20,000 Leagues Under the Sea" and it was my first movie. My little brother didn't get to come with us because he was just a kid. My parents and my big sister Judy sat in the middle of the row with me between Mom and Dad. We were in the middle of the Liberty Theater and Dad kept telling me to use my little voice. I didn't understand why and found it impossible to hold back all the questions running through my mind.

Dad bought a big white box filled with popcorn. It had red letters that said Majorette Selected Pop Corn over a picture of a girl in shorts shooting a gun. The popcorn kernels were bigger than the ones Mom popped at home and it tasted like butter. Dad let me eat all I wanted… Judy got a box of her own.

There were three theaters in the business section of town, and they all had a Romanesque style of architecture and were beautiful. The Liberty, Capitol and Yakima had domed interiors with balconies. Mr. Mercy owned most of them, and built them to be vaudeville houses. When the Liberty was built, she was the grandest and most luxurious the city had ever seen, and her murals were gorgeous.

There were lots of great movies to see beside "20,000 Leagues Under the Sea". "Davy Crockett" and "Peter Pan" were a couple of really good ones that were popular when I began going to the movies.

When Mom and Dad allowed us to attend movies on our own they had several rules they expected us to obey. The first rule was no movies at the Roxy or Avenue theaters. They were in the middle of the blocks known as Skid Row. Although they cost fifteen cents to attend just like the nice movie houses, they were very different. The smell of dirty clothes and urine was strong. Many of the chairs were broken, and bubble gum was stuck everywhere. The reason we knew all about the Roxy and Avenue was we broke the rule. We would get dropped of in front of Liberty, Capitol or Yakima theaters and pretend to buy tickets. When our parents drove off, we would pocket our money and walk the three blocks to the banned theaters where they showed Lash LaRue movies.

A year or two after I watched the Jules Verne movie, I had become a big fan of cowboy movies and loved Lash LaRue. LaRue was different from the usual cowboy hero. He dressed in black and spoke like a gangster with a "tough-guy" accent like Humphrey Bogart. His use of a bullwhip was what set him apart from other cowboy stars such as Roy Rogers, who played the guitar. After watching one of his movies we built our own whips and would snap bats out of the sky on warm summer nights.

The other great thing about the movies in the 1950's was the cartoon. Before the movies all theaters showed at least one, and there were lots of them for the theater to pick from. Disney started it all in 1928 with "Steamboat Willie." The ones I remember had characters like Mickey Mouse, Donald Duck, Bugs Bunny, Daffy Duck, Porky Pig, Popeye, Woody Woodpecker and Tom and Jerry. There were lots of others and I loved them all. Some times a theater would show two cartoons. When that happened we felt really lucky.

Besides the cartoons they would have newsreels and maybe one preview...not the forty-five minutes they show us today.

I still love movies...so do my kids. I'm not sure what the magic is but I do know that once I'm in my seat with my popcorn and pop... all the problems of the world are somewhere else.

GYMNASIUM 1954

Locker rooms smell. I would have thought that a bunch of elementary kids would have smelled better than older boys. They didn't. I began spending time in locker rooms when I turned out for sixth grade basketball. I didn't know much about the game, and did know that the guys who played were cool and loved to play.

I was tall for a kid and Father Queen, our coach, encouraged me to join the team. He was fresh off the boat from Ireland and didn't know the game, but had a book all about it rolled up in his hip pocket.

Mom got me a pair of white low top Keds. Choosing between the low and high tops was difficult. Mom wanted me to have the additional support of the high top but when I saw the Ibach brothers wearing low tops, my decision was made.

We had great maroon colored uniforms with gold numbers that we wore when we played games. The rest of the time we wore red shorts and t-shirts that said something Catholic. When we scrimmaged, one team would put on red tank tops and the other would be shirtless and called "skins."

The locker room at St. Paul's was located in the southwest corner on the ground level. The gymnasium was one flight of concrete steps above the locker room and was full of maple wood. The floor was painted with bright colors to mark the court boundaries and in the center a maroon circle with a growling cougar praised our team image. On both sides of the court there were bleachers that remained closed until game day or an assembly meeting. On the south end of the court the stage was hidden by long maroon drapes. It was on that stage I played a green elf with tights on St. Patrick's Day. I didn't like wearing tights. I thought my legs were funny looking and the tights made them look worse. The north side of the gym had half a dozen steps leading up to the double glass doors that led into the school's main hall and the second floor classrooms.

Most of the Catholic kids in our school were of French and German decent. There were a few Irish tossed in, and I don't remember any kids of color.

I also don't remember the girls at St. Paul's having structured team sports, but I do remember them being cheerleaders. Our cheerleaders attended all our games and wore fancy maroon and gold sweaters that displayed our school mascot.

The Ibach boys had been basketball stars at St. Paul's for years and we had two of them on our team. They weren't really brothers, but were cousins. They knew how to play the game. The rest of us, with the exception of Bobby Cole, made lots of noise and tried to act like basketball players. Bobby and the Ibachs taught us the moves and we all tried hard to play like them with varying degrees of success.

Every day after school we practiced for a couple of hours and I loved it. I was tall and strong but never really great at basketball. Being tall it was assumed that I work well under the basket. I didn't. Many times I remember getting the ball and thinking, "all I have to do is jump up and lay this ball over the rim." I would jump, shoot, and have the ball arch away from the basket as if some invisible defender had swatted it away. I hated that.

The Catholic school across town was St. Joseph. It was in the northeast section of Yakima and many of the folks in that area were poorer than us. We all knew that poor kids were better athletes because that had to fight and that made them tough. Thinking about playing ball against them was always stressful, and my first game proved my anxiety to be well founded.

Before the game started and while both teams were warming up the guys from St. Joseph's acted like they had already won. They laughed and sneered at us and didn't miss any of their practice shots. The game was hard. They were stronger and faster than us. Their coach was tall and athletic, while ours was skinny, short and could barely speak English. We were lucky and when we got down to the last few minutes of the game we had managed to catch up with them. Their center, a big kid who had been pushing me around for the whole game, fouled me. "Shit." Now with almost no time left, I approached the foul line for two shots. I was the center of attention and was rotten at foul shots. Following the instructions I had received from Father Queen I prepared to shoot. I spun the ball in my hands to get a good feel for it, squatted down and swung the ball down between my knees and then back up and towards the basket. My first shot bounced back off the rim and landed back in my hands. The second went under the rim barely brushing the net and bounced up the steps towards Sister Superior's office. I wanted to disappear. A few moments later the buzzer sounded and we lost the game.

Failing was a big deal to me. My teammates were quick to accept the loss and after shaking hands and whooping with the other team they were on their way down the steps and to the showers. I was left standing alone and not knowing what to do next.

I was never really great at any sport, just adequate. I liked shooting drills and scrimmage but the pressure of games was hard on me. Most often when the contest was over I would be happy whether we won or lost. Not making a fool of myself in front of my teammates and all the people in the stands was the important thing. That day I felt the fool and hated it. I always felt that way about sports. I think I still do.

FORT STEVENS 1954

The Japanese lobbed several bombs of some type or other at Fort Stevens during WWII and there wasn't a drop of blood shed until I arrived. It was our first vacation in Oregon and we had set up camp next to the Crimins who had traveled with us from Yakima. They had a rented trailer and we were using an old military cook tent from World War II that has served us well on other vacations in Washington. My sister, Judy, was more interested in avoiding my brother and myself, so she kept herself busy sweeping sand out of the tent. Steve, little brother that he was, tried hard to keep up with Johnny and myself, but found he had more fun playing with Bruce, John's brother. The big day of the blooding came when we decided to tour the military fort. I was more than under-impressed with the size of the fort and had a hard time understanding why the Japanese bothered wasting any of their shells on such a puny base.

There was mostly sand and beach grass around the buildings and the absence of tanks, jeeps, trucks, howitzers, airplanes, U-boats or anything military added to the boringness of it all. Fort Stevens was nothing more than a few half buried bunkers.

My interest was somewhat lifted as we wandered the under ground passages between the bunkers where massive howitzers had once been bolted to the floor. All that was left of the howitzers were massive bolts that extended several inches above the concrete slab floors and this is where the blooding started.

Slipping into my fantasy world, John and I became great warriors charging from one bunker to the other. The brightness of the coastal sun and the darkness of the bunkers made seeing inside difficult. Having found the remnants of a weathered 2x4, I considered myself armed with my M1 and charged with abandoned courage towards the slits in the bunker wall to spy on and possibly shoot the advancing enemy. Pain shattered my forward motion and dropped me to the floor with my rifle sliding across the floor. I grabbed my foot and felt blood flow over my hands, staining my new flip-flops. I couldn't believe that I had stubbed my scantly clad foot on a howitzer bolt. I couldn't believe the pain. As always, Mom was soon at my side and sacrificed her yellow scarf to design a temporary wrap for my toe. I lost a large hunk of flesh and later John and I spent hours looking for it.

Shortly after Mom had attended my injury I felt the need to show the full assembly of families how I had sustained this war injury. While everyone watching I again picked up the 2x4 and walked into the dark entrance of the tunnel. With a fearsome battle cry I turned around and charged towards the same bunker slits that had been my initial goal. Again I found myself on the cold hard floor with not my left foot in my hand, but with the right. In front of God and all the family I had sacrificed my other big toe to the protection of the homeland.

HIGHLAND GROCERY STORE 1950

The first time my Mom rolled me through the doors of the Highland Bungalow Grocery Store in my stroller, Gordon Webster was behind the counter and he remained behind that counter for the fifteen years we lived on Fourteenth Avenue. The Bungalow was a family owned and operated grocery, and it was typical to see Gordon's wife or son working with him.

The Bungalow was unlike the stores of today. The floors were wood and smoothed with years of traffic. Each individual board was different from the other. The space between them was evident and the occasional patch of metal covering an unused hole was obvious and covered by the same dark stains that had protected the wood for years. Shelves being moved from time to time displayed wood that had spent years covered and sheltered from dirty shoes and bare-footed kids.

Just inside the door and to the left was the meat department. The white enamel and glass-faced coolers displayed the butcher's meat. The windows on the front were fixed and the sliders on the back made it possible for Gordon or his hired man, when times were good, to pull from the case and present for my Mother's approval a piece of meat she had pointed out. The coolers framed the area used to cut and wrap beef, pork, chicken and the lamb my mother never bought. Steel runners with massive meat hooks were suspended from the ceiling and tracked deep into the walk-in-refrigerator where they suspended large pieces of uncut meat. Against the back wall stood a butcher-block cutting table with knives and other carving tools mounted on its front edge. This table and the large square butcher block in the middle of the floor were sloped and rounded like the back of a camel.

The scale was on top of the front cooler and had a large glass face on its side that spun and settled when meat was placed on its stainless steel tray. Upon seeing the weight and the price per pound stuck in the meat with little stainless and red plastic clips, Mom would have him take or add a little more. The meat was then wrapped in brown butcher paper and sealed shut with wide paper tape dispensed from a machine with a large metal arm attached to its side.

The cash register sat on the sales counter and was faced in a textured looking metal. White tin tabs with large black numbers would pop into the glass window and could be seen by Gordon and my Mom as each item was priced and placed into a paper bag. Behind the register the cigarettes and chewing tobacco were displayed. Lucky Strikes, Camel, Chesterfield, Old Gold and Raleigh were a few of the popular brands in the 1950s.

Gordon kept a variety of paper bags on shelves below the cigarette display. The display was made of wood and had slightly angled slots that held twenty or more packs. When he sold one he would take it off the bottom and add fresh packs to the top. Mom smoked Camels and Lucky Strikes when she was young and in the late fifties switched to Viceroy that had filters and were better for her.

Next to the sales counter there was a freezer with a glass-sliding top that kept the Popsicles cold. There were also some boxed quarts of ice cream on the side but we always wanted Popsicles or sometimes the five-cent Yakima Big Bar.

Each of the three isles had two-sided display shelves that held all the dry goods and a single shelf on the back wall. They weren't tall and Gordon could keep an eye on kids who weren't taught to be honest by their parents. The long sidewall was where he kept the produce. It wasn't a big section and only a small part of it was refrigerated. As the seasons came and went so did Gordon's produce. I was always happiest when the apples were fresh and the Red delicious, Golden delicious and Jonathan were in season. Mom liked to cook pies with the Granny Smiths and Winesaps.

The best shelf in the store was the one closest to the sales counter which held all the candy. There were boxes and boxes of penny candy and a big selection of five-cent candy bars. Nik-L-Nip Wax Bottles, Bubble Gum Cigarettes, Sugar Lips, Chewing Gum, Clark Bars, Oh Henry Bars, Slo-Poke Jr. Suckers, Candy Buttons, Bubble Gum Cigars, Necco Wafers, Black Licorice Pipes, Chuckles Jelly Candy, Walnettos, Charms Sweet Pops, Reeds Root Beer and Butterscotch Candies were a few that made their way into my pocket and mouth.

We always walked to the Bungalow and if we needed a home delivery, Mom could call Mr. Webster and read him our grocery list. He would bring everything we wanted to our house and never charged us for the service. If money was a little tight for Mom and Dad we could charge. I remember charging popsicles and penny candy for all my friends and Mr. Webster asking, "What's your Mother going to think when she sees this bill for candy?" My reply was, "Don't worry Mr. Webster…my Mom likes us to eat things that are good for us."

BIKES 1950 - 59

What I remember about the bikes on our block was the absence of new ones. My bike was an excellent example. Dad had bought it old and had cleaned it up at his service station. He added a new seat and applied a two-tone paint job. He sanded all the rust off the chrome and hand painted it with a silver coat. After he added the new handlebar grips and aired up the fresh balloon tires, he called it "new." My father was an excellent craftsman and if he hadn't told me my bike was rebuilt, I wouldn't have known.

Some of our bikes had black tires and a few had whitewalls that were more than two inches wide. Even though our bikes were beat up, you could still appreciate the two-tone frames, built-in horn compartments, torpedo-shaped lights and shock absorbers.

One day we were amazed when some kids from Fifteenth Avenue rode by with playing cards attached with a clothespin to the fender braces of the bike's rear wheel. The card or cards, if you wanted to be extra loud, were stuck into the spokes and make a big noise like a motorcycle. When I saw what they had done, I wanted to do it better and have the hottest, noisiest bike around.

I got my first bike when I was six. It wasn't big like my permanent bike and the bars between my legs sloped down to the pedals. Some of the kids tried to tell me that it was a girl's bike, but I knew that my father wouldn't give me a girl's bike, even if it was a starter.

The world opened up to me when I started riding bikes. I learned to ride quickly and discovered that I could travel great distances despite Mom and Dad's rules. They didn't need to worry about me or know where I was. I rarely rode alone and preferred traveling in packs of three to five kids. We felt safe on our block and were always a bit on guard when we rode through other neighborhoods or downtown.

Biking as a kid was not a direct trip from one location to another. A good bike ride required jumping off of curbs, kicking rocks with dangling feet, quick turns and slides to further hone riding skills and avoid collisions with each other. We didn't keep watch, but we saw a lot.

One of our favorite places to ride, outside of our own neighborhood, was the Medical Center. It was a new brick medical complex of single story buildings covering several blocks and a short distance south of St Paul's School on Twelfth Avenue. The word was out and very clear that the Center didn't want kids on their property, especially kids on bicycles. It was a difficult rule to obey because the Center had excellent sidewalks with ramped curbs. We would lined up three or four in a row and peddle up a ramp, down the sidewalk and across the parking lot of the family practice section and then do it again by the ophthalmologist's offices. We always prided ourselves on our ability to avoid pedestrians and yet move at high speeds as we explored one medical department after another.

Most always we would, within ten minutes of entering the Medical Center, spot the arrival of a patrol car. We never knew who called and were always suspicious of the tall skinny woman with the black glasses who stood behind the counter in the pharmacy building. She never smiled and most often had a phone against her ear.

Once the police spotted us and drove in our direction we would begin displaying exceptional peddling prowess and our knowledge of the neighborhood.

During an escape we liked to stay together as we dashed through yards, up alleys and down streets. Sometimes, if the police were persistent, we would have to implement plan B and separate. We had a neighborhood code, kind of a "one for all…all for one," but sometimes a hot pursuit left us no other option.

Don't think we were looking to bait the police…we weren't. We knew someone might call them, but the fun of riding around in the Center was so over powering that the fear of being caught was placed in the backs of our minds, like most other consequences of our behavior.

Some of our bikes had kickstands that were never used. We all knew how to slide up to the feet of a friend and step away from our bike as it fell to the ground without tripping us up or hitting anyone. Our bikes would lay in piles in front of the home or yard we were playing in until it was time to move on to our next adventure or food.

Upon occasion we would violate the rule all our parents agreed upon which forbid our biking across town or down to the river. The river was dangerous and our parents wouldn't have allowed us in it even if they were along. Older kids who owned cars would inflate truck tubes and ride the river. They were bigger and stronger and still several would die every summer.

Our adventures were not for swimming but capturing critters. We would hang bags off the springs of our seats and fill them with food and the empty jars we would need to transport our captured specimens. Our rides would take hours of riding to avoid the city traffic as we worked our way across the tracks and down to the northeast part of town where the lumberyards cut and stored their products. These outings were rare and although exciting we felt uncomfortable, off our turf, and weren't often willing to put ourselves in harms way for a few frogs or salamanders. We also knew that if we were caught the punishment would be gigantic and endless.

It wasn't until I got my drivers license that I parked my bike in the carport and watched it slowly work itself to the back where all rarely used things ended up. In later years I bought a Motobecane which was French and beautiful with candy apple red paint and skinny tires. Although I loved my road bike with the little leather pouch behind the seat, it was nothing like my rebuilt and repainted American big tire bike.

YOUNG NUN 1954

She was a young nun and pretty. I liked her and felt sad to see her standing on the metal enclosures that held the heat registers. They were about three feet high and at the base of the windows. She had opened one of the windows and was crying as she said, "If you children don't stop I will jump."

Our fourth grade class was on the third floor of St. Paul's Cathedral School and we were the largest Catholic school west of the Mississippi. I don't know what Dominican nuns were trained to do, but it couldn't have been teaching. In my eight years of elementary school I did not meet a single one who was good at it. What they were good at was being mean. We had seventy-two kids in our class and most classes were large like ours. Maybe they were mean and poor teachers because their workload was so large.

The school was new, or close to new, when I entered the first grade in 1951. It was a four story building shaped like the letter L with the cafeteria and gymnasium on the short end. The top floor of the long part was where the nuns lived and us kids called it the nunnery. The three floors below the nunnery were filled with classrooms. The halls were wide and the class doors were kept closed. The building had the same concrete color inside and out. At the end of each hall there was a glass-enclosed area where you could go up or down the steps. There was asphalt everywhere outside with little play equipment except a Jungle Jim and the Tetherball poles.

The cafeteria wasn't big enough for all of us, so we ate in shifts. The lunches were hot and we had to stand in line for long periods of time as we watch for the nuns and played silly boy games. The women who worked in the kitchen wore nets on their heads and acted like nuns.

When I think about how mean everyone was at St. Paul's, I have to wonder why our parents paid to send us there. No one liked our school and it is no wonder that poor nun wanted to jump.

NAILS 1954

The street was narrow with concrete sidewalks and curbs. Over the years the hot summers and cold winters had expanded and contracted the concrete causing many sections to fracture and separate. We all knew that stepping on a crack would break our mother's back and we, without exception, jumped every one. The narrow parking strips sandwiched between the sidewalks, where we chalked out hopscotch games, and the curbs, grew grass and had a tree or two. The types of trees varied. Most were maple like the pair in front of our house. These exceptionally beautiful trees shaded our yard and provided us with more than enough fall leaves. They also supplied me with one of the most painful physics lessons a young boy of ten could imagine.

The problem was my desire to climb the tree and its lowest branches being ten feet above my head. My solution was found in my father's garage where hammer and nails were easy to find. The plan was a simple one and I was confident that in ten or fifteen minutes I would be securely perched high in our maple tree yelling down to the neighborhood kids gathered in admiration around the base.

I knew that both of my hands needed to be free in order to scale the tree's trunk and implement my plan. I had watched the men from the phone and power companies climb their poles and remembered that they had big belts that wrapped around the pole and hooked on both sides of their hips. I didn't have the belt but did have a heavy piece of rope Dad had used to tow Uncle Don's truck out of the ditch last winter. I had also noticed that the pole climbers had leather belts with slots and pockets to carry their tools. With a little searching I found an old canvas nail pouch hung on a support post in the corner of Dad's garage. The pouch was stiff and wrapped two times around my small boy belly. I filled the pouch with the big shiny nails Dad and Grandpa had used last summer to build the addition on the house. I was fearful that I might drop the hammer on one of my friends and found an old cord Dad had saved after restringing Mom's Venetian blinds. I attached one end of the cord to the hammer sling on the pouch and the other end around the neck of the hammer. Dad had kept this particular hammer when Grandma was giving away Grandpa's tools after his death.

I was ready! Dressed only in shorts and canvas shoes, one untied, I approached the larger of the two trees. The kids in the neighborhood began to gather around as I took my hammer and drove the first nail into the tree's trunk. I placed my foot on the deeply driven shaft and tossed my safety rope around the tree and tied the ends together behind me. I drove nail after nail as I climbed the spike ladder and soon I was within easy grasping distance of the lowest branch. Then, as if God had turned his back on me, the unbelievable occurred. The nail I had just driven and placed my foot upon bent. I began to slide down the bark with such force that when my foot hit the nail below…it also failed. If I hadn't lashed myself to the tree I would have taken my chances and pushed myself away from the trunk hoping for a clean fall. I had become fairly accomplished at jumping from the flat garage roof in the Cook's back yard and was confident that I would land without harm. Now the only hope of avoiding damage from the several dozen nails protruding from the tree like anxious meat hooks was to…with all my strength… stop my fall.

Squeezing and screaming I dropped the hammer, wrapped my arms tightly around the trunk and slid down until my rear bounced off the green grass and I collapsed in tears. My Mama, who was never more than a deep breath between screams away, was at my side and freeing the rope that had forced my self-mutilation. I couldn't look and could tell from my Mother's face that my injuries were more serious that the bee sting I had gotten the week before. I was off the grass and on the kitchen table quicker than our cat's dash across the yard after Dad drove over its tail.

Over eighteen nails had pushed their heads into my legs and chest. Most of the gashes were minor and several should have been stitched. My protests at being taken to the Doctor were so great that Mom complied and taped me us as best she could. When I pushed our wooden screen door open and stepped into the bright summer sun my blood stained bandages shone like badges of honor.

Today there are several scars on my legs that remind me of the physics lesson I was taught on that hot summer day.

CHINAMAN 1954

"Do you hear the bells? It's the Chinaman…it's the Chinaman." Fourteenth Avenue was a narrow street lined with maple trees. With cars parked on both sides, it was a tight squeeze for anyone else driving up the street. Hopscotch drawings covered the sidewalks and family dogs barked at noises they rarely heard.

The vegetable wagon was a weekly visitor so the dogs got to bark. The Chinaman pulled his wagon with an old horse. The wagon was green and tiered to display his homegrown vegetables. They were all there, tomatoes, potatoes, peas, beans, lettuce, onions, beats, squash and watermelons. Each was curbed by its own wooden slat and washed to brightness. The back of his box was stuffed with fresh cut flowers. Bells were hung across the bottom of his wooden seat and they announced to the neighborhood and its dogs the coming of the Chinaman. He tossed fresh peanuts on the street for us kids and not a one was left uneaten.

The tires were rubber and filled with air while the horse was a big old guy with lots of white hair around his hooves and muzzle. The loud-gated clunk of his steel shoes added to the magic of the visit. Yellow stained teeth were shared by the horse and his owner, as was slowness in their movements.

Hanging on the back of his wagon was a neighborhood skill and despite his disliking our hitching he never stopped to knock us off.

I think my Mom was afraid of the Chinaman. She would never buy his produce, not even when he stopped in front of our house. He would invite the women, who would often sit on a blanket in our yard, to come and sample his wares. Most of the others would go, but not my Mom. She was careful with what she didn't understand and she didn't understand the Chinaman.

CAN CRUNCHING 1954

Properly crunching a pop or beer can with a full sized American made bike required skill, adequate speed and body weight. If all three were not in place the can would not properly detach itself from the tire on its first passes through the bikes front yoke and the rider would be catapulted forward over the handlebars.

The steep graded road beside the school was the Pike's Peak of can crunching. My Schwinn had a spring loaded front end that enabled me to raise its front tire higher than traditional bikes. My buddies, Butch and John, would place cans in the middle of the street and hold them in place with small pebbles. We had heard stories of less experienced bikers performing this stunt without ample speed and they had catapulted themselves over their bikes and down the concrete street. We were Fourteenth Avenue Boys, who were born with skill and not concerned with the mistakes of others.

John and Butch placed several cans in place, twenty or so feet apart from each other, and when they saw I was ready, they stepped up on the curb and waved me forward. I rolled my weight over the bikes handle bar and balanced myself on both pedals. Seeing the signal I began pumping down the hill. I hadn't quite reached sonic speed when I jerked my fifty-two pounds back against the length of my extended arms. The front of my bike lifted and seemed to float for the longest time and then under my practiced guidance began its quick and decisive decent upon the first of the three cans. The tire struck directly upon the Lucky Larger label and the can was crushed. As if time had stopped I watched the can cling to the tire and refuse to release as it jammed itself into the yoke and stopped the rapid rolling of my front tire. Why this occurred is a mystery that remains unanswered today and in less then a microsecond I was catapulting. I flew so high that if I had worn my cape, prolonged flight would have occurred. Capeless…I quickly descended, grazed the concrete street and rolled to the curb leaving chunks of knee, elbow and scalp.

Despite being tough…my tears and wails escaped. My life was gushing from my body as I leapt to my feet and attempted to stop the flow of blood while running to my mother's arms. She was in the front yard and running towards me by the time I passed Johnny's house. Mom had an uncanny ability to know when my injuries were life threatening. She grabbed me up and together we examined the injuries. She was pretty upset with the ripped out knees of my new jeans. Once we were home she concentrated on pouring iodine into all my open wounds.

I returned to the front yard wrapped like a soldier of war and proud of the medicine stains that looked a lot like blood. Butch had walked my bike home and we three huddled around it to see how the unthinkable had happened to one of the Fourteenth Avenue Boys.

THE ARTIST'S HOUSE 1954

"Wake up kids," Mama whispered. "Come into our bedroom." It was the middle of the night and we were never invited into Mom and Dad's room. Rubbing my eyes I jumped off the top bunk and landed beside my brother, who had just pushed his bare foot out from under his cover. Mom wrapped a blanket around both my little brother and myself and led us to their room. The blinds were up and the window was the color of orange and sunlight.

Judy was already sitting on the bed as Steve and I climbed up beside her. The house across the street was on fire. In front of our house several people were silhouetted on the sidewalk as two more fire trucks joined the one that had arrived several minutes before. Firemen were hooking up hoses and the house was in complete flames. All the windows had exploded and fire was pushing out of them like fingers on a monsters hand. Judy had her arms wrapped around herself and started to cry. Mom and Dad sat beside us like bookends. None of us said anything as we watched.

The crowd outside our window grew and we began to talk. Mom said the Crooks were out of town and thanked God they were away and safe. Dad talked about the loss of all the paintings and how hard Don had been working in preparation for his art show. He also thought that all the artist's oil and solvents might have contributed to the fierceness of fire.

We watched the firemen drag hoses to the house and direct their water into the windows and on the roof that had just opened like the burner on a stove allowing the flame easy access into the night air. Sparks wound themselves around the streams of water and refused to submit as steam rose with the flames until the home collapsed into the rectangle formed by the block foundation.

Two of the trucks backed away leaving only one to spray a soft mist of water over what had been the home of Don Crook and his young family. Mom slid us off her bed and back into our bunks and kissed our faces as beams of morning light peeked through our bedroom curtains.

GARAGE 1954

Dad's garage was filled with great stuff. It was an old building with a warped wooden floor for most of its length. Spaces between the planks were wide enough to devourer small nuts and screws carelessly dropped. The floor sloped to the dirt at the back double doors where a car could be pulled smoothly inside, although Dad's car never saw the inside of his garage. Saws, screwdrivers, hammers, nails, drills, grinders, scroll, table and skill saws and tons of other tools filled the garage. I loved it.

I crushed my thumb, cut my fingers, sawed my hand, banged my head and stepped on nails in this temple of creation. I made apple box scooters, military and space weaponry, boxes, crossbows, wooden toy cars, buildings, wagons, traps, racecars and a few gifts for my mother.

The hub of this Mecca of manufacturing was the workbench. It was thirty-two inches tall and had a power grinder, scroll saw and vice bolted to it. Behind the bench was a bank of small pained windows that allowed the creator moments of reflection. There wasn't much light. At each end of the forty-foot building there was a light bulb that hung from rafters on two wires that were wound around each other. A flat black knob on the brass socket was the on/off switch. Turning on the bulbs was never a problem. Care was required turning them off to avoid the heat of the one hundred watt bulbs that could easily burn a boy's skin.

The shop was entered from the side through an eight-board door. Once inside the dark room I would find the apple box, step up and turn the switch on. The shine from the bare light bulbs freed my imagination, which was limited only by a shortage of material. This material shortage was the cause of much pain in my childhood. I viewed all family and neighborhood personal property as usable. I didn't consider value or ownership when my creative juices were flowing. My sister's jewelry box could easily be converted to the blower on the make believe motor in my new wooden street rod, or Dad's fishing pole could be its whip antenna. Mom's pie pans were perfect hubcaps, and our metal camping cups were just the thing for headlights. I was so innocent in this process that I would display my creation to the family with pride and was always shocked when they would roar with anger over my misuse of their treasures.

I never grew tired of my father's garage. When we moved to our new home on Thirty-First Avenue, we had a carport. A carport isn't good for creating much of anything. For several years I was without a Mecca of manufacturing, a temple of creation. At the age of twelve I began to work in my father's business. He owned a tool-filled garage that specialized in auto and truck repair. I was back home.

BEE'S IN THE PANTS 1955

"No, no, no! Don't take off my pants off," I screamed as Mom tried to pull them down in front of the neighborhood girls. My tightly fastened leather belt with the cowboy buckle and my thrashing from side to side protected what little modesty I had left. I was shamed and in pain as I rolled around on the grass with both of my hands squeezing my crotch.

We were really innocent of wrong doings, except possibly trespassing. The Palmer's home was across the street and closer to the Catholic School. They had a couple of kids and were the only couple I had ever known who were getting a divorce. Their house had a basement that wasn't a dirt tunnel system like my Dad had dug under our house. It was big and the walls and floor were concrete. All the kids in our neighborhood had seen the basement but none of us had ever been inside. Their house had windows in the foundation and if you pushed the flowers to the side and crawled up to the glass you could rub away the dirt and have a good look.

My house was built close to the ground and we had a one-step porch. The Palmer house, like a few others in the neighborhood, was taller because it had a basement and that is where my problem began.

The Palmer's front porch was big and made of concrete. It had four maybe five steps and a flat porch before the front door. Like our street, the concrete had cracked and in that crack... there were bees. We didn't know what kind of bees they were but they were yellow and there were lots of them.

We had decided that morning that we would take some of our pop bottles down to the Bungalow Grocery Store and buy balloons rather than the Bazooka Bubble Gum or jawbreakers we would normally get. We planned to fill the balloons with water and stage a World War II attack on those dirty bees. We felt OK about picking on them because, we know they weren't honeybees, and were pretty sure they were yellow jackets. I had also heard one of the kids at school say that yellow jackets would, from time to time, gang up and attack kids. We wanted to beat them to the punch.

The trip to the grocery store was uneventful and Mr. Webster, the owner of the market, warned us to be careful when we shared with him our plan. The balloons were kept in a box and Mr. Webster let us choose the colors we thought would be most effective.

Johnny, Butch and I talked a lot about our attack plan and our little brothers, Steve and Bruce, tried to chime in, but we didn't pay them much attention. On the way to my house we stopped by Butch's and got a cardboard box out of his garage to carry our water filled balloons. I guess it was our ammo box. The balloons weren't as easy to fill as we thought. Sometimes when we stretched the end of the balloon over the end of the garden hose they tore. We still tried to fill them up but found it difficult to tie the knots. When we were done we had eight red balloons, four yellow ones and a killer black one. It was the only black one Mr. Webster had in his box.

Our armed balloons were heavy so we put the ammo box in our wagon before we filled it. One by one we carefully placed them in the box and pulled it across the street and down the sidewalk. We didn't want to park the balloons too close to the porch's crack, knowing that the bees, with one poke from a stinger, could pop our limited supply of weapons. With our wagon safely in place, we each took one balloon and approached the enemy.

We were crafty and knew that these attack bees would be after us, so I planned my escape. Across the street there were two trees that had branches I could reach and quickly climb to a safe height. Bees knew that people lived close to the ground and wouldn't find me if I was high in a tree. We made our little brothers stand on the other side of the street and when we felt everything was in place we made a three point attack. Like fighter planes we charged the crack and tossed, with amazing accuracy, three red balloons. Johnny and Butch ran across the street and I executed my plan by climbing the tree and watching from my sniper position.

After two attacks we realized that our balloons were ineffective. The bees acted as if a rain bird sprinkler was splashing the entrance of their nest and continued their work. Within minutes we had discharged all our weapons including the killer black bomb with no effect.

Butch decided to uncoil the Palmers garden hose and attack like the army guys with their flame-throwers. He put the nozzle on the most powerful setting and we all, with hose in hand and one behind the other, approached the nest. Suddenly, as if some wind had blasted them out of the crack, the bees were upon us. It was a major counter attack. I didn't see where Butch and Johnny ran, but I headed back to the tree.

Quickly I climbed to one of the higher branches and settled in to watch. Suddenly…I felt a searing pain high on the inside of my thigh. "Oh, God! I've been infiltrated by bees," I squealed as I tried to climb down and was stung several more times. I grabbed the crotch of my jeans hoping to squeeze the bees to death and protect myself from further pain, when I lost my balance. With one hand I broke my fall by grabbing another branch and began screaming my distress call. "Mama.….Mama!" She was at my feet in no time, urging me to let go and fall into her arms. After several pleas and the loss of my strength I, fell into her arms. That was when she laid me on the grass and began to pants me in front of the girls.

It might have been OK if the audience was the guys, but Patty and Judy Immely had heard my scream and came running with their mother, as it seems, did every other mom on the block. My Mom was quick to recognize my predicament and was pretty sure I had the bees squeezed between my hands and the denim. She swiftly picked me up and carried me into Johnny's house, where I let her remove my pants. As if to hoist a final flag of victory, my captured yellow jackets, when I released my grasp, stung me where no little boy should be stung.

Johnny's mom shooed the bees out of her house as I tossed my jeans across the room saying that I would never wear them again. I didn't.

CARROL'S HOUSE 1955

Catholic kids pretty well knew how one should pray to God and were fascinated with the damning and dangerous religious practices of others. The Carroll family, who were very active in another faith, lived across the street from us on the corner of Tieton Drive and Fourteenth Avenue. As a kid I didn't know what their faith was...just that it wasn't Catholic so must be wrong. It was interesting that the Immelys and our family were the only Catholics on the block, and yet I had figured out a way to accept all my friends. Thinking back I don't remember if any of them went to church, except for Easter when everyone did.

The house that the Carrolls lived in had a tired old wire fence on two sides of their lot. Shrubs had grown and wound their branches through the wire, offering the fence more support than the cedar posts that had rotted away. There wasn't much paint on the house, and the lap siding had pushed itself past the thin finish giving the home a dark brown appearance.

Johnny, Butch and I liked to hide behind the Carroll's hedge and toss dirt clods into the Titeton Drive traffic. We were pretty good with our timing and could hit a car's windshield most all the time. We would lob them high in the air and let them fall to their target. This style of lobbing requiring greater skill than a straight shot and allowed us time to hide before they hit the car.

One day David, the Carroll's boy, joined us and straight shot a rock rather than a clod. We couldn't believe it when he hit and broke the windshield. It was the last time we let him play with us.

Two women, who kept their hair tightly wound around their heads like my German grandma, raised David. He dressed like the rest of us while the women and Peggy, David's sister, didn't. They wore simple dresses that were always buttoned at the neck and hemmed well below the knees. The only shoes I ever saw them wear were clunkers like my grandma's and even Peggy, who was just a girl, wore them.

My sister Judy was Peggy's best friend. They would spend nights together at our house and some times at hers. I don't remember anyone going into the Carroll house except my sister and all the other people who attended church there on Sunday and Thursday nights. These people smiled and laughed like everyone else and would have passed for good Catholics except for the way the women dressed. Sometimes they would have picnics in the front yard and everyone would sit on blankets and eat fried chicken and potato salads just like my family did.

My buddies and myself had a wonderful day playing baseball in the street and were still full of adventure when the sun set and our neighborhood began to tuck itself in for a good night's sleep. We had gotten permission from Butch's mom to sleep in their back yard and were in the process of setting up our camp when cars began pulling into the Carroll backyard for church. We crept between Butch's storage shed and his garage where we squatted down and watch. It was dark between the buildings and we enjoyed not being seen as car after car unloaded. Butch and Johnny had on dark shirts and I was concerned because mine was yellow and easy to see. I knew that if we were going to be really sneaky, I would have to be careful.

It wasn't long before the screen door closed and the sound of some church song filtered itself through the screen and into the yard where we were hiding. The people were all in the front of the house and we couldn't see them. We knew we had to get closer. On our elbows and knees we crept, like the soldiers in the newsreels, closer and closer until we were under the dining room windows. The three of us sat in the flowerbed and leaned against the side of the house as we whispered our plan. We decided that if we waited until they sang again and were all looking at their songbooks we would be able to stand up and take a good look. With our plan in place we waited and when they began singing a song about an old rock, we all stood up and put our faces against the window. It was great…we could see everything except the woman playing the piano. I had smeared some mud on the glass and it was blocking my view. I pulled my yellow sleeve over the palm of my hand and tried to rub the mud away. It was then that their God attacked me. The glass I was rubbing clean shattered and shards scattered into the house. Women screamed and men yelled, "What's going on."

Without stopping to see if we had injured ourselves we ran and ran. We finally landed in Johnny's back yard and dropped to the grass. We talked for a while and developed another plan. It wasn't safe in Butch's back yard, so we all went home. We told our Mom's that we were pretty sure it might rain and had decided to sleep in our own beds. Everything went well until the next evening when I heard my father talking with someone at the front door. He said, "Don't worry. I will be over in the morning to measure and replace the glass." How did they find me? How did they know it was me that broke the window and not Butch or Johnny?

I stepped out of my bedroom and looked at my father who asked me what I had been up to when I broke the Carroll's window. I denied doing it or any involvement at all. My father's expression was one of disappointment, but for some reason he didn't pressure for the truth.

The next day my father installed the Carroll's new window and thirty years later, I fess up.

KELLY'S LIES 1954

Kelly was a liar and I told him so. He went to public school and was in the fourth grade with Butch. He was a big blond headed boy who wanted to impress Butch and us kids who attended the Catholic school. One day his parents visited the family who lived two houses down from us and let all of us sit in their new Oldsmobile. While sitting in the car Kelly, who really wanted to impress us, told me where babies came from. He was stupid to believe what he was telling me and I wasn't dumb enough to believe him.

The kids on my block played doctor. Doctor was a once-in-a-while game that us boys and the girls seemed to like. It didn't involve much medicine, mostly exploration and peeking. I think the girls were as interested in peeking at us boys as we were at them. We seemed to know that we weren't supposed to be looking at each other and did it anyway. I don't know what the girls thought about me, but I do know what I saw and what Kelly was telling me didn't make sense.

He was telling me that my Dad would put his dick in between my Mama's legs and that was when a baby was started. He also said that after the baby got big it came out the same place. How stupid! I knew that babies grew in Mama's stomach and came out the belly button. I wasn't sure how babies got in there but was pretty sure it was because they got married. It made me mad that he felt so sure about his opinions. He must not have played doctor with the girls in his neighborhood.

Enemy Airplanes 1955

Most of the folks in Yakima thought that the tower crew at the airport was the only outfit doing the hard work of watching for enemy airplanes. The kids in my neighborhood knew differently. We had joined the cold war efforts and were prepared to warn our community of all unidentified aircraft that dared to fly over 416 South 14th Avenue or Johnny's house, which was next door. We called ourselves the Air Guard and our outlook post was built between our garage and the neighbor's, which was four feet away.

We started construction with a can of used nails, assorted in size, 2x4's in varied lengths and old fencing boards that had been stacked in the corner of Dad's garage. Although we wanted our viewing platform to be above the peeks of both garage roofs, we had to settle for the height of the roof overhangs due to a material shortage. The lower level was the office of information and records. It had a door and could be latched from the interior to protect the staff from sneak attacks. Inside, and assisted by the light that came through the picket fence, you could see our identification clipboards hanging on nails. Short sections of 2x4s were nailed directly on the neighbor's garage wall and were the steps we used to climb up to the middle level. Adults would have had a difficult time getting up to that floor, but all the members of the Air Guard were kids, so it was easy.

With the help of a knotted rope, we hung from the garage rafter that extended several feet beyond the outside wall, we were able to climb through the hole in the second floor ceiling and reach the observation deck. Once on top you could see from one end of the valley to the other. It was great.

Our main concern was that our location would be conspicuous so we utilized military camouflage. Green and brown paint was smeared on our deck in random shapes that blended well with the neighbor's vegetable garden. We didn't have the money to buy a real pair of binoculars like the ones Butch's brother brought home from Germany, but we knew that if we were going to be effective, we needed to isolate our vision. To do this we utilized cardboard toilet rolls that we taped together with black electrician's tape and painted camouflage.

To know which crafts passed through our air space proved to be our most difficult task. We cut pictures out of Life and Look magazines and pasted them on butcher paper with the critical data written below in black or blue crayola. We knew that crayola would protect the information from damage during the occasional rainstorms that passed through Yakima and that was important.

Finding good pictures of the enemy's crafts was far more difficult. We were unsure who the enemy was, although we did know they were all Communists. We also decided that there could be spies flying small crafts like Pipers and bi-planes. We kept detailed records of all our observations and planned to deliver those records to our partners in defense, the Yakima Airport.

I don't remember when our neighborhood Air Guard was decommissioned. Maybe it ended with the summer of fifty-five.

Thirty years later I drove up the alley between Thirteenth and Fourteenth Avenues and discovered that the nail holes left by that lonely outpost that kept the Yakima Valley safe during that dangerous summer were still there.

FOOTBALL 1956

It was one of the first manly sounds I loved. The shoes were black. Some were high tops; others low. On the bottom of each shoe there were half a dozen yellow colored cleats that had metal caps. Dressed in our maroon and gold uniforms, which tightly covered our shoulder and hip pads, we sounded like a herd of wild mustangs as we ran down the sidewalk towards Larsen Park where we practiced.

Boys had to be in the sixth grade before they could join the team and I was anxious to become one of the young men I had spent years watching as they ran by my house on their way to play football. We all felt grown-up as we, with helmet straps loose, waived at the neighbors as we passed by. My Mom was often on the porch smoking a cigarette, rubbing my little brother's head and waving as I jogged by, trying to keep a smile off my face in front of my teammates.

There was a lot to learn about being a football player and being friends with Jim Ibach and Bob Cole was helpful. They were natural athletes and I wasn't. I watched how they rolled their socks, put the pads in their pants, added the metal cup to their jockstrap, put tape around the ankles, and tied double knots in their shoelaces and other subtle moves that made them jocks.

I was an exceptionally tall kid with some meat on my bones. Although I couldn't throw or catch the ball, I could run over kids that were half my size. I remember Grandma, who lived in a little house next to the school, always said that spotting me on the playground was easy because I was a head taller than anyone else.

Doing the team warm-ups was fun and running with the ball felt great. What I didn't like was having my hand stepped on, or the wind knocked out of me. I really loved our games. When it was muddy, it was extra fun. Trotting home with dirt all over my uniform filled me with pride. I was even proud of the cuts and bruises, once they quit hurting.

With game or practice completed, we would all hang our uniforms up in our lockers and shower together. Lots of towels were snapped and the camaraderie between us boys grew. It was a very good thing.

Red Flyer 1956

The four seasons were as much a part of Yakima as apples and the State Fair. There was snow in the winter and the summer days were long and hot. I remember winters when the snow stacked in the middle of Yakima Avenue was so high it was difficult to see cars on the other side. St. Paul's hill was where we did most of our sledding and on rare occasions we would hike up to the Franklin Terraces beside the Junior High School. They were steep and very dangerous.

The area Junior High was named Franklin and it was built on ten city blocks of property with the terraces on the north side of the football field. There were two sets of terraces separated by a forty-foot wide flat decline. That decline was where the test of a boy's courage began.

I remember well the first night I stood at the top of that fifty-yard decline with my new red flyer in tow. There were round oil pots burning on the streets edge and traffic signs blocked the cars. Adults brought wood, built hand warming fires on the frozen ground and had thermoses filled with coffee and hot chocolate. I was delighted to be there with my family and didn't lose that feeling until Dad and I walked to the edge of the hilltop and realized the bottom was fifty yards away and the decline was close to forty-five degrees.

Dad wanted me to have fun and didn't push me to exceed my comfort level. He offered to push me and gave me that "its ok if you don't do it" look. It was the first time that I remember been afraid to do something adventuresome. I had made a big deal of asking Dad too take us to this hill and felt I had to conquer it or shame myself in his eyes. Mom looked at me and smiled. Mom never smiled when there was danger around so I felt bolstered.

Encouraged by my parents' confidence in my ability, I slowly dragged my sled to the edge of the hill. "Do you want to sit or lay on you sled, Son?" were Dad's words. What a choice! I could break my legs or my head. I chose the prone position knowing that my head had proven to be pretty hard in the past. I was tightly wrapped with two pairs of gloves, thick socks, a couple pair of pants, three shirts and a hat that looked like a baseball cap with flaps.

As I lay down, I tucked my towrope under my stomach, centered myself on the sled, got a good grasp on the wooden guides and took a deep breath. Dad said, "Are you ready, Son?" "OK, Dad," I said, "Let's go." My father was very strong and could do everything better than other Dads. He gave me one hard push and I was on my way. As I slid at rocket speed to my right I checked my steering and it was slow but effective. I was less than a third of the way down and ten feet right of a straight decent when I spotted a ramp that several high school boys had build as a truck tube jump. "Oh God!" I screamed. That was something that Dad would say when he was upset, and as I drew closer to the jump…I was upset.

I tried to miss the jump and hit it at an angle with one of my runners. The sled, with me holding on tightly, left the snow and flew through the air. At first I kept my eyes closed. When I felt myself roll in the air, I peeked and saw the sky through my runners. For a few moments…time disappeared. I knew that I had crashed and that I had slid, apart from my red flyer, to the bottom of the hill. I know that I cried for a while and I also know that Dad ran all the way down the hill in his zipped rubber galoshes. What I didn't know at the time was that the other kids thought my crash was cool. When I shared my adventure with Butch and John, they were very impressed and for a while, I was the sledding Evil Knieval…a small price to pay for fame.

Franklin hill provided me with years of winter pleasure. When I was sixteen, several of my high school buddies and myself built a jump in the middle of the run for our truck tubes. Keeping the little kids off the ramp was our biggest problem.

GO CARTS 1956

Dad was a mechanic. He knew how things worked and how to maintain and repair them. He had strong feelings about Steve and I not choosing his profession, but did want us to know about motors, cars, and trucks.

We were always trying to talk him into helping us build something we could drive up and down our street. It was before the days of go-carts, but we knew our Dad could help us create something with a motor that would be fun.

The undertaking started with an old reel mower that had cut its last blade of grass some years before and was shoved into the back of the carport. It had a good motor, so Dad, with our help, knocked the blades off and mounted a couple of 2x4s to the front of the mower with nuts and bolts. Dad would drill the holes, and then Steve and I would push the bolts through and tighten them up.

Dad's week was hard and we understood that he was often too tired to work on the cart. He did set aside several Saturday afternoons and a Sunday or two, and together we built a marvelous rig.

It ended up looking like a soapbox derby racer with a lawn mower chasing it. No one had ever seen anything like it. It wasn't handsome... but performed very well. Steve and I spent many hours grinding the rubber off its little steel wheels ripping up and down Thirty-First Avenue. Several times Dad took the wheels to a tire retread shop and had new rubber wrapped around them.

We would start the motor by yanking on the pull rope, and then we would jump in, grab the steering ropes, and stomp on the gas. The centrifugal clutch allowed the motor to idle without moving the cart. It went pretty fast and if you weren't careful turning, you could flip it on its side.

Dad rigged up a simple wooden plate for braking. There was a handle on the side and with a hard, pull the plate would drag under the cart and you would stop...kind of. We didn't use the brake much, but were glad it was there for the really big emergencies. Like everything mechanical, the old mower motor died one day. It could have stopped because of its age, or our being too anxious to drive it and not checking the oil.

Steve and I were hooked. We wanted another cart...bigger and better. Dad agreed and began drawing pictures of our new rig. He tried to involve us, yet would most often do what needed to be done without our help. Steve and I would boast to our friends that we had built it with our Dad, but what we did most was watch, and that wasn't bad.

The second racer went through many modifications before it looked like most of the go-carts you could buy in stores. We hadn't seen the factory made carts, so our first prototype didn't look much like them. It was long and high not low and short. Dad didn't want its bottom dragging across rocks, and wanted to drive it himself, having space for his long legs. Unlike the mower, this cart was metal with real wheels and inflated tires. The motor was a yellow Briggs and Stratton two and one half horse that we bolted to the metal frame and ran a chain to the left rear wheel sprocket. The steering wheel looked like it belonged on a real racecar and didn't have ropes.

We would pick up and push our cart into the back of Dad's pick-up, drive to the school grounds and race. It was great fun taking turns and learning how to power slide and wind through the boxes we would set up for our skill course.

When factory go-carts became popular in 1956, we realized that we didn't look like the other guys and I felt embarrassed when we showed up to race at the new cart track they built by the river. Appreciating the better design of the factory carts, Dad took ours back to the welder, lowered the frame and made it so short he had a difficult time driving it. Now we were competitors and compete we did.

After a summer of racing, we took our cart apart and rebuilt it. Because I was older and more skillful with my hands, Dad taught me how to port and relieve the little motor, and we got a different carburetor. We gave it a new paint job of bright yellow paint and when the winter weather passed and the racing started again, we were quick and pretty. I remember sliding around the corners and reaching back behind myself to adjust the fuel in an effort to capture its maximum speed.

After my twelfth birthday I began working Saturday mornings at Dad's station cleaning up and changing tires. On Saturday afternoons, after Dad and I had worked the morning, we would get Steve, load the cart in the pickup truck, and drive to the track. Other carts would show up, and we would often beat them. We were extremely proud of our bright yellow go-cart.

Things changed when the factories made live axles and added bigger motors. Winning became difficult. I remember one day when I couldn't catch some kid in his hot new cart. We went around and around the kidney shaped track, sliding on every corner, and I couldn't pass him. Finally on the last lap of our race, I cast all caution to the wind and tried to take him on the outside of the last corner in front of the grandstands. There was a little gravel on the track and I lost control. When my cart left the track I was probably close to my top speed of forty mph. The front wheels didn't negotiate the corner and I hit the 1x8 inch fence that protected the folks in the stands. The board snapped, smashed my hands, and pushed my steering wheel over before it slapped against my chest and broke the back of my seat. I landed on the benches not ten feet from my father. I couldn't breathe. Dad was beside me in a moment and flipped the cart to the side. I had torn flesh off my chin, and the motor's muffler had burned my forearm.

A lot of fuss was made. Before long though, I was reliving my accident to an audience of boys and their fathers who were glad to listen, and happy that I was OK. We repaired the damage to our cart and raced some more that year. During the winter months, like the mower we started with, the cart worked itself to the back of the carport and wasn't used again.

Both Steve and I learned a lot about the workings of mechanical things during our cart seasons. Several years later, Dad gave it away. I was always disappointed that we never took a picture of it.

BOY SCOUTS 1956

Many of my friends were boy scouts and I wanted to be one. Learning about camping and surviving in the woods sounded like great fun. I also thought the uniforms were neat, with their merit badges, and I wanted to make a clasp for my scout scarf out of a cow vertebra my uncle had given me. My friend, John, had joined a troop that held its meetings at Nob Hill School every Wednesday night, and that was just a couple of blocks from my house.

I joined to discover that scouting was what I had hoped it would be. Our scoutmaster and his assistant were smart men who knew almost as much about the outdoors as my Dad. They wanted us to have a good time and learn something while we were at it. I did, and I also discovered the troop bully.

I wasn't an aggressive kid. I liked to play, laugh, and have fun. Being tall and having weight on my bones gave me an older look, and that must have threatened Darrell. He was a couple of years older than me and didn't like me from the beginning.

I liked my new shirt and the red and gold scarf I kept tied around my neck with the newly varnished vertebra. With my shirt and tie freshly washed and pressed by my mom, I was proud to stand tall and straight as we scouts stood in line and recited the pledge of allegiance and the scout motto.

After a couple of weeks my shyness passed and I felt comfortable being myself. I had developed new friendships, felt accepted, and it was easy for me to lean towards leadership. It was then that I found myself at odds with Darrell, who had been running the show for a long time. He began with a little bumping and pushing. I felt forced to defend myself and pushed back. That wasn't OK with Darrell. He grabbed me by my ironed scarf, pulled my face close to his, and threatened me until the scoutmaster intervened and pulled us apart. "I will get you after the meeting," were his words as we were instructed to break it up and get along with each other.

I hated the thought of fighting and didn't think I would be very good at it. The balance of that meeting I spent with a knot in my gut, fearful that I would not be able to charge out the door fast enough to escape Darrell. I knew that if I got to the end of the walkway, I could disappear into the darkness. Getting out the door would be the difficult part.

If my scoutmaster had known about my plight, he would have given me a merit badge for my quick attempt to escape. But I wasn't fast enough and found myself pinned between the bricked wall of the school gym and Darrell. Two quick punches to my soft boy stomach and I was on my knees. I hated the weakness of my tears and knew that the others were watching. Darrell walked away from me that night satisfied that he had conquered me and he had. It was my last scout meeting with that troop, and my only memory of being beaten.

MOUNT CLEMENS 1957

Even though my first experience with scouting had ended with my being attacked by the troop bully, my desire to be a scout hadn't diminished. I found a new troop at another school, Mom bought me the blue scarf they wore, and I went on my first outing. It changed my life.

The Mt. Clemens mountain range framed one side of the Yakima Valley, and the scouts were hiking it in the middle of August. The hills were very dry, so there was much talk of snakes, specifically rattlesnakes. The hills were filled with them, and knowing how to identify dangerous snakes was a part of our educational experience.

With pride we wore our tan shorts with our scout shirts and colorful scarves. One of the guys carried our troop standards on a shaft, and we walked in line as best we could. We were a handsome group of boys. When something of interest was observed, like a horned toad or a lizard, we would stop, circle round it and inspect. The weather was beautiful and we saw lots of animal life as the sun baked the rocks and dirt that compose the range.

Our day had been full and we had accomplished many tasks that would earn us new merit badges. After the last break and before we descended the mountain, we were told that we could find our own way down if we stayed in pairs. Mack and I lived on the same street and were best of friends, so we teamed up to begin our descent towards the cars that were parked at the base of the mountain and looked like little toys.

Snakes love hot rocks and they also like the protection of ravines. Mack and I knew this, but were more interested in being the first to the cars than being cautious. We stopped in the bottom of a ravine half way down the face of the mountain to drink from our official Boy Scout canteens when we heard disquieting sounds. We froze. It was the same sound our scoutmaster made when he shook the snake rattle he had brought in his pocket. It was the warning. It was the announcement of your death.

We were standing beside several hot slabs of basalt and on the basalt were snakes. These snakes were coiled up, looking at us while their tails rattled. The scoutmaster had said that if you come upon a snake...stop and slowly back away being careful to not fall. Both Mack and I screamed and ran. There were snakes everywhere. My feet did not touch the ground for the next five hundred feet, as we flew down the hill, escaping with our lives. I had never before had such strength and grace as I skimmed rocks and tumbleweeds on my descent. We were covered with sweat and gasping like distance runners when we reached the parking lot. We hadn't talked since seeing the snakes. The only sound that had escaped our mouths was our conjoined screams. Mack grabbed me by my arm as he bent over and gasped for air. "Did you see that Jim? There must have been a million of them!"

I always enjoyed, and continue to appreciate the beautiful mountains around the Yakima Valley, and never again felt comfortable hiking them. In my teenage years I drove my yellow jeep across those ridges, but never stopped. I seemed to have lost my interest in hiking around snakes.

Ahtanum Creek 1957

Shortly after we moved from Fourteenth to Thirty-First Avenue, we discovered Ahtanum Creek. Johnny and his little brother Bruce had moved to Thirty-First a year before our family, and introduced us to several other guys who were always looking for an adventure.

During the summer months, we slept out in each other's back yards and filled our days with bike rides and swimming. We were pretty free to do what we wanted after we mowed our lawns and took out the garbage. Sometimes we would help each other mow so we could escape sooner and do something fun. It must have been entertaining for our moms to watch three boys with their own mowers cutting one yard at the same time.

Eight or nine blocks south of our home and next to the airport, there was a small creek. It wound between several farms and the commercial builds attached to the Yakima Airport. Unlike most of the land in the valley, both sides of the creek were natural and overgrown with a variety of trees and underbrush.

The ride from my house to the creek was a little over a mile and easy. It was mostly down hill, and the only busy street we had to cross was Nob Hill Boulevard. Once across the Boulevard, we would ride a couple of blocks west then down Thirty-Fourth to a farmer's field beside the creek. We would hide our bikes in the corn and hike through the weeds and trees on a path that was hard packed by other kids, who had visited the creek before us. The best swimming hole in the world was just a hundred yards down the stream.

Some kids in years gone by had blocked the creek with boulders and smaller rocks. As the years passed, debris filled most of the space between the rocks and formed a dam. Behind the dam a deep and cool swimming hole developed with all the natural wonders such a pool should have. Beside it, a stately and sculptural Madrone tree gripped the bank with widely spread roots that held the massive forty-foot tree in place. One of its branches reached across the pond and to it, a rope was tied. The rope was big and bleached by years of use and weather. Massive knots were tied on its end and strands of it dragged through the water with every swing.

While the valley suffered day after day from temperatures above one hundred degrees, we would escape to swimming, searching for fish and crawdads, swinging on the tattered rope, and loving Ahtanum Creek.

We could spend hours catching little fish and crawdads. A variety of jars and cans were packed with us to transport our catch back to our homes. I remember digging a hole in Mom's garden and filling it with water to create a new home for my freshly captured crawdads. They always died. Many animals I experimented with died. It was never my intention to do them harm, and I always felt bad.

When I turned twelve, my Dad took me to work with him during the summer months and I stopped visiting Ahtanum Creek. The recollections of swinging to the middle of the swimming hole and dropping into its cool water will always be a favorite memory.

PINK PONTIAC 1958

Washing the car was a good thing. Washing it with Spic & Span wasn't. Mom and Dad loved their 1957 Pontiac Chieftain. It was the closest to new they had ever owned. The four-door car was capped with a white hardtop. The body was painted a fabulous Carib coral, and a wide stripe of white ran down the sides. Carib coral looks much like pink and was beautiful next to the super chrome package the car sported. I was fourteen and when I sat behind the wheel of the Chieftain, I felt like a grown man.

I don't remember how I manipulated my parents into allowing me to drive their car...but I did. My trips weren't long, but they were exciting. I would always find the car locked and in the middle of the driveway. Both Mom and Dad liked to park it in the same spot. I would open the door and easily slide behind the smooth round wheel. The horn ring was chrome, and in the center of the wheel was a sleek oval design sporting the golden word...Pontiac. I would then slip the proper key into the ignition, next to the lighter, and to the right of the large round instruments below the speedometer. One turn of the key and the powerful V8 would leap to life. It never failed me. Slowly I would check all the mechanics; fuel level, charging amperage, oil pressure and water temperature. The steady click of the signal indicator assured me that all lamps were in proper working order. Behind me was Thirty-First Street, and down the drive and past the house was the carport. In total the driveway was sixty-eight feet long and twenty-one feet wide. It narrowed to twelve feet by the side of the house before it opened up again and ran into the carport.

Mom would often stand in the front window, with her arms folded over her chest, and watch me through her rhinestone-edged glasses. I always began the same way. I would lower the driver's window and place my left arm on the top of the door being careful not to burn myself if it was a hot summer day. Then, I would grasp the long fluted shifting shaft on the right of the wheel and move it into reverse. With my foot on the brake, I would glance in the rear view mirror, apply pressure with my foot on the gas peddle, and slowly begin backing until I felt the rear wheels settle into the concrete rain gutter between the street and the drive. It was then that I would know that I had reached the maximum driving distance in reverse. Next, I would move the shifter to drive and slowly move down the driveway until I reached the gates Dad had built on the front of the carport.

It always felt good when I had successfully driven the full driveway. I would repeat my trek from the curb to the carport countless times. Mom was liberal with my driving time and wouldn't ask me to stop until the tires, for some unknowable reason, would begin to squeal.

The only damage the car experienced under my care was the loss of its shine when I washed it with Spic & Span rather than car washing soap. For that I was eternally sorry.

FIRST CAR 1960

It was new or very close to new when Mom and Dad purchased the 1953 Ford. Dad owned Clarks Service Station, so he knew the Ford experienced seven years of easy driving and regular maintenance. She was a pretty little car with a tan top and bronze body. My father prided himself on keeping his cars stock and refused to hang the fuzzy dice I purchased him on the rear view mirror, although he thought they looked fine in the old truck we used as a service vehicle at the service station.

When the Ford became the family's second car, my big sister, Judy, drove it around for a year or two. When she went away to college and I got my driver license, the car became mine, or that was the thinking in my head. My parents probably still considered it the family second car, but no one else ever sat behind the wheel again.

She was washed and waxed and wiped down daily with a special rag I kept in the trunk. Slowly her appearance began to change. The Ford hubcaps disappeared, and baby moons with deep chrome rings replaced them. Black wall tires were replaced with white. An OOO GAH horn found its way under the shiny hood. The three vertical lines on both sides of the bullet-like grill were painted tan to match the roof, and the parking/signal lamps were replaced with amber bulbs shortly before the tail light lenses were improved with the addition of the long, pointed Cadillac lenses. New seat covers with a roll and pleat pattern were installed. The column shifter disappeared and was replaced with a Hurst floor shifter and a custom ball. The quiet hum of the V8 flathead motor my father enjoyed was replaced with the intoxicating roar of duel pipes with Cherry Bomb Glass packs. A pair of gorgeous chrome pipes rode just below the bumper that wrapped itself around the rear of the car. A welder's torch found itself cutting coils out of the front suspension, dropping the bumper within inches of the street. Custom frames surrounded the license plates, and a fuzzy brown dog with flashing red eyes sat in the rear window, letting everyone behind me know where this young buck with the cool little Ford was going.

For sixteen months she served me well, and her steamed windows knew many of my girlfriends. For unknowable reasons the rear tires would lose their rubber in months, and the rumbling of my pipes always informed all our neighbors that my dates were over and I was coming home.

When I began to purchase my own cars, Dad didn't know what to do with the Ford. He wouldn't be seen in it, and Mom thought it was impossible to drive. Johnny, my childhood buddy, made Dad an offer and it sold. I watched it sit in front of Johnny's house, where he, and then his little brother, Bruce, used it until it was tired and only good for junk yard parts.

HIGH SCHOOL FOOTBALL 1961-63

He had the name of a gangster and wasn't the easiest guy to like. Coach Dutch Schulz was his name, and he was short, wide and from one of the blonde-haired-blue-eyed countries. I respected him. His assistant was Glynn Moore, a noisy man who was much easier to like.

I had played football for several years when I joined the A.C. Davis team, and had always played in the backfield. I was big, so it was hard to bring me down. I didn't have the talent to throw the ball, but I could hang on to it and run over my competitors.

Dutch was quick to appreciate that the only thing I had going for me was my size, and at this level of the sport, there were lots of guys bigger and better. I became a tackle, with number eleven emblazoned on my jersey. We were Pirates. Our school colors were black and orange. On the sides of our orange helmets we sported white skulls and crossbones. The vertical black and white striped knee-high socks locked in the Pirate look. That year our basketball team wore the same socks. I've never seen socks like them on any other team, and I think that is probably a good thing.

I attended Central Catholic High School for my ninth grade year, and when I decided to move into the public school system, I got to pick between Eisenhower and Davis. Davis was a racially mixed school, and all predictors believed that they could be state football champions. Eisenhower was a very white school, and had an unexceptional team.

Johnny had moved up to Thirty-First Avenue before our family, and chose to attend Eisenhower. Butch and all of my other childhood buddies went to Davis and I, after years in Catholic schools, was finally able to attend public school with them.

The high school was on the west side of Lyons Park and the old Yakima Creamery. Down the block and on the south side of the park was a concrete building that was constructed under stadium seats. That was our locker room. It stank. I had never, before or since, smelled a locker room as bad as that one.

After class we would file into the building and begin the process of suiting up. There was lots of white tape, Tough Skin, and additional pads that were worn. We practiced on the field next to the locker room. It was there that we perfected our plays and pushed the tackling sled, with endless shoulder blows. Our games were played in the new stadium next to Eisenhower High School…our cross-town rival. We worked hard. Some of us excelled…other didn't. Some of us loved the game… others played it for different reasons.

What made playing great for me was the black letterman jacket with the big orange D and my name across the chest. There were many cold winter days when my hands and fingers threatened to shatter under someone's grinding cleat or when the coach would hit me and push me in the direction I should have pushed my opponent. I would have preferred being with my girlfriend doing anything else, but I endured. The game changed us and friendships grew. Dutch was known to say, "In your life there will be difficult times and you will remember what you accomplished on this field. You will remember that you are capable of doing difficult things. You are capable of victory."

When I was a junior, we had an excellent team, but in my senior year, we lost to Eisenhower…despite our being the city's toughest team.

GIRLFRIENDS 1960-64

I discovered girls in a handholding way when I was twelve. It seemed that the boys in our Catholic school were interested in kissing and dark room parties a year to two before my neighborhood buddies that attended public schools. The first girl to move my heart was Patricia and it occurred when she kissed me. Patricia was, like me, taller than most of the other students. She had a birthday party at her home and invited me to come. She played records on her phonograph, and we danced to Elvis. I think she liked it that I was taller than her. We played all the games, and ate the cake and ice cream, and then, just as I was leaving, she kissed me. I couldn't believe it. I peddled my bike home and charged into our house interrupting my mother and several of her lady friends saying, "She kissed me Mom. She kissed me right here on my lips." Mom and her lady friends smiled.

Several years later Punkie, one of the senior cheerleaders at Central Catholic High School, decided, even though I was only fifteen, and a sophomore, that I was worth her time. We attended school dances, games, and caught an occasional movie together. My buddies couldn't believe that she was willing to pick me up and run us around in her car. I felt very grown up. Our scandalous relationship came to an end after a few months, and shortly before we would have been ushered into the Headmaster's office.

Later, because of love, I did end up in the Headmaster's office. Her name was Sue, and she had the most beautiful eyes and glossy black hair. We walked everywhere together and were a serious item in the halls of our school. Sue liked to live on the edge and that was what I liked most about her. She wore makeup and her Scarlett Johansson lips were exceptionally wonderful with red lipstick and smiling.

Suzie broke many rules and the one that got her in trouble had to do with wearing hose without seams. She thought that her ninth grade legs looked good in seamless nylons and I agreed. She was called into the Headmaster's office and warned. Towards the end of our freshman year, she wore the nylons for a second time, and they expelled her. She didn't seem to care, but I was indignant and complained to the Headmaster. He wouldn't change his mind, so I and withdrew from Central and began a new academic career at A.C. Davis High School.

Sometime during the summer Sue met a guy with a car. Although she loved me, he had something I couldn't offer her, and he took her away. Again I suffered the pains of love until I met Randa, a blue eyed blonde haired beauty, who came into my life just about the time I got my driver's license. Randa was my drive-in sweetheart. She liked kissing more than most and loved hanging out with me. She was also the girl who discovered with me the freedom of having a car. We parked everywhere and were always fearful that someone would catch us behind our steamed up windows.

I loved girls and was never more that a week or so out of a relationship. Some relationships were short and playful, while others were more serious and lasted months. They were all filled with youthful laughter and adventures and, although I enjoyed steaming up car windows, I was never willing to take the chance of being a dad. I surprised myself when my twenty-first birthday arrived and I still hadn't.

The love of my high school years was Suzie Gould. She was a year younger than me, and was one of the Eisenhower cheerleaders. She was tall, blonde, with a gorgeous smile that filled her face. Her parents liked me, and saw as much of me as they did of their daughter. Suzie and I were inseparable. We took long drives in my fifty-three Ford, and later we drove off road in my old yellow Jeep that I named Suzie II, in big black letters across its front. Hours were spent dragging the gut and waving at our friends and stopping at Don's or the Dairy Queen. We watched movies and parked at the drive-in. Once we drove to Portland, Oregon where she marched in the Rose Parade. We danced the Hand Jive, Locomotion, Twist, Mashed Potatoes and the Stroll. I wasn't a masterful dancer, but once the floor started to fill, I would take my place and do my best at being cool. Suzie was always cool, and I was proud to be with her. We also spent lots of time looking for the perfect place to park and neck. I remember driving home after walking her to her door with lips that were numb from use.

At the end of the summer of sixty-four, I had completed my first year of junior college and she left Yakima to attend the University of Washington in Seattle. Our relationship ended, and I grieved for several weeks before I began to date again.

Women continue to delight me. There is something about the way they are in the world that keeps me interested and wondering. Loving women has brought me great joy and devastating sadness. The price has been well worth the paying.

OLD YELLOW JEEP 1961

I found the Jeep, a 1946 Willys CJ2A, on a lot behind the bottling plant on South First Street. It wasn't much to look at, although the body was in pretty good shape, with a fresh yellow paint job. The top, an old bolt-on, was painted white, with little square windows on the sides and back. Military lugs were on the rig when I bought it. They were old and badly worn. The front seats and the two-person jump seat in the back had been reupholstered in red vinyl. With the yellow exterior, the Jeep looked like it belonged to the Denver Nuggets. The motor was a four cylinder flat head covered with dirt. It started with the first turn of the key and push of the foot starter.

I had sold the 1953 Ford to Johnny and was looking for a new adventure. Several of my friends owned Jeeps and were spending their weekends off road in the mountains driving over and through country that was rarely seen. I wanted to join them.

I bought the Jeep for a few hundred hard-earned bucks, and began the same "fix-it-up" process I had done with the Ford. The first thing that disappeared was the top. Other than the winter days I drove up to White Pass to ski, I kept it off and stored in the back room of Dad's shop. Sun, rain, snow and cold had easy access to me, and I liked it that way. It was fun driving by folks who were trying to keep themselves warm in their cars and me with my head in the wind bundled up like an Eskimo. Their smiles and slight headshakes encouraged me to tough it out, no matter how bad the weather got.

Two months after I bought her, the Jeep looking like a different rig. She had reversed Mercury wheels with wide lugged tires. The welder created a custom roll bar that I painted black. The muffler was removed and replaced with a heavy steel four-inch pipe across the back. While in town I kept drilled out caps on the ends and when we were in the woods, I would remove them and enjoy the rumble of the motor. The sheet metal shop made some custom half doors that kept the draft away from my legs, and I bolted the tailgate shut, mounted the spare in the middle, and added matching red five-gallon fuel tanks on both sides. With new recessed taillights and a 1955 Buick wheel cover on the spare, the rear end looked great. A very long whip antenna with a large coil base was also mounted on the back. The Cadillac radio I had salvaged from a wreck sounded great, and impressed my girl friends when we were high in the mountains or deep in the woods.

During the 1960's Jeeping was a great Yakima sport. There were several clubs and lots of owners who fancied up their rigs and prowled the countryside. I remember hot summer days and driving across the twisted dirt road that laced itself across the top of Ahtanum Ridge. With my windshield down and lashed to the grill, I drove at foolish speeds and delighted in the squeals of my girlfriends. There was never a sign of life on the ridge, besides a few snakes and the plume of dust rising behind my speeding rig.

In the spring, when the high mountain snows began to melt, a couple of buddies and I would begin to break through the snow on Clear Lake Road. Every weekend for weeks, we would drive as far up the road as we could, in an attempt to reach the lake. The road was covered with massive snowdrifts. We would take turns and spend hours driving our Jeeps against the snow until we were able to punch through and take on the next drift. The first Jeeper to reach the lake's edge received great honor.

The games we played in high mountain meadows, chasing each other around and attempting to crush each other's five-gallon gas tanks, would today be criminal offenses. Then, we were just a bunch of rambunctious boys playing games in the woods.

BOB DYLAN 1962

There were many wonderful songs in the early sixties. "Surfin' U.S.A." by the Beach Boys, "Sugar Shack" by Jimmy Gilmer and The Fireballs, Skeeter Davis's "The End Of The World," "Rhythm Of The Rain" by the Cascades, "Hey Paula" by Paul and Paula, and Bobby Vinton's "Blue Velvet."

I loved them all! One weekend I drove to Ellensburg, Washington to see Peter, Paul and Mary perform "Puff the Magic Dragon" and "Blowin' In The Wind." It was my first concert, and fabulous.

In 1962 I discovered Bob Dylan and considered myself extremely cool to be one of the first to love his music. His voice wasn't much but his protest songs rang true in my heart, and continue to do so today.

SKI CLUB 1963

Only a handful of Davis High School students were interested in skiing, and I was one of them. Tom Dills, Bill Mullen, Sue Day, and I formed a club during our senior year, and took several trips to White Pass.

I bought myself a pair of Fisher downhill skis that stood seven feet tall and had long thong heel bindings and Marker toes. They were yellow, and I felt very like a professional packing them from my car to the ticket booth. When strapped to my boots, I discovered that, at my skill level, they were almost impossible to turn.

Tom had been skiing for years and was willing to spend a small part of his morning teaching me the ropes on the Bunny Hill. Tom liked to drink and presumed that skiing was impossible without a little wine. As we scooted across the snow towards the hill he hung a full wine bota around my neck. "This will make learning to ski much more fun," were his encouraging words.

The day was clear and beautiful. The sky was robin egg blue and the snow was crunchy corn and easy to slide across. Tom showed me a couple of basic turns and quickly took off with Sue to the chairlift to make a couple of runs downhill.

I wasn't much of a drinker, and appreciated the additional pad the bota offered during my numerous falls. With twelve or thirteen runs up and down the Bunny Hill behind me, Tom and Sue showed up and asked me to join them for lunch. They both commented on my accomplishments and encouraged me to take the chairlift to one of the easy mountain runs.

Courage wasn't my problem, so in no time at all the chair swept behind Tom and me and we were on the way up the mountain. The ride was a wonderful adventure in itself. When the time came to ski off the chairlift, I delighted myself when I did it without falling. Tom led me across the top of the mountain to a well-packed trail that wandered into the woods. "Just follow me and do what I do and you will be OK," were his words, as he and Sue shoved off ahead of me. Again, I did well and loved being in the woods, skiing down a narrow path that rose and fell much like a small roller coaster as it wound itself down and through the trees.

The trail lasted for several delightful minutes and my confidence was high. I was a skier. Suddenly the trees were behind us and we were standing on the top edge of a huge white bowl that was steep and dangerous looking. It was much steeper than the Bunny Hill and I didn't know how to stop. Tom reminded me of the stem turn I had been doing all morning and said, "If you need to stop just keep your feet apart, put the tip of your skis together and squat. You will stop." I trusted Tom and shoved off behind him and Sue. They both fearlessly zipped down the hill and stopped at the bottom of the bowl. I was only half way down when I heard Tom's voice, "Let your skis run and snow plow when you get close to us." I straightened them out and it was thrilled to go fast.

There were several dozen people standing with Tom and Sue. They were at the entrance of a catwalk that zig zagged down a very steep cliff and were waiting their turn to ski it and give me further instructions. My speed had accelerated and when I began to snowplow, I didn't slow down. The snow was hard packed and my edges weren't cutting in. I dropped to my butt and screamed, "Get out of my way! I can't stop!" I then grabbed the base of my poles and jammed the tips into the snow behind me as I stretched out on my back. It was in this position that I flew beside and beyond Tom and Sue. They watched as I flew off the cliff screaming like a lost soul dropping into the pit of hell.

While falling I looked behind myself and could see skiers working themselves down the cliff on the catwalk and wondered if I would survive the drop, and which of them would reach my body first. My first contact with the snow occurred hundreds of feet below the point where I, in a full prone position with outstretched arms, launched myself. Both skis came off and began beating me, as the leather straps I had wrapped around my boots did their job and kept the skis from running free and hurting someone else.

I bounced, rolled, and slid until I came to a stop so far from the beginning of my jump that the people standing at that point were too small to recognize.

I was OK. The only problem I had was the absence of air in my lungs. I gasped and gasped as I sat up and tried to compose myself. In moments the ski patrol was at my side asking if I was OK. They may have thought that I was a master skier who had lost his luck upon landing. With my assurance that I was OK, they skied on, with their body basket empty and in tow. Shortly Sue and Tom joined me as I lashed my skis back on my boots. "Wow!" said Tom. "I have never seen anyone ski off that ledge before." I thought it was kind of him to describe what I did as skiing.

MGA 1963

Standing back with a smile on my face and hands on my hips I said, "Ohhh! Look at her." My high school days were over. I was about to start college, and I had purchased my dream car. Following a long summer of hard work, saving as much money as I could, and selling my beloved Jeep, I bought a mint green 1961 MGA roadster. Her wheels were spoked with knock-off hubs, after factory chrome bumper bars had been added to the front, and a powerful road lamp was mounted on the driver's side of the grill. Within weeks of ownership, I added white racing stripes to the driver's side, like the Le Mans racing cars. The Tonneau Cover, soft canvas top, and matching fiberglass hardtop were like new. The interior dash was covered with instrumentation, and I soon added more. I installed a state-of-the-art radio, and extra switch panels.

The car was so cool I could hardly stand it. When I sat behind the wire spoke steering wheel, I loved being alive. The motor had a wonderful rumble, and the short shift gearbox made driving feel like racing.

Girls loved the MGA, and so did my little brother, Steve. At night, after I had returned home from my dates, my little brother would sneak out of the house, unlock my car and roll it down the street. He had made a copy of the car's key, and wouldn't start the motor until he had rolled down the hill and out of hearing range. He continued this behavior for the several years I owned the car and didn't fess up until he was in his thirties. Once he bent the bumper and spent the entire night in one of his friend's garage, repairing the damage that I never noticed.

I took many trips in this car. Several times I drove down to San Francisco to visit my sister. Other times, I found myself zipping up and down the Oregon and Washington coasts. I would clip a luggage rack on the top of the trunk lid, fill it up with suitcases, grab a travel mate, and drive down the road with my sunglasses on, a smile on my face and my head in the wind.

I would have kept this car for years if it hadn't been for the high cost of the insurance, which punished me for being young and driving a sports car. When I sold her, my heart broke as I watched someone's young daughter drive her down the street. I heard that she lost control of the car on a sharp corner and totaled it. Sad.

A.C. DAVIS HIGH SCHOOL 1960-63

Twenty-four years before I strutted down the worn and rolled hardwood floorboards of my high school, my father had walked there before me. When he was sixteen the building was new, and it stood on high ground west of the railroad tracks and above the valley floor. In his day they called it North Yakima High. Between 1961 and 1963, and today, it was and is A.C. Davis High.

The building was exceptional and would have reminded you of the castle Arundel in South West England without a moat. Tall octagonal towers and crenellation ramparts built around the buildings top gave the school the appearance of being ready for battle.

Several massive maple trees lined the parking strip, and two-inch metal pipes were welded and bent to form a fence that protected the lawn, and led to the entrance. Fourteen wide steps with sweeping brick banisters framed the building's main entrance. I never knew why the school looked like a castle, but it did, and I loved it.

The basement had concrete floors and held the lunchroom, drafting classes, and the art department. The windows were close to the ground, and the classrooms lacked the smartness of those on the second and third floors. Wooden banisters smoothly opened the wide steps, allowing hundreds of students to move from one floor to the other. The ceilings were exceptionally high, with massive metal lights. Window encasements, mop boards, doors, crown molding, steps, and rails were made from clear lumber. Black boards were black, and chalk was white.

The students that attended A.C. Davis High were a diverse group representing many races and economic backgrounds. The girls wore knee-length skirts, blouses, and sweaters. Flats and low heeled shoes were normal with peds, seamless nylons, and, from time to time, anklets. Hair was almost always short and full, while eyeglasses were often dark and horned rimmed. The guys wore tan slacks, shirts with button down collars, white sox with black or brown loafers. Hair was most often short, with the occasional long-haired rebel, with forehead curls and ducktails.

The basement halls slightly varied in height and were ramped from one level to the other. They wrapped themselves completely around the lunchroom, which occupied the entire middle of the basement, and were full of lockers. It seemed that the kids that clicked together had their lockers together. Most of the guys I hung out with had their lockers on the outside of one of the long halls. The girls we socialized with hung out on one of the end runs that were shorter, and had much more space. They would gather together and share what girls shared, while us guys would circle around them and visit on the edges. There were lots of school cliques, and sadly, we rarely spent time with each other.

I remember my early morning arrivals at school and driving my 1953 cherry Ford. I would keep it in low gear, loving the sound of the barking pipes when I let up on the gas. I would rumble past the school entrance, and then up a nearby street to park. Dust never settled on my cars waxed finish, and I was proud. I would park, slide out from behind the wheel in my letterman's jacket, and feeling good about myself, as I teamed up with my buddies and flirted with the girls.

I know some of the kids were sexual in high school, but girls would pay a high reputation price if they slept around, and most didn't. The guys I ran with respected NO and, as a result, we were pretty virtuous also.

Rarely did we hear of anyone using drugs, but drinking beer and wine seemed a part of passage for some, and was seldom abused by others. The sophomore, junior and senior years all brought new benefits and responsibilities with each year. The group of kids I ran with did well with their studies and was involved in sports, theater, and music. We were also on the look-out for weekend "stomps," and loved dragging the gut.

Our Junior-Senior Prom was a big deal. Most students dressed up and attended…even the leather jacket guys with their long hair and their girlfriends that weren't afraid of riding in their hotrods, or on the backs of their bikes. The guys would rent tuxedos and buy expensive corsages for our dates, who were beautiful in their formal gowns and fancy hairdos. Dinner at one of the town's good restaurants was part of the evening and we all felt grown up, and ready to conquer the world.

At the end of it all we found ourselves in caps and gowns marching proudly forward to receive our reward for twelve years well done. Our high school life came to an end with the All-Night Party, closing the door on three memorable years.

COLLEGE OR TRADE SCHOOL 1963

"That's right son," my father said, "You get straight A's this quarter and I will buy you a new Corvette." I was an average high school student and graduated in the middle of my class of three hundred. I didn't lack the ability to be a good student…just the interest. I loved girls, cars, art, sports, and working hard for pocket money. If I had been graded for these interests, I would have been in contention for class Salutatorian. Even though I academically shortchanged myself, I like the choices I made and enjoyed my youthful life.

Many of my friends planned to attend college. Some were going into the service and others were going directly into the work market or trade schools. My Dad, who worked with his hands, didn't want me to follow in his footsteps. He wanted me to use my mind more than my back.

Concerned with my less-than-stellar academic performance, Dad decided to expose me to the local trade school. He drove me down to Perry Trade School, where we walked the halls and peeked into the classrooms. Even though, in later years he would teach small engine courses at this school, he discouraged me, so I left my tour motivated to study harder and attend the local junior college. I wish he had pushed me towards the trades rather than discouraging me. I had always loved working with my hands and had an ability to understand the working of things.

My Dad's word was as good as gold. I wonder what he would have done with a straight A report card.

CUTE STORY POORLY CRAFTED 1963 – 1965

Sitting on a stool behind one of my abstract oil paintings, I tried to push away the shame of the C- grade that was scrawled across the top of my first attempt at writing, which was stuffed in the back pocket of my blue jeans. One of the required courses I was taking at Yakima Valley College was Creative Writing 101. My lack of spelling and punctuation skills had discouraged my professor, who jotted below my grade a tad of encouragement with the words, "cute story poorly crafted."

I don't remember the story, but I do remember it being about a bowl of pea soup that was served at a dinner. The pee soup I wrote about still makes my head drop as I imagine that aged professor trying to make his way through my two-page effort.

I loved sitting behind a potter's wheel, weaving fabric, carving wood, drawing pictures, painting canvases, and learning how to be more skillful. The required courses I was mandated to attend served as background noise as I sketched my nudes in the room's last row. It wasn't until my second year and a well taught history class on world civilizations that I expanded my interest and learned something not taught in the art department. The guy that taught the course would have looked like most of the guys I smoked and shared coffee with at the Pizza house we frequented, and he brought history to life. He painted the course and sketched us into the love, power, loss, and importance of what we studied. I ended his course with my first A in a class other than the arts.

All of my college courses were the same. I excelled in the arts and those that were well taught. The others…wouldn't hold my attention and kept my GPA average.

FIRST WIFE AND USMCR 1966

I first spotted Patty, my first wife and the mother of my two children, during a High School drawing class taught by Mr. Canon. She was eye-catching and had an air about her that was different than the girls I normally dated. Years later I would realize that I was often attracted to women who had a bit of gypsy about them, and she had plenty of it. She seemed to go against the flow and had few friends at school, other than Sue Day and Kay Robinson. The fellows she dated were older and attended schools in the lower valley where most of the guys were tough farm boys. We flirted and I asked her out a couple of times and was always disappointed when she told me she was going steady with some guy I didn't know.

I was working myself through college and spent many hours selling shoes at Miller's Department Store. The store was a 1950's modern building with lots of glass. The shoe department, where I spent most of my time, was in the back of the store beside the steps that led to the mezzanine and women's apparel. One day, while trying a pair of Nine West heels on a woman my mother's age, I glanced up to see Patty coming down the steps. She looked great and had on some sexy thing that knocked me over. She confessed later that she had hoped to catch me working and said "yes" when I asked her out for the third time. I was thrilled.

The Viet Nam war was raging and I, like most young men, was subject to the draft. The Draft Board considered me fair game because I wasn't a senior when I started my fourth year of college.

I had been dating Patty for several months when I joined the United States Marine Corps Reserve. I hoped to avoid the draft and fighting a war I didn't support. Several months before I departed for my basic training, I asked Patty to marry me, and she accepted. I didn't want to leave her behind and have another guy snatch her up.

I was twenty-one and she was the first woman to share a bed with me. I was crazy in love and, despite my parent's disapproval and the worrisome comments of most of my friends; I wanted her to be my wife.

She had just ended a serious relationship with another guy who found himself having to marry a girl who was pregnant with his child.

Patty was devastated and I, in reflection, must have been her rebound guy. We married shortly before I left for San Diego, California and the United States Marine Corps boot camp.

It surprised me that I was proud to be a member of the USMCR. My arrival at Marine Corps Recruit Depot San Diego was an experience much like Alice and the rabbit hole. Once in the hole, another world, unlike any I had experienced, opened and became my reality.

Bald heads, yellow sweatshirts, unbloused utility pants, and black boots were everywhere. The Marine Corps told us we were being transformed from boys into Marines. Upon arrival we receive our first haircuts and initial gear issue, which includes items like uniforms, toiletries, and letter writing supplies. We were given a full medical and dental screening. DI's were screaming at us and our heads were bleeding from the shortest haircut we had ever received. During this era of long hair, it upset me to look at the guys beside me, and I am sure they were upset looking at me.

Our Drill Instructors were callous men who pushed us to perform and verbally abused us in ways I had never imagined. Some of my fellow recruits failed and disappeared like road kill, while others rose to the surface and became glory boys. I remained in the middle with my eyes frozen in the forward position.

We drilled and drilled. At first we were sloppy and unable to follow the DI's screams. As the days and weeks passed, we became well-oiled machines performing synchronous and complex drill movements. Our DI's wanted to instill discipline, pride, and unit cohesion and, despite our hippy hearts…they were successful.

As our training continued, I was horrified when we experienced combat water survival. Their intention was to develop a recruit's confidence in the water, but when we, in our utilities and combat gear, which included a rifle, helmet and pack, jumped into the pool…I knew I was about to drown.

Our physical training was very demanding. We ran obstacle courses and went on forced marches up to ten miles in length with our fake M-14 rifle and pack. We learned to shoot rifles, toss hand grenades, fire machine guns, and stab dummies with bayonets. Most of us enjoyed the academics and the breaks the classes offered us from the hot San Diego sun. The recruits in our unit were mostly college students and the classes on history, customs, courtesies, and lifesaving procedures were interesting.

MCRD was asphalt, sand, desert trees, and yellow stucco buildings, with red tiled roofs, metal Quonset huts, ice plants, and DI's in bad moods. Our unit was billeted next to the airport, and my heart attached itself to every plane that was flying away.

After eight weeks of boot camp I was allowed to return to my home and my new wife. I was in the best shape of my life, and my body was hard. I tried to remember and respect the hippy in my soul, yet was proud to be a Marine.

When my six months of active duty was completed, I returned to Yakima, where Patty and I played happily married and created our daughter, Jamie.

Shortly after the birth of our beautiful daughter, Patty informed me that she was not happy in the marriage and wanted a divorce. Sadly, I wasn't her Gypsy guy. I couldn't let the marriage end. I wasn't willing to be a part time Dad. I truly believed that if I loved and supported her enough, our marriage would survive and I would win her love. For the next twenty years we played happily married and weren't. I tried everything I could to win her love, and didn't. Those years were filled many good experiences and too many sad stories, that are better left untold.

YAKIMA POLICE DEPARTMENT 1966

There were a handful of off duty cops who worked security during the Christmas season in my department store. Although their pay was good for off duty work, it was boring, and they would often find themselves standing in my shoe department shooting the breeze. "James, the department will be hiring several new patrolmen…you should take the test," was the invitation they offered me. I had never considered being a cop, but I knew that the financial demands of family life required more money than I was making while I attended college and worked in the department store. Almost as a lark, I took the test and scored well. I was offered the position and accepted.

It was an amazing job! If it wasn't for my wife's dislike of life in Yakima, and the hours I had to work, I could have happily made it a life career. My months as a rookie introduced me to the formidable power of the job, and the ugliness that exists in people and in our city.

O.A. Nye was my first training officer. My months with him exposed me to old school law enforcement and street justice. What he taught me didn't fit with my image of a peacekeeper, and I didn't adopt much of his training, although, as the years passed, I did appreciate the effectiveness and simplicity of his style of law enforcement.

I was a capable Patrolman and rapidly developed a reputation as being clear headed and well grounded. During my three years on the force I investigated too many deaths by accident, auto, suicide, and murder. I participated in high-speed auto pursuits, investigated many auto accidents, family disputes, burglaries, robberies, assaults, deceased persons, and thefts. Many emotions were experienced doing my job, and the stress related to most of them was high.

Although there were moments of extreme excitement, the bulk of my time as a Patrolman was spent in traffic control, security, and endless paperwork.

POSSIBLE DISEASED PERSON 1967

It was Thanksgiving Day and I was on patrol. At the end of the month I would celebrate my twenty-fourth birthday. I had completed my first year as a patrolman for the Yakima Police Department, and was working another holiday. Our shift sergeant, appreciating the importance of family, had modified the schedule so we could all have a long dinner break with our relatives. Fifteen minutes before it was my turn to enjoy a warm turkey dinner, I received a dispatch, "possible diseased person."

Most new cops want to experience difficult calls early in their careers. There's a hope that once it's behind you, you will know what you do when your anxiety is high, and, in the future, be more skillful in your job performance. I had many of my first experiences behind me: fatal auto wrecks, suicide, murder, assault, family beefs and high-speed chases. I had not had an unattended death.

Like most November days in Yakima, it was cold and sunny. Traffic had been light and other calls were few and uneventful. There was a skeleton crew, and I was responsible for the entire northwest section of the city. I knew, as I drove towards Willow Avenue, that I wouldn't expect back-up assistance unless I made the request.

I wondered if this call would be false, or if I would shortly be looking at a dead person. Would it be a normal death, or the result of a crime? Would I be able to control my guts? Or would I puke, like I did after my first fatal auto accident? Most often calls don't turn out to be much, so I presumed that this would be another "call unfounded."

The kid had a wild-eyed look that flashed with fear. He couldn't have been much older than thirteen, and when he saw my patrol car turn down the street, he ran across the yard waving his arms. I parked and quickly opened the door. The kid was going to be by my driver's door in seconds, and I hated to have people standing over me when I got out of the car. It didn't feel safe. The voice that came from him didn't make sense, and I quickly realized that this young man had learning disabilities. He was extremely excited. As I calmed him, I was better able to understand his speech.

His name was Josh and his parents had been driving through the neighborhoods looking at "For Rent" homes. The house we were standing in front of looked like it was under remodel. It had caught their eye. They had thought that maybe it would be available when the project was finished.

Josh, with his parents, had parked their car across the street and had walked around the house peeking through the windows. The windows were not draped, and as they walked around the back they discovered that the door was not locked. Thinking that it was probably no big deal, they opened the door and entered. The kitchen was on the west side, and on the other was a closed door to a bedroom. They opened that door, and that was the reason I was now standing in the yard of this old house on Willow Avenue.

Josh's parents were very upset and ran to the neighborhood grocery store to call 911 rather than drive. They instructed him to wait for my arrival, and hadn't yet returned when I drove up the street.

I asked Josh to remain outside the house when I entered. It was early in the afternoon so I had not carried my flashlight with me. I was surprised by the darkness in the back of the building, but instead of returning to my patrol car for my flashlight, I reached into my pocket for my lighter. I pushed open the bedroom door, unsure if it would be empty or not. My eyes had not adjusted to the darkness and seeing into the room was difficult. I held the lighter in front of my chest and stepped inside. Even though it was darker than the inside of a cow, I could see that the windows were covered with old blankets nailed to their frames. Against the wall there was a cot with something piled on it. I stepped closer and held the lighter over my head. I took a startled breath as I identified arched arms above the cot. With three cautious steps forward I could see, by the flicker of my Bic, that there was a man in the room who had been dead for a while. Without taking a greater inventory of the room I backed out and returned to my car to call for assistance and to get the flashlight.

The owner of the house had made a deal with the carpenter. "You can stay in the house for six months if you repair its problems and clean it up." He hadn't heard from the carpenter for several months and had presumed he had moved on. It had been five months, and the owner's work in Walla Walla had kept him from returning to Yakima.

Working on the house had provided the old handyman with shelter and a place to store his tools until he could find a full time job. He had fixed the little back bedroom up with a cot, hot plate and tacked blankets over the windows. He had only worked two weeks or so into July when he died. His body lay there for four and a half months while nature had her way claiming his remains. I was glad that it was close to freezing and that there wasn't heat in the house.

It had scared me to see this mummified body with his arched back and arms locked above his chest. The lighter's flame had added to the horror of the death, and the expression on his face should have been kept under the lid of a coffin.

My Sergeant soon arrived, and we called the funeral parlor for body removal. There was no crime here, just a man who had died and was denied the protection and privacy that burial offers. I had kept my cookies that day, and developed a knowing about death that few have.

Three hours later, I sat at the family table looking at a drumstick and all the traditional fixings. My appetite was poor that year.

BEING A COP 1966 – 1969

I think I loved it. It was a man's job in the 1960's and was filled with responsibilities and powers most guys in their mid-twenties didn't have…maybe most didn't want.

There were hundreds of applicants who wanted the job and I got it. I was one of three new officers who were hired by the Department and during my first year as a patrolman I received excellent training in many different aspects of law enforcement. The mid sixties were transitional times for America, and for the Yakima Police Department. Our senior officers were grudgingly learning a new way to enforce the law, and us young pups were receiving new age information.

I was the perfect different kind of cop, and quickly was appreciated by the brass. I knew I was a rising star and enjoyed myself when the city mayor, or other community members of importance, would ride shotgun with me on my evening patrols.

I liked the way I looked in my dark blue and gray uniform, with the Indian-head emblem on my sleeve. Around my waist I wore a black leather belt and clamshell holster. The belt was heavy and packed my handcuffs, pepper spray, Diamond Back pistol, with twelve extra rounds, and a holster for my heavy-duty flashlight. I liked the two additional inches in height I gained wearing my black Wellington style boots. I even had a whistle and silver chain attached to the flap on my shirt shoulder and the front pocket button. It added a little extra bling.

I was clean-shaven, two hundred and ten pounds, and in great shape. I kept my hair short, and would wear reflective mirrored sunglasses that looked very coppish.

I spent many months walking Skid Row. It was an amazing education for a peaceful, middle class man. I saw brutality, degradation, racism, and experienced many dangerous situations. Most often I had a partner on my rounds; occasionally, I worked alone.

One night while walking in front of a tavern I spotted a fight, or some disruption, in the back of a building by the bathroom. They spotted me when I walked through the door, and moved behind a panel that blocked the view of the bathroom entrance. My heavy-duty flashlight came out of its holster and onto my shoulder, with its face shining in front of me as I walked towards the back of the room. I had slipped a piece of tight fitting tailpipe over the battery shaft and wrapped it in black tape. It was an effective weapon when needed. I stepped behind the panel, into the small bathroom and immediately knew I wasn't where I wanted to be. Blades were out, people were drunk, there were too many of us in the room, and I was pretty sure they all disliked me more than they did each other.

I stretched myself up to my six foot six inch height, including my big boots and tall cop hat, puffed up my chest, dropped my voice to its deepest range and barked, "Back off, boys, before I have to hurt someone." It was quiet for a moment. Then, as I moved towards door, they, thank God, stepped back. I backed out, and continued backing half way through the tavern before I turned and quick-footed out the front door. By the time I radioed for assistance and returned to the tavern with a couple of other officers, it had calmed down, and the bathroom was empty.

Another night I was on patrol in one of our high performance 440 Plymouths with a police package. I had just returned to service, following my dinner, and was driving west on Yakima Avenue towards the Dairy Queen, when a new GTO convertible pulled out of the parking lot with it's tires spinning.

It was close to midnight, so to hear the squeal of tires wasn't an abnormal experience during those days of super hot cars and excessive drinking. I punched the throttle of the Plymouth and zipped past the Dairy Queen as the GTO, at a high rate of speed, rushed up the avenue, and out of my view.

A little tire noise was tolerated, but this guy was driving way too fast. I flipped on my overhead lights, siren, and increased my speed. The road was open and my performance motor had me at 90 MPH in a moment. I caught the flash of the GTO's taillights turning north up Sixteenth Avenue. The traffic light was in my favor when I hit the intersection and power slid the corner. The GTO was blocks ahead of me and I had no idea if he had spotted me behind him or not. I knew he was speeding well over a 100 MPH as he blew the lights on the next two streets.

I couldn't safely catch this guy and began to back off when I watched him blow his last light at Fruitvale Boulevard. His car struck the 5th wheel of an eastbound semi. By the time I reached the accident the tractor and trailer had been pushed across the road divider and had jackknifed several times before spitting the chomped car out and up the street.

I ran to the red convertible, which was no longer recognizable as a car, and discovered a young, drunk and dying man conscious and quite in the middle of the steaming mess of metal. I climbed up beside him and rested his head on the fold of my arm as I, unfoundedly assured him that he would be OK. He didn't say a word and died without closing his eyes.

I climbed off the wreck and staggered to the gutter where I puked up my dinner before investigating the accident.

He was a preacher's son, twenty-one years old, had just returned from Viet Nam and was getting married the next day. I was twenty-four, hardened by a fatality accident and confused.

There was much about law enforcement that was black and white and yet a lot to be confused about. Attempts to make since of loss, abuse and inhumanities seemed a waste of time. Learning how to keep your cookies down and maintaining faith in mankind while observing it all... seemed a sensible effort.

I wore a shield for the Yakima Police Department for three years. I saw too much and left the department following a long and ugly civil service hearing. An old school Sergeant ordered me to issue a citation to a guy I hadn't seen drive. I refused and he filed charges against me for refused to follow his orders.

My wife hated my being a cop and hated living in the Valley where she felt people had been unkind to her. When I ended and won the hearing I resigned and moved with her and my daughter to Shelton, Washington where I went to work for Safeway as a box boy. It was a big change.

JAMIE TRICIA HEINTZ 1968

She was little. I could hold her head in my hand and her little butt would bump against my bicep. I loved breathing the same air she did, and lost hours of sleep waiting for her to take her next breath. I held, loved, wiped, fed, nurtured, and prayed for my daughter. Watching her blow spit bubbles and blink her blue eyes when I played with her nose enchanted me.

I was twenty-four and very ready to be a Dad. I had total confidence in my ability to love and nurture her. All my life I had envisioned myself a father, and now I wanted to offer her a relationship with God that was better than mine…but I didn't know how to do it. I wanted her be strong, wise, capable, beyond limitations, fearless and loving. I wanted her to devote her life to changing the world and to making it a better place for her children…my grandchildren.

SHELTON 1970

It was a small mill town of six thousand people nestled on a southern finger of the Puget Sound. Unlike Yakima, where springs were fresh, summers hot, falls crisp, and the winters cold; Shelton was coastal. I loved walking in the forests above the Yakima Valley, but in Shelton the undergrowth was so thick that walking was almost impossible. The sun that never disappeared in Yakima was gone for weeks, sometimes months in Shelton. Rain was rarely seen in Yakima and would drown you in Shelton. It was a big change, and stimulating. I learned a great deal about moss, mold, wind, and water.

The town, with its densely forested hills, was wrapped around the Oakland Bay with endless docks reaching far into the water. Most of the mooring areas were commercial, with heavy wood pilings wrapped with thick ropes, and sea life growing on everything. Some of the docks were new…others were old and collapsing into the salt water.

On one end of the Bay, a galvanized building sat on pilings with massive mounds of oyster shells nearby. Inside the building, over long metal tables, folks would work all day shucking oysters. Their hands were quick and jars were filled with tasty morsels and shipped all over the world.

The Florence Yacht Clubs docks were filled with attractive power boats and sailboats. The boats celebrated of the glory of the Sound with sails, flags, and banners. Its clubhouse was blue and constructed with T-1-11 like many buildings in the area. The trim was white. It stood on a high spot beside the long and well-maintained dock.

Our first house in Shelton was on a hill above the city. It was an old two-story place with an unfinished swimming pool. The pool wasn't much, but we made the best of it, and had some interesting pool parties with old friends from Yakima.

The next year we moved to Harstine Island, renting a waterfront house on several acres. During our years there, we collected two old horses owned by a friend, and a couple of teenage boys. The boys were living in an Olympia halfway house for convicted felons and came to our place, with their house manager, to play in the bay. They stayed with us for a year or two, and were a real mixed bag. We loved them, and we paid a high price for the scars they had received before they reached our place.

Patti taught at Shelton's elementary school, and I did what I could to make a buck. Boeing Aircraft in Seattle had lost several major contracts, which tossed the Northwest into high levels of unemployment. It was hard to find work. My first job was with Safeway Grocery Stores. I had many entry-level responsibilities, and spent much of my time filling grocery bags and packing them out to cars in the parking lot. Although I enjoyed the friends I made at Safeway, the pay was poor, so when the mill had openings, I applied.

The mill was the area's largest employer and they paid well. I was lucky, got hired, and went to work in the plywood plant. Working the night shift, I was assigned to a grading table, where I pulled thin sheets of veneer off a wide belt and stacked them on carts behind me.

Less than a month on the job, I found myself in the lunchroom having a discussion with my Foreman about how wings are attached to airplanes. I thought we were having a friendly difference of opinion, but soon discovered he didn't appreciate my view and fired me on the spot. I paid a high price to be right about something I didn't know much about.

I tried to make a living as a freelance photographer, Christmas tree harvester, country grocery store manager, handyman, life insurance salesman, and finally, I drove to Olympia, Washington and got a job driving a Doxel Propane truck.

Although my marriage continued to be difficult, I loved living in Shelton. The summers were fabulous with warm days, blue skies, and lots of butter clams that lived inches under our rocky shoreline.

We would build a fire on our beach, fill a canning kettle with sea water, heat it up with a tub of butter melting in the coals on the fires edge, and steam buckets of freshly dug butter clams.

Many hours were spent fishing on the massive rocks beside the bridge. We didn't catch much to eat but the dogfish were fun to hook and my little dog, Dr. Irish, loved swimming after them. He would catch them by their tails and drag them back to shore where he would chew on them until they stopped moving. He was the size of a small terrier and the sharks were often four to six feet long. I admired his fearlessness.

My daughter was three. She loved playing on the beach and being in front of my camera. My photo albums still have pictures of her…they were and remain excellent.

We built boats, sailed with orca, raised rabbits, horses, and chickens. The stories around all of these adventures are endless. I loved turning myself from a city kid to a small town boy.

FINDING VIRGINIA 1972

I was trained by New York Life Insurance to develop a contact base by comparing the local telephone book with the high school annuals of people that would be in their mid to late twenties. Most of the matches would be married, have children, and hopefully, I would be able to convince them that they had a need for the products I was trained to sell. Most young families moved away from Shelton to larger cities where employment was easier. I was able to find several names that matched the company's criteria. Ken Martig on the top of my list. The address was in a nice neighborhood, on the hillside above the Shelton Yacht Club. I parked my car in front of the Martig house, picked out a pamphlet I thought would be of interest, and walked to the door.

I wasn't a big fan of cold calls, I don't think most salesmen are, yet I had been told that it was an important part of insurance sales. Because they were difficult, I usually started my day with these calls to assure myself of getting them done. When I knocked on the door, I heard movement inside and positioned myself back from the door so I wouldn't make the initial contact uncomfortable. Salesmen often come on strong and end up with rejection. I didn't want to be that guy.

The door opened, and a woman in her late fifties or early sixties stood before me. She was tall and elegant. Her long dark hair was streaked with gray and pulled back into a bun. She had a large smile and eyes that looked at me as if I were a dear friend who was returning from a holiday. With one hand she held the screen door open and with the other she held her glasses and a book against her chest. I smiled and said, "Hi, my name is James Heintz and I have an idea I would like to share with you." She smiled and said, "Hello James, are you a Baha'i"?

I had heard of the Baha'i Faith from friends in Yakima who had attended several Baha'i meetings. They had pamphlets and we had spent time looking them over and discussing the ideas they contained. I had stepped away from my Catholic upbringing when I was sixteen and wanted to find a spiritual path for my three-year-old daughter and myself. The Catholic and the protestant churches I had exposed myself to had not satisfied my spiritual needs, and I didn't want to pass them on to my child.

"No." I said, "I am not a Baha'i, but I have heard of it and I am interested in knowing more." I don't think another word was said about insurance and we did talk a lot about my life and my spiritual needs.

Virginia Martig was the mother of the Ken I had found in the school annual, and was married to Ken senior. She had been raised in the Baha'i Faith and had devoted her life to sharing its teachings. My ordinary cold call had become an extraordinary visit with a remarkable woman.

For five days we talked. I had many unanswered questions and I learned that there were many people who believed as I did, and they called themselves Baha'is. Each morning I would arrive at Virginia's home shortly after their breakfast and would remain with her and her husband Ken until dinnertime. I would then return to my family and spend the evening talking with my wife about what I had learned. She was unsure of my involvement with these people, and even more uncomfortable with their belief that Jesus had returned. She firmly believed that if Christ had returned, she would have known it.

At the end of five days, I knew that I was Baha'i and that my spiritual search had a new direction. I declared my belief in Baha'u'llah, the Prophet founder of the Baha'i Faith, on the twelfth day of February 1972 and have remained eternally grateful that my cold call resulted in my meeting Virginia, my warm and charming teacher.

JORDAN GABRIEL HEINTZ 1975

His mother wanted to name him Jordan and I chose the Gabriel...so Jordan Gabriel Heintz it would be. Seven years had passed since Jamie's birth, and his coming was a surprise. I was shocked and delighted when Patty told me she was pregnant. Although I wanted another child and maybe more...I didn't think it would happen. My marriage had been hard and my Faith had helped it survive. I would often say to myself that it was by our tests that we grew and that my marriage was my greatest source for tests. He was conceived in a little house on Pickering Passage, a few miles closer to Shelton than the Harstine Island home. By the time Patty was ready to give birth, we had packed up all of our belongings and moved back to Yakima. It was the birthplace of both Jordan and Jamie, as well as their parents.

The world of medicine had changed. When his sister was born, I sat in the hall with the other fathers and talked about sports, hunting, and other manly interests I didn't have. With Jordan, I got to be a part of the birth. Like his big sister, he was beautiful and had bright and inquisitive eyes. I wasn't a boy anymore and wanted to teach my son a new way of being a man. I wanted him to be strong, gentle, understanding, patient and vibrant. I wanted him to know himself, and to make choices about his life that respected himself and those around him.

BUS 1978

Jordan was three and Jamie ten. We had sold our Tumwater, Washington home, made a profit, had money in our pockets, and wanted an adventure. My high school buddy Larry Keeler had done all the hard work of converting of an old five window Dodge school bus into a rugged motor home he used for hunting and fishing. We bought it from him and adapted it for our escapade.

I added shelves, additional storage, extra beds and a surprisingly good looking brush paint job. The body of the bus was gloss white with grass green bumpers, molding and the name above the side windows. The green turtle I painted in front of the name, La Tortuga Blanca, added the finishing touch. She was beautiful with her storage box on top and the heavy duty bike rack on the rear door.

We packed her up with too much personal stuff and headed down the road to San Francisco where we visited for several days with my sister Judy, her husband, Mag, and their three boys. We then drove south through Los Angeles and San Diego where we visited the Zoo.

Spending time in Mexico was our goal even though everyone warned us of Banditos and sickness…we were determined. Crossing the border was easy and driving through Tijuana exciting. We had the address of some Baha'is so we drove around until we found them in a poor area of the city where streets were dirt paths and our bus was view by the children as a luxury filled motor home. They couldn't believe we had a refrigerator and running water. Their home didn't have either.

Our trip took us south on the Baja Peninsula to Ensenada where we stayed a week with another Baha'i family. Patty got sick so our day or two stop turned into more. Her stomach was unwell for most of the trip and rarely did she venture far from the bus.

We weren't in a rush and slowly camped ourselves eight hundred miles south until we reached Cabo San Lucas. Throughout our journey, we enjoyed fires on the beach and were delighted with the people we met along the way. Sanitation was poor and we were always dismayed by the used toilet paper in the baskets beside the toilets. The roads were always under construction, but drivable, until we made our trip from La Paz to Cabo. We had been using the coastal road beside the beautiful Sea of Cortes and decided to drive inland. I spotted on our map a road running down the center of the peninsula. The one hundred mile trip looked like a straight shot, and we wanted to see the inland part Baja. Several days before our departure, I filled two five gallon reserve tanks with fuel and strapped them on top of the bus in the storage box. With extra water and the gas tanks full, we headed south. After less than ten miles, the road quickly turned from asphalt to dirt. For miles and miles we slowly rolled down the road, enjoying the occasional shack with wide-eyed occupants standing nearby staring at us. They rarely responded to our wave, which we found disconcerting. The folks on the coast had been extra friendly. We didn't feel concerned and yet I wondered, as the number of shacks became fewer, if we were driving through Baja's version of Deliverance. Soon the shacks disappeared completely and shortly after that the road, which had blended down to a pair of tire tracks, also disappeared. It was extremely hot...well over one hundred degrees. Patty became upset that I has selected this route and wanted to return to La Paz. We had driven a long ways, used lots of our fuel, and I had no idea how much further we needed to drive before we would reach Cabo San Lucas.

I decided to back track and climbed up onto the back of the bus to unload the extra fuel. Both cans were feather light and almost empty. I had no idea where the fuel had gone, but knew that we couldn't make it back to La Paz. The bus had a compass and I reasoned that if we kept driving south, we had to run out of land and see Cabo. Patty was in tears and the kids were crowded around me, seeking reassurance, as we continued our slow drive between cactus, and across the uncharted land.

Jamie got towels wet and hung them around my neck. The fuel gage, which was pretty accurate, showed empty. There was nothing ahead but more of what we had spent the last hours driving through. Patty retreated to the rear of the bus, acting like a prisoner on death row. Suddenly the land sloped downhill and our windshield filled with the beautiful sight of the ocean. Like driving out of an undeveloped lot we pulled onto the asphalt road and zig zagged downward towards the city. Halfway down the road we ran out of gas and coasted into a gas station at the bottom of the hill.

Our weeks in Cabo were wonderful. We parked for free on a sandy section of beach with lots of other travelers. It was the perfect tropical place to be. There was only one hotel. Food was close-by in the village, which had a bakery that made the best bread I have ever eaten. Having day after day to bask in the sun with your kids is the best it can be.

We decided to take a ferry from Cabo to the mainland, docking at Puerto Vallarta. It was an overnight sail and not as expensive as I had expected. I had fears of getting seasick on the eighteen hour trip, but didn't. When the ship was drawing close to land, I could smell the jungle. I had become accustomed to the dry desert climate of the peninsula, and was delighted with the humid and alive smell of Puerto Vallarta.

We drove off the ferry and a few miles north of the city center, where we found an RV park on the beach. It was cheap, close to shopping, and our new home for several weeks. It was here that we build impressive sand castles. I painted a canvas or two under palapas. The kids and I took bike rides on cobblestone streets. They rode a pony led by a kid not much older than Jordan, and I watched the Mexican youth adore my blonde headed children. I fell in love with Puerto Vallarta and have returned several times. Our RV park was destined to become a resort like most of the beach fronts in the tourist areas of Mexico.

Our next destination was Lake Chapala. We were on our way to Guadalajara and wanted to visit the largest lake in Mexico, and the villages that lined its sides. The temperature was cooler and there was much to see. In one of the resorts I had the opportunity to eat my first fish taco and passed. The word on the street was the lake wasn't healthy and I presumed the restaurants served fish caught in its waters.

When we got to Guadalajara we bought tons of tiles, ceramics and stained glass. Shopping there was a delight for me and the kids. We visited several pottery shops, a massive and hell-like building that manufactured blown glass, and we walked the beautiful city, that had horse drawn carts and many gorgeous churches and public buildings.

With many weeks in paradise behind us, we began our trek north. Close to Nogales we camped in a park that provided Jordan with his first memory. The park was full of giant bullfrogs which Jordan found easy to catch. I delighted watching him grab one after another until he got a good grip on one the size of a small dog. He packed it into the bus where Jamie and Patty screamed at him as it emptied its quart sized bladder all over the floor. Jordan and I loved it. The girls didn't.

It was wonderful to cross the border and see an American flag flying over a McDonalds. We drove towards Tucson and then on to Yosemite National Park where we stayed a week and explored much of what the park had to offer while we adjusted to living around fir tree and toilets that flushed paper.

On our way back to Tumwater, Washington we parked by Fern Ridge Reservoir outside Eugene, Oregon, and fell in love with the beauty of the area. We returned home, packed everything up and moved to Eugene.

HANDYMAN 1978

I was raised in sawdust. My father liked to fix his home and I remember being under foot to watch his every move and hand him tools. I bought my first home in 1968 and discovered that, like my father, I enjoyed remodeling. As years passed and my abilities grew friends asked me to help them out with their repairs or remodel projects. Although I have been diverse in the work I have done...building has been my favorite.

I remember having a small single-wheel trailer that I designed to open up to provide a work table as well as a storage pack for my tools. I hooked it up to my MGB and must have been an unconventional sight driving from lumber yard to worksite with the top down. Over the years I had many vehicles that helped me pack my tools around. Most were more traditional than the MGB.

I loved remodeling bathrooms and kitchens, and always thought that woods and tiles produced a beautiful finished product. Pop a skylight in here, add new cabinets, sinks, tubs and lighting. It was great fun, and elicited a swell of pride as I admired it at the end of the day.

For years I would break out my tools between my traditional jobs and was always able to make a buck. I probably would have had a productive and enjoyable work career in the building trades if I had apprenticed with a home builder and learned the profession from someone who really knew what they were doing.

SHRINE 1980

Italian marble feels cool under the bare foot. That coolness is one of the precious memories of my Pilgrimage. "Good morning" was the guard's greeting as he opened the iron gate and slightly dropped his head, as if I were a member of a royal family. The gardens around the Shrine of the Bab were closed to tourists in the morning. Only Pilgrims were allowed.

My first view of the shrine came at the end of a long bus drive across the arid and parched land that only Bedouin could survive upon. The bus rose to the top of Mt. Carmel and there She stood. I had expected Her to be sitting high on some knoll, and was surprised to see Her below me on the side of the mountain surrounded by green. The dome rose like an unopened tulip sitting on a white marble pedestal. The gold leaf finish captured the bright Israeli sun and reflected prisms of light. Words slipped past my lips, "Oh God! There She is! She's beautiful, so beautiful."

I had seen many pictures and lots of slides from others who had made the Pilgrimage, but was still shocked by the beauty of the building. Like a child whose sight is captured by a butterfly landing on a flower, I was unable to take my eyes from the vision that was growing before me. A prolonged hush fell over all in the bus until it was interrupted by the driver's amplified voice telling us what we all knew we were seeing.

We wound down the hillside and stopped at the Pilgrim House. My desire to dash past every one and to wrap my arms around a pillar was not containable, yet my hunger would be unsatisfied for a short time longer. We were escorted into the house and someone, I don't remember who, talked. Their words were lost to me. I knew that I should be respectful of protocol, but I felt like a thirsty man watching water bubble from a fountain. Soon I am sure, although it felt so very long, we stepped back into the gardens and walked down the path to the guard. He has seen the look in my eyes before.

I wasn't the first in the parade of pilgrims and it didn't matter. Moving quickly didn't matter. The fragrance of Its flowers drifted across us all and we didn't talk. We didn't hold hands. We all walked silently and alone in our group to the Shrine. I saw that shoes were left on the marble skirt that surrounded the building and I quickly slipped mine off. "Sweet Baha'u'llah…I am home."

The world could have folded in upon itself and I would have smiled knowing that I was in the palm of God's hand and His will was my will. I was slow to enter the Shrine and happy to walk around it on Its cool marble apron. My head was dropped in prayer and yet I felt guided in my steps as I passed by others who had joined me circling in adoration.

Friends had asked me to pray for them in the shrine and I knew I would but now…I felt elevated above the world. All that existed was God and me.

Some of the Pilgrims had visited the interior of the Shrine and had returned to the Pilgrim House. I stopped my prayerful circling in front of the white, metal doors that opened into the resting place of 'Abdu'l-Baha. The step up was slight and the door easily opened before me. The color of apricots and rich Persian carpets greeted my eyes. Two steps across the rug I fell to my knees and inhaled.

Serenity Lane 1985

I really wanted to do something for myself. I had spent the bulk of my adult life postponing my interests and concentrating on Patty's needs. During our years together she convinced me that I had problems and needed help. We rarely counseled together because she was doing just fine and the problems were mine.

I began therapy when I was in my mid twenties and worked with a variety of therapists. Some were skillful; others weren't. Month after month and year after year I worked on myself, trying to figure out why I was unlovable, or at least why I couldn't make my wife happy.

I wasn't successful with Patty, but I did grow to appreciate the personal growth process. When I heard about an Internship with Serenity Lane, an alcohol and drug treatment facility, I committed.

The yearlong internship was fabulous, and for the following nine years, I worked as an inpatient and family counselor. I wasn't recovering from an addiction and, despite that difference; I was successful in the counseling process. The first four or five years I worked exclusively with inpatient clients and the last few years my attention was directed towards the family members of addicts and alcoholics.

There is much that is exciting about the recovery process and it's tough. I watched many of my coworkers enter and leave the job because of the stress and endless heartaches that are an unavoidable part of the experience. After nine years I succumbed and left the career. I was out of gas and was trying to suck wisdom and energy out of an empty vessel.

I began the Internship in the last year of my marriage with Patty, and it was there that I meet my second wife. Shirley and I worked together in Serenity Lane's Family Program. She was very proper and while I was married kept a distance between us. We were just friends, and she kept it that way.

BROKEN HEART 1988

I was foolish in thinking that if I set aside things that were important to me and devoted my energy to bringing happiness into my wife's life…I would be successful and loved. I wasn't. In later years I would wonder why I did what I did. Why did I put my life on hold? She didn't ask me to do that. She would have probably appreciated it if I hadn't. Early in the marriage there must have been something that allowed her to marry me. Whatever it was disappeared and she couldn't or wouldn't recapture it. Maybe it was a rebound marriage. Anyway…my refusal to give up landed me on a surgeon's table receiving a triple bi-pass.

My cardiologist said I had no family history of heart disease and yet I was a mess. He attributed it to STRESS. I attributed it to a broken heart.

SECOND TIME AROUND 1988

I was getting a divorce, recovering from by-pass surgery, out of the house and needed help. Shirley was a co-worker who told herself that her four kids were enough and although she didn't like being a widow, she wasn't willing to mess her life up with a man who had children. She also was absolutely unwilling to get serious about a guy who couldn't or wouldn't share her Foursquare Gospel spiritual path.

She wanted to help and offered me a bed in her home. I accepted and didn't leave. After twenty years with little affection and a freshly open chest, I lacked wisdom and was vulnerable. We both, like foolish children, tossed aside our shared concerns and fell in love.

It didn't start out well, but we pretended it didn't matter. Her family liked filling the hole left in the family by their dad's death. My kids were confused and hated the change when I completely ended the "My Man Friday" relationship with their mother.

My relationship with Shirley became a marriage when my divorce with Patty/Jesse was completed. Patty had changed her name to Jesse during the years, so I truly married one and divorced the other. To this day I wonder where the girl I married went. Maybe she was never there.

Shirley and I took off like charging horses strapped together. We wanted to change our histories and live better and more fulfilling lives. Together we entered real estate sales and eventually became brokers. We bought homes and commercial properties. We remodeled everything we owned and created good investments and attractive businesses.

One grand project was the purchase, remodel and creation of The Ivy Street Coffee Company. It was a tired old building that we gutted and molded into a very cool restaurant, serving three meals a day and outrageous coffees. We also added a caboose coffee drive-through across the street with its own bright red paint job and brass bell. The Coffee House hired both of my kids and several of hers. We expanded into the old theater next door and created the Montage. We hired a skilled baker and built an exceptional bakery, flower shop, ice cream parlor, gourmet grocery and gift shop. People raved about our creation and we loved it.

What we didn't love was the discord that developed between Shirley and my kids. She had said at the beginning of our relationship that she didn't have room in her heart for more kids, and she didn't. She had also said that she wouldn't marry a man with a different spiritual path than hers, and I was a Baha'i, and was unwilling, despite her continual encouragement, to step away from my Faith.

With ten years of marriage behind us I reached a point when, despite my affection for Shirley, I could no longer live with the family disunity and was heartbroken being inactive in my Faith.

We separated and eventually divorced. It was a difficult process and we lost all the material things we had worked so hard to gain.

DAD'S BIRTHDAY WISH 1990

Knowing my own mortality, my thoughts of my father on his birthday are nudged with feelings of urgency and my need to reflect before his inevitable demise. My thoughts quickly rush to my child years and the memories of times perhaps more important than the moments we share today. My today is full because the man who gave me life loves me and is only a moment away. A three-hour drive can put me in his arms, allow me to smell his smell and look into his tender brown eyes. With a phone call I can hear his laughter and talk of motors, cars, politicians and world affairs.

The foundation of my relationship with my father was built when he was a young man and raising me. Recollections of his being big and strong are mixed with memories of his huge and hurtful hands that caused pain if not carefully managed. His voice was and is deep and capable of being heard miles away even in a whisper while his hugs, with rough whiskered cheeks, scratched my young boy face. Dad's laugh and caring for others were mixed with my hearing time and time again, "Oh Johnny, what a wonderful fellow you are."

I remember Dad's big chair leaned back with his pigeon toed feet elevated, and the roar of his snore. His Adam's apple was famous throughout the neighborhood as was his head, which has always been hairless, and most often covered, except when indoors where it could display its shine and the recent injuries it had received.

His hard work and honesty stood like pillars beyond questioning and his judgementalness was nonexistent. As a kid, surf fishing, clamming, being caught behind tide pools, sleeping in the mountains was all made secure by his confident voice or his nearby snore. His garage was filled with tools, manly tools, which I abused and lost. In his service station, I entered a world where he was god and kindhearted with his employees. I felt pride because I was Johnny's boy, growing up to be like him.

At home Dad's world was remodeling, barbecues on the patio, and the beautiful yard with Cindy grapes on the green arbor. He kept everything in good working order and took pride in all he built. We raced go-carts and enjoyed driving the truck to the track where we smelled the heat, oil and gas of the sport. We took trips to Kent, Washington to watch Hann's Ferrari race and to doing manly men things. With his friend, my Uncle Don, we would hunt pheasant in the early morning and shoot skeet on hot summer afternoons.

My greatest awareness is my father loving me and accepting me for who I was and am. What more could a son ask for.

MY FATHER'S BIRTHDAY 1991

Dear Dad,

When you were a man in your late forties, did you find yourself looking at your reflection in the mirror, think about how you are in the world, how you think others see you, how you work, laugh and play? Did you compare yourself to your dad and find there seems to be more of him in you every year?

As a child I was small, you were big. I had hair, you didn't. You worked and I played. You were responsible. I had no responsibilities. The differences between us were great. We were beyond compare.

The idealism I possessed as a young man served to maintain our differences. I had an edge on life. I had vision and understanding. I was in my twenties, a glorious and egomaniacal phase of my life. You had passed through those years and supported me as I began my way.

With each passing year of difficulty, tests and loss, I looked to you and wondered what your tests had been when you were twenty, thirty, and forty? What caused you pain? What did you learn? I wanted to know. You had something I needed. You had been where I was, where I was going.

Quickly I had children, raised them and watched them go. I could see their mistakes, their pain and growth. I knew that you knew about me, as I knew about them. I am one step ahead of them; you have one step on me.

Today dear father, I feel mortal, closer to the close of my life than feels comfortable. The man in my mirror is graying, thinning and the blush of youth has been replaced with crowfeet, skin tags and sags. You have been here; I can see it in your eyes.

It pleases and honors me to follow you through life. You are my father and I am your son and the man in our mirrors often looks like one.

I love you Dad. Thanks for leading the way.
Happy Birthday! James

HE'S DEAD, DAD 1999

I had concerns about the drive and the inclement weather I had experienced on past mid-winter trips, and was pleased with the dry road conditions. It was February and I was on my way back to my childhood home. I had lived in Yakima for seven months following a failed marriage, and then had moved back to Eugene, where I had lived for thirty years and raised my children. My plan was to pack my truck with a final load of tools, which I had stored in my brother's shop, and visit with my parents and brother.

Steve, my brother, was disappointed when I left. We had talked about buying and fixing up a couple of old houses and doing a little car restoration. These plans vanished when I decided to move back to Eugene. I felt badly that, after being apart for so many years, I had abandoned him again. I had tried putting my life back together in Yakima, but was not successful. Being close to my mom, dad, and brother was important to me; however, my life would be easier in Eugene where I had business contacts and friends.

It was cold on Satus Pass with a blue clear sky. The traffic was light and the drive across the end of the Yakima Indian Reservation was beautiful. Winter on the high desert is stark with a total absence of green foliage and ample amounts of sage and tumbleweeds.

I found myself anxious to see the folks and was surprised when my cell phone rang and I could see that Dad was calling. "Hi Dad, I am just about to drop down into the lower valley. I will be there soon." Dad relied with "Good son. We are anxious to have you here. We're a little worried about your brother and will talk about it when you get here."

My brother had been separated from his wife for several months and had been struggling with depression. He had made a suicide attempt ten years before, when his second marriage ended. Friends who found him in a pile at the base of his basement steps foiled that attack on himself. He spent the next year in counseling and improved his view of living. Most of that year he lived with the folks. It was a hard year on all three.

During my months of living in Yakima, Steve and I walked and talked a lot. He was fearful of his depression, so when he separated from his wife and began exercising, praying, eating better. He visited his physician and received a prescription of anti-depressants. Steve and I liked to walk and talk together, and as our relationship evolved and trust developed, the flavor of our walks changed. He believed that he had made a mistake leaving his wife. He became obsessive about moving back in with her. "Damn it Jim! She can't keep me out forever. I love her, and once she realizes that, we will get back together. When that day comes, I will spend the rest of my life showing her how much she means to me." "What if she doesn't, Steve? What if she is unwilling to give it another go?" I would say and he would respond with, "Well...I don't know. I can always take a handful of pills." It was his idea to separate from his wife. He didn't realize he was walking through a one-way door.

Driving through the lower valley is a culturally rich experience. The towns of Toppenish and Wapato are on the highway and the Indian heritage is everywhere. Murals of tepees and horse-riding natives beautify many old buildings. The Yakima Indian Cultural Center and grounds give those passing by an appreciation of whose land this is, and has been, for a long time. There are endless acres of cultivated land owned by both Indian and white. Like the Yakima valley, the lower valley has many fruit trees, and unlike Yakima, lots of grazing land for horses and cattle.

When I pulled my truck into the folk's driveway around noon, Dad came out to meet me. Maybe he didn't want to talk in front of Mom. I didn't know. He began by telling me that shortly after 9:00 a.m. Steve's work had called and expressed concern. He had not shown up at work and was always reliable. His recent behavior had them feeling a bit edgy. They wanted us to check on him to make sure that he was OK. They liked him. Dad and Mom had taken a drive up to his duplex after the call, and didn't get an answer to their knock. Being more than a little worried, Dad walked around the building and tried to peek in the windows. He didn't see anything, and the doors were all locked. He decided to return home to wait for my arrival because I had shared

Steve's duplex before my move back to Eugene, and Dad presumed I would have a key.

"I don't feel good about this, Jim," were Dad's only words as we drove to Steve's. I didn't feel good about it either. It was a strange feeling, much like approaching a moment of punishment. I felt hollow and bound in fear. I pulled the truck into the driveway and got out with a foreboding urgency. The key slid into the knob and released the lock. The duplex had always had a smell of staleness, and that was my first sense as I walked through the door. Steve wasn't a very tidy housekeeper, so the clothing on the sofa and floor seemed normal. "Steve, are you home? Are you here Steve?" Dad's voice came in behind me "Son, are you OK?"

I walked through the kitchen and saw prescription bottles, many prescription bottles on the counter. Steve's bedroom door was open and as I glanced into the room I saw what no brother wants to see. Steve was slumped on the carpet with his face turned down and away from me. "He's in here, Dad, in the bedroom," I said as I knelt down beside him. I reached out and touched the small of his back, which was exposed between his jeans and shirt. He was cold. I looked back over my shoulder at my father and said, "He's dead, Dad." My father tossed his head back and to the side as if he had been struck. "No... No...I knew it! Oh, Steve."

We both immediately grabbed action as a retreat from the unbearable moment and called 911. Other calls were made, I don't remember to whom. When we stopped and before all the people arrived, I returned to my brother's side and cried.

A year has passed and I have spent hundreds of hours trying to box up my brother's death. I have been unsuccessful. Dad said, "Don't try to make sense of it, Son. You can't."

CARDS 1999

Old business cards line the shelves beside my computer monitor. At first glance you would presume that they are used for easy reference. They are, in fact, reminders of times past. My little brother died a year and a half ago. His card is yellow with simple black print "Steve's Body Shop."

Beside the Body Shop is my nephew, Bryan's card. It was a quick computer business card printed by the office staff at Lyons & Gustafson PS Attorneys at Law. They hadn't ordered his permanent card when he first began his law practice.

Below Bryan is Dad's. J.M. Perry Institute is typed across the top with the logo. Dad's name is in the center "John Heintz, instructor, small engine repair." Dad liked has last job. It followed half a dozen years of his sitting in a booth on a gas station lot selling fuel. His back had failed and he was not physically or emotionally able to practice his profession as an auto mechanic. The years before Perry were difficult for Mom and Dad.

Beside Dad's card and to the left is my old Charles Ellis Realty card. A photograph with lots of hair and a beard remind me of younger years.

A later photo has me beardless and older. Heintz Counseling, addiction services. I lived on my farm then and had converted the front third of the barn into an office and counseling space. I had worked with Serenity Lane, an alcohol and drug treatment center, for nine years, which was one year too many. I was overwhelmed by peoples' problems and needed a change. I went into private practice for about a year. It was a fun effort at a very difficult time in my life. Several months later I rented my office space to an old lady who lived and later died there.

Several other cards mark my past, including Coldwell Banker Realtors in Yakima, Washington. I had tried to make Real Estate work for me following my failed marriage and was short of funds. I ended up returning to Eugene. I had been gone from Yakima for many years and wanted the comfort of familiar friends and places.

The homemade card on the bottom has always pleased me. James D. Heintz, Entrepreneur, "the one man who can solve all your rental maintenance problems." I drew a hammer, saw and trowel crossed in the center of my circled name. Working with my hands has always pleased me.

On the other side of the monitor are two cards from daughter, Jamie. The top is a black background with the faces of Jamie and her friend Setti. The card reads "Once Upon a Time" Wedding & Portraits

Photography. Jamie looks great with her sweet smile and long blond hair. Below it is the only full color card and it is one of Jamie's fabulous rodeo photographs. A young straw-hatted woman is riding across the card dressed in leathers on a young pinto. On the left of her face in white letters it says "Jamie T. Heintz" and on the right "Photographer/ Artist B.A. Fine Arts, Specializing in Western Themes, Animal / Owner Portraiture." It's a very cool card that reminds me of a wild and difficult time for my daughter.

I have other cards that I keep in my Rolodex, but the ones hanging by my computer are easy to see to keep my memories alive. There is a little stained glass box that has my current card in it. It reads "Heintz-It" James D. Heintz Properties, Remodel – Maintenance Repairs." Some day I will tape one of these cards beside the rest.

COFFEE HOUSE 1994 to 1998

I owned a coffee house. My second wife said, "You will love it, James ... just wait and see."

It was an old stucco building which had spent the last fifty years being used like a cardboard box. None of the businesses it served cared much about the appearance, except someone in the sixties who wrapped, like a wooden tutu, a shake mansard around its fascia. It was in the middle of the block on the city's main drag...Ivy Street.

The last owner, an optometrist, had walled the interior off into many little box rooms filled with lettered signs and professional equipment. Back in the 1920's it had been a café with a neon flower on the ceiling. It was cool and well remembered by the old folks who visited our coffee house. When the café closed the ceiling was lowered and the light disappeared, until I discovered it fifty years later.

When we closed escrow, my first project was to rip off the mansard and expose the tall stucco walls. I had designed art deco signs that complimented the design of the building. We papered the windows and stored the signs until just before opening day, wanting to keep the new business in town a secret.

I gutted the building back to the original two room café it had been. The larger front area was for dining and the smaller room became the kitchen. Shirley's son, Doug, helped with the remodel, and her daughter, Molly, added her extremely talented artistic touch. Even the neon tubes on the ceiling helped out by lighting up when the power was connected...except for two pedals that were probably broken when the lower ceiling was built.

I built a coffee cup and saucer big enough to hot tub in, and hung them on the front of the building, above the black and gold art deco sign. Black canvas doorway and window covers were mounted and looked great against the cream colored walls. A great mural reflecting the windows of the coffee house was painted on the wall across the courtyard by Shirley's daughter Molly. The folks in the mural windows looked like they had lived in another era, and resembled all of the family members, including a few friends like Bob Dylan and Eric Clapton.

We hired heating and air guys to put in a good used system and paid carpet layers to install the rich wine colored carpet that looked like the floor of an elegant turn-of-the-century hotel lobby.

After the kitchen was built, floors tiled, walls and coved ceiling repaired and painted, cabinetry and counters built, dining tables formicaed, sofa and chairs bought, and art work hung on the walls... The Ivy Street Coffee Company was ready to open.

On opening day everything was fresh and clean. It was an ultra cool art deco coffee house with seating for thirty-five. The sound system played blues and the coffee was the best we could buy. Modern lighting gave the room a soft glow and the small table lamps that illuminated a high shelf above the windows showed off cool collectables from the thirties and forties.

Early every morning we baked fresh pastries and always had customers waiting at our door when we opened at six a.m. I loved making Lattes, Caffe' Mochas, and my favorite, Cappuccinos, and learning the art of making other fancy drinks behind our three-head coffee machine.

As the years passed, we paved the court yard and added umbrellas, tables and chairs, and began making soups and sandwiches for lunch, Italian dishes for dinner, and impressive breakfasts. We hired several great women, who worked full time, and a bunch of the part-time kids from the high school. It was very successful, and so much fun that we set our real estate business aside and accepted a lower income.

In time, my daughter, Jamie, became the manager and son, Jordan, when he was home from school at Whittier in Los Angeles, was the coffee Barista. When my marriage with their mother had ended, the family was damaged. The coffee house gave me the opportunity to repair damage and to spend quality time with both of them. For that, I have always been grateful.

Jamie was quick to learn the business and won the respect of all the employees. It pleased me to watch her, dressed in company-required white long sleeved shirt and black slacks, work the front counter and treat our customers with respect and humor. At five foot ten inches she was striking with her bright blue eyes and blond hair. I appreciated it when she would take an employee to the side and firmly, but fondly, teach them a better way to do their job or treat a customer. She was skillful in resolving employee problems and able to keep the operation running smoothly.

Anyone who has worked in a restaurant during lunch hour rush knows the dance the employees do as they smoothly pass around each other placing, then picking up orders, and serving the customers. Jamie was the best dancer I had ever seen. I also found it interesting that when Jamie was on duty, more young cowboys came by for coffee.

Jordan turned out lean and tall like my father, with thick auburn hair and a five o'clock shadow by noon. He was quick and dexterous behind the espresso machine, spinning cups on his fingers and artfully creating drinks with hot foam stacked high. High school girls would stand around the espresso counter delighting in his skill and friendly manor. I would often tease him about his following only to have him reply with, "Just friendly kids, Dad, no big deal."

One summer break, Jordan brought friends home with him who wanted to work and check out Oregon. I was able to hire Erica, who was great to work with and became his wife several years later. I enjoyed watching them together and wasn't surprised when they got together in Europe and later decided to marry.

On special days, like the Junction City Car Show or the Scandinavian Festival, we would be packed and knocking out drinks a fast as we could grind the coffee. We turned the music up, laughed, and enjoyed the party we made in the coffee house.

The only difficulty with the coffee house was Shirley's struggles with my kids. She was quick to find fault. It was easy for her to love and accept her own children and almost impossible for her to love beyond blood.

Despite Shirley's problems, I loved working with my kids. I was proud of them, admired both of their work ethics, and enjoyed being close to them.

As time passed, we purchased the old theater next door. Years before someone had gutted it and poured a slab of concrete over the sloped theater floor. With a double wide garage door cut into the alley entrance they were able to use it for old car storage, and lots of junk. After the old owner got his property out of the building, we cut openings between the two buildings, which shared a common wall. We rebuilt the heating and electrical systems, and created a market place that had a bakery, ice cream parlor, art gallery, flower section, gift items, fancy food items and collectables. We were also pleased to develop a food prep area and additional dinning space for the coffee house. We spent lots of money making the Montage into an extraordinary place, including thirty five thousand dollars of wall art and murals. It was magnificent to see with massive paintings on the walls and the smell of fresh bread.

Sadly, we violated a basic real estate rule…location, location, location, and lost most of the money we had worked so hard to earn during our ten year marriage. Folks who visited the Montage loved it. There just weren't enough of them.

LAST HUG 1998

I don't remember when the last hug occurred. Others have said it was the same for them. We all agree that the last intimacies between two people should be marked with remembered moments and not the hazy memories that leave those moments feeling inconsequential.

"You son of a bitch! Get thou out of my sight, you servant of Satan." I remember that moment. I remember standing in the doorway to the utilities and looking back across the room to the part of the kitchen I had designed to use the old soda fountain stools. We had loved them. She saved them from an old ice cream store she had owned in Veneta.

She sat on one of those stools that day, and flashed a facial expression that matched the vile words she spat at me.

I knew, ten years before, that this woman was very different from my first wife. She liked the way I looked and felt. Patty didn't. She enjoyed my humor and my boy-like attitude towards living life. Patty didn't. She wanted to partner with me and to spend all her time with me. Patty didn't. I thought we fit together like two pieces of a puzzle. We did, but the puzzle was stood on end not flat and stable.

Early in our relationship she had said, "I didn't want to marry a man who has children or a different religion." I had also thought it important to marry someone in my Faith and was surprised when I didn't and also went against the teachings of my beloved Faith to do it by not waiting the required year between ending my last marriage and entering into this one.

I knew and she knew that we were breaking the rules. These were rules that we had lived our lives by, her rules, and my rules. Together we believed that we would be the exception. We weren't!

A dying relationship is much like a prolonged disease. Everyone knows when the symptoms surface that death will follow. Symptoms like "I hate your children, I hate your Faith." And yet the occurrences of remissions, a nice outing, or good talks on long walks, cast the illusion of health and prolonged life. The death itself is expected, and yet we find ourselves surprised, and are disappointed that we didn't remember the last intimacies…the last intimacies of a relationship that wasn't created to die.

BEST FRIEND 1999

"Hi, James. I'm going to be driving through Selah tomorrow and was wondering if we could get together for lunch." I hadn't expected to hear Suzanne's voice and was delighted. Suzanne has been my friend for thirty years and has always stood beside me…even during some difficult times.

She was good to see and reminded me how much I loved Eugene and my many friends in the Baha'i community.

We walked and talked as we wandered through Sportsman Park and enjoyed the beautiful day. She said that her divorce was close to complete and I shared that I had started mine. We talked about lots of things that we valued together and agreed to see each other soon.

She valued her Faith, which was the same as mine. She loved my children, who she has taught in Baha'i classes for most all their lives. I like her boy who hung out in the Baha'i Center when we were remodeling. I taught him how to nail and use a hammer. She likes to travel…so do I. Humm!

LETS TRY IT A THIRD TIME 1999

We didn't want it to be fancy and we did want a celebration. We both felt pretty beat-up by our past marriages and wanted number three to be lucky. We bought a home in Florence, and I moved in and began to remodel. Suzanne would drive over from Eugene and we would work together, and have a good time counting our blessings.

We set a date and invited all our friends and family. Just off the ocean's edge a wide and long run of flat beach separates the water from miles of rolling dunes. The day before our wedding, in a hollow between dunes, we found a perfect spot and at its base we built a big fire pit. The entrances between our dunes and the nearby parking lot were delightfully obvious when we placed twenty-foot arches wrapped in colorful flags and banners. Vibrant standards on tall poles were jammed into the sand and added to the festivities. The B-B-Q, coolers filled with drinks and lots of extra firewood were stacked to the side. On the face of one dune we marked a spot with smaller arches and made it the point where we would stand and face our witnesses and share our vows. We loaded up all the party things we weren't comfortable leaving on the beach overnight and drove to our new home. Everything was perfect.

For months before and months after our wedding, it didn't rain. On August 7th, 1999 we dressed up in our matching Hawaiian outfits, dashed through the rain towards our truck and squealed, "Come on, Baby…lets do it." Our friends were all there. Umbrellas of every color and size were over lapped as we, soaked to the skin, stood before them and committed our marriage to God. The flags and banners swirled then drooped towards the ground when the gusts of wind passed. The fire tried to push its flames through the rain and succeeded in filling our little holy hollow with smoke. It was, almost all of our friends proclaimed, one of the happiest weddings they had ever attended.

We didn't stay on the beach long, and appreciated the help as we loaded it all up and drove home, where we set it up again in our front yard with the B-B-Q under the porch and the arches across the driveway. Inside our dry home we celebrated and danced the day away.

MOTHER'S DAY 2000

"Good morning, Sweetheart. How did you sleep?" She turned towards me as she passed the office door, rubbed her eyes and responded with, "Good, Baby. How about you?" I had gotten up a couple of hours before and had made coffee and eaten a little toast with peanut butter. On Saturday and Sunday mornings, I like to drive to the market where I purchase the Register Guard Newspaper. After breakfast I picked up my prayer book and perched myself on the outside swing where the morning sun peeked through the branches of the Linden tree and warmed the swing's wood. Elway, my hundred pound Shepherd, licked my hand and curled himself beside the swing's base, where the wisteria vines began their climb up the support timbers. By the time my sweetheart got up, I had said my prayers and talked with my mother and her caretaker in Yakima.

Today is Mothers' Day, and cooking a special breakfast for Suzanne was my goal. I made her fancy French toast and peaches that we ate on our oak table. The morning sun warmed us as we took extra time to enjoy our food and the paper. Suzanne prefers a slow to start her day, and today, before she showered and dressed, she sat by the pond and fed the fish.

We had planned to take our little blue and green fishing boat out on Munsel Lake to gather water plants for our pond. I knew that her shower would take a while, so I fixed our windsocks that had tangled during a recent storm. When I finished the sock project, Suzanne joined me in the garage and proudly announced that she was ready to go boating. I hooked the boat to our truck, and we loaded the shovel and buckets we thought would be helpful in our plant gathering. Florence has lakes all around the city and Munsel Lake is only ten minutes from the city center. The boat ramp was empty, so, with my improved backing skills, the boat was floating in minutes.

Our dear friend, John Flaherty, sold us the boat last fall and the Honda motor has always started on the second pull. Today was no exception. We explored the water's edge, dodging old fallen trees, and soon entering a shaded cove filled with water plants. I was shocked at how deeply they were buried in the muddy lake bottom, and the large pineapple-looking base was a further surprise to me. We spent two hours on our water adventure, and picked up several types of plants.

The expedition was followed by another impressive display of trailer backing skills and boat loading. Suzanne was happy to be back home, and watched the time as she waited for her son, Jason, and his friend Shawn. We had plans for a weenie roast on our favorite piece of beach, just off of Ocean Way. Jason didn't arrive as planned, so I took advantage of his delay to curl up on the sofa with an old James Bond movie, followed by an afternoon nap. When I awoke, I found Suzanne in the front yard dead-heading the rhododendrons. We sat on the benches in the yard and talked about how pleased we were with our efforts and what our next project might be. Several hours later, Jason and Shawn arrived, and we quickly drove to the beach. The entire day had been filled with sunshine and now, with our beach event at hand, massive clouds laced with thunder and lightening moved in from the ocean, determined to drown out our picnic. We persevered, built our beach fire, and roasted our weenies. True Oregonians never let a little rain discourage any event. We cooked, ate, and enjoyed our very wet party. When we got home, the boys and Suzanne hopped into the hot tub, and I sat down with my computer to record a delightful day in my fifty-fifth year.

HOLIDAYS 1999

Holidays are for children. At another time, they were for me, but not now. All is in order in my life, except I will not be with my parents or children this Christmas. Jamie is with her husband in

Eugene, Oregon, Jordan is with his wife and mother in Whittier, California, Mom and Dad are in Yakima, Washington, and I am in Medford, Oregon. If I were the grand weaver of wishes, we would all be together in some great lodge filled with color, warmth, and music. The smells of good cooking would float through the Christmas tree boughs and mix in our nostrils, tantalizing all our senses. Pans would rattle with spoons, and laughter would blend together with soft and private conversations, punctuated with giggles and cries of delight. We would move from one group to another, sharing our past accomplishments and hopes for tomorrow. Our children would be joyful and filled with the excitement of our celebration. Those whose hard days had ended and needed rejuvenation would take naps and our loved ones, who have passed beyond, would parade through the rooms and tell of their new adventures and assure us of their well-being and their hopes for us. Our dogs and cats would share space on the hearth while awaiting their venture out to the snow. We would ski, and sled, and roll snow into snowmen, while the children would make angels and pick holly for the fireplace mantel. When the sun traded places with the cold winter moon, we would all come inside and drink hot chocolate and coffee. The table would be massive and we would all gather around and hold hands while we thank God for all we have and will receive. Our dinner would be endless and our sharing the same as we talked of memories the old ones and the making of new. Yes, all this and more would come to be, if I were the grand weaver of wishes and dreams.

CHRISTMAS EVE 1999

This night, Christmas Eve, is drawing to an end and has been filled with new people, new experiences, new traditions, and laughter. Suzanne's mom is ill. The cancer that she thought she had licked eight years ago is back. Her time in this world is short. Suzanne's dad passed away eighteen months ago. We're all making an effort at "Merry Christmas," but not always successfully. I have, to some extent, appeased my holiday appetite with phone calls from my parents and children. I just read the "Holiday" piece I wrote the other night to my wife's son, Jason.

He said that his Christmas days have also passed. He's only seventeen. His Christmas mornings were once filled with married parents, loving grandparents, and gifts upon gifts rolling out from under the decorated tree. He remembers a spotlight of attention being directed upon him, and feeling special within his little family. He also remembers furniture that has been given away, people who have died and traditions that are no longer practiced. He agrees that holidays are for children.

I HATE IT 2000

I hate it. I hate it. I hate it. I have just returned from taking Mom to see her physician. She appears to be in pretty good health. He is upping her anti-depressant and cutting off the muscle relaxants. I will be attending a meeting for the family members of Alzheimer's patients this afternoon at two.

This morning my time with Mom was terrible. She's so damned angry. She's directing that anger towards me with a toxic mix of..."I love you and I know that you are doing the best you can and I hate the life you are forcing me to live." She keeps talking about having a place of her own. She wants control of her life. She hates all those people who are trying to help her. She is sweet and tearful when she talks of being a burden for me… then refuses to enter the Care Center after the doctor's visit. She hangs on the door and won't let go. "Mom we can't do this," I moan. "I have to go to work. I can't leave you in the parking lot." She screams, "I won't go into that place. You can't force me to go where I don't want to go." I pulled her hand from the door and rolled her wheelchair into the lobby. I said, "Goodbye" and walked out through the door. She was right behind me trying to force her way through the opening. I pushed her back and closed the door. I hate it. I hate it. I hate it.

WEDDING 2000

Yesterday I experienced a momentous and eventful day. It was the marriage of my daughter. I loved it. The wedding place was an elegant restaurant on the banks of the Willamette River. The decor was a mix of expansive windows, expensive carpets and tasteful furnishings. The fabulously creative ceiling chandeliers, which celebrated the best of the 30's, and the vogue wall hangings added to the atmosphere. The restaurant wrapped itself around the courtyard that framed its view between columns of stone and fall painted trees. It was on the terra cotta patio that the service was held. Its ceiling was open and framed by wooden over-hangs that pushed warm heat down on the late morning gathering. The sky was blue after the lift of early morning mist. On the river side, just inside the courtyard, stood four white fluted pillars. Each was capped with a bouquet of roses and foliage that captured the glory and elegance of a country garden. The height of the pillars varied and between them yards of broad gold cloth that was gathered here and there with clasps of roses was draped. The corners were bound with large plush tassels and cords that hung below the bouquets.

Around 11:00 am people began to arrive and all were given an agenda printed on paper of soft pink and white roses. Music, that was light and had a hint of an Irish countryside floated between conversations. Hugs and kisses were everywhere. The women were dressed with elegance, and the men had ties, and freshly pressed suits. The bride was in her secret place with the women and girls. What they did and said was unknown to those of us who were so anxious to see her.

"The bride is ready." Visiting calmed and everyone walked outside. The courtyard was quickly filled and all faces turned and waited for her arrival. I stood between the pillars and handed the cord to the white brocade runner to Jason, who slowly rolled it out over the terra cotta stones. Mothers, and grandmothers, with their escorts, slowly walked to their places. Hardly noticing, the music changed, and the powerful sounds of Bolero filled the courtyard. The groom, in his flawlessly tailored suit, seated his mother and stood at the head of the runner. He adjusted his silver blue silk tie and waited. Everyone stood when they saw her. The gasp of delight could be heard above the music. A quick "Oh, look" passed Chuck's lips as a smile spread across his face.

She stood on the far end of the runner. Her satin slippers were invisible under her dress. The aisle was filled with satin and lace. Her bodice was covered with white sequins that spilled across her skirt. Her skin was tan and rich. The veil was edged with seed pearls and draped over her bare shoulders. Her blond hair was high in a French twist, and a small tiara held her veil in place. She was beautiful!

As her eyes glanced across the gathering and ended on her husband to be, she began to cry. It was an adorable mix of smile and tears. Standing beside her and holding her arm was her brother, Jordan. At his lead they began the slow walk across the white brocade. Smiles were everywhere. Jamie took her place beside Chuck. He was dark and handsome; she, fair and luminous.

As the Bolero soundtrack ended, I heard my voice welcome the Friends. "Jamie and Chuck are delighted that you have joined them today. This is a Baha'i wedding, and thus is completely a creation of Jamie and Chuck. They have selected Holy Writings from the Baha'i Faith and the Bible. They have also asked several friends to sing. The "I do" moment will be when they say to one another, "We will all, verily, abide by the will of God."

Vida stood and walked to the center of the aisle. She turned and faced the gathering. In her voice, which is an enchanting mix of English and Persian, she read the opening prayer "He is God! O peerless Lord! In Thine almighty wisdom thou hast enjoined marriage upon the peoples that the generations of men may succeed one another in this contingent world, and that ever, so long as the world shall last, they may busy themselves at the Threshold of Thy oneness with servitude and worship, with salutation, adoration and praise. I have not created spirits and men, but that they should worship me. Wherefore, wed Thou in the heaven of Thy mercy these two birds of the nest of Thy love, and make them the means of attracting perpetual grace; that from the union of these two seas of love a wave of tenderness may surge and cast the pearls of pure and goodly issue on the shore of life. He hath let loose the two seas, that they meet each other: Between them is a barrier which they overpass not. Which then of the bounties of your Lord will ye deny? From each He bringeth up greater and lesser pearls. O Thou kind Lord. Make thou this marriage to bring forth coral and pearls. Thou art verily the All Powerful, the Most Great, the Ever-Forgiving." Abdu'l-Baha.

Joseph and Debbie then filled the air with their voices and his guitar. "Give yourself to love" was their song, and their voices mixed beautifully. They stood at the base of the brocade runner and faced Jamie and Chuck with all the friends looking in their direction. Chuck then explained the Marriage Quote and I read it. "In this glorious Cause the life of a married couple should resemble the life of the angels in heaven - a life full of joy and spiritual delight, a life of unity and concord, a friendship both mental and physical. The home should be orderly and well organized. Their ideas and thoughts should be like the rays of the sun of truth and radiance of the brilliant stars in the heavens. Even as two birds they should warble melodies upon the branches of the tree of fellowship and harmony. They should always be elated with joy and gladness and be a source of happiness to the hearts of others. They should set an example to their fellow men, manifest a true and sincere love towards each other, and educate their children in such a manner as to blazon the fame and glory of their family." Abdu'l-Baha

Darya and Eric sang a Marriage song they had written. Their style was very different than Joseph and Debbie. As "Give yourself to love" has a folk sound the "Wedding song" was smooth jazz. As Eric played his guitar, Darya would raise her hands in delightful expression. Chuck explained the meaning of the importance of God's light and guidance in our lives.

I then read the 36th Psalm. "Lord, your love reaches to heaven; your fidelity to the clouds. Your justice is like the highest mountains; your judgments, like the mighty deep; all living creatures you sustain, Lord. How precious is your love, O God! We take refuge in the shadow of your wings. We feast on the rich food of your house; from your delightful stream you give us drink. For with you is the fountain of life, and in your light we see light. Continue your kindness toward your friends, your just defense of the honest heart."

The next reading was the 37th Psalm. "Trust in the Lord and do good that you may dwell in the land and live secure. Find your delight in the Lord who will give you your heart's desire."

Following a short pause Diane stepped to the end of the runner and began to sing "Perhaps Love." Her rich deep voice carried out over everyone, and all eyes were torn between the lovers and Diane.

Chuck talked about his father and dedicated the 23rd Psalm to him. "The Lord is my shepherd; there is nothing I lack. In green pastures you let me graze; to safe waters you lead me; you restore my strength. You guide me along the right path for the sake of your name. Even when I walk through a dark valley, I fear no harm for you are at my side; your rod and staff give me courage. You set a table before me as my enemies watch; You anoint my head with oil; my cup overflows. Only goodness and love will pursue me all the days of my life; I will dwell in the house of the Lord for years to come." I then shared with the friends that Chuck and Jamie had chosen their vows and they would now recite them before God and all present. They turned to face each other. I handed the vows first to Jamie, then to Chuck. "I Jamie, take you, Chuck, to be my partner in life. I will always celebrate our friendship and our romance. I will cherish you and respect you, comfort you and encourage you. I promise to always be honest with you and trust when I misunderstand. I will love you forever, always giving thanks that we have found each other." Jamie then slipped the wedding band on Chuck's finger and said "We will all, verily, abide by the will of God."

Chuck slipped the band on Jamie's finger, as he shared the same vow. He then wrapped his arms around Jamie and kissed her with all the class of Clark Gable.

Following the kiss I shared with the friends that we had one more prayer and also a song that Chuck had picked out for Jamie. It had touched his heart, and he hoped that it would touch the heart of all that were present.

Suzanne stepped to my side and read "O my Lord, O my Lord! These two bright moons are wedded in Thy love, conjoined in servitude to Thy Holy Threshold, united in ministering to Thy Cause. Make Thou this marriage to be as threading lights of Thine abounding grace, O my Lord, the All-Merciful, and luminous rays to Thy bestowals, O Thou the Beneficent, the Ever-Giving, that there may branch out from this great tree boughs that will grow green and flourishing through the gifts that rain down from Thy clouds of grace. Verily, Thou are the Generous. Verily, Thou art the Almighty. Verily, Thou art the Compassionate, the All-Merciful."

As Suzanne returned to her seat the room filled with the Joshua Kadison's song, "Beautiful in my Eyes." As the song played, Jamie and Chuck stood close to each other and delighted the friends with their hugs and kisses. I stood behind my daughter and her husband and watched her embrace him, oblivious to her surroundings, and whisper in his ear, away from the sight of all but me "I love you." He turned her face to him and said, "I love you, Jamie."

I then raised my voice and said, "May I be the first to introduce Mr. and Mrs. Coy." At the couple's request, they remained where they were for photographs, and everyone entered the restaurant for a delightful lunch with toasts, a very precious dance with Chuck twirling Jamie in her wedding dress, and cake cutting. It was a momentous and eventful day that I will always cherish.

HAPPINESS IS SINGING 2000

I remembered last year standing on the third row of risers and singing great old show tunes for appreciative spectators. This year I was part of a charmed audience and wondered how I happened to be sitting and not on the risers in my black slacks, starched white shirt with a green and yellow scarf draped around my neck.

My wife and I saw the signboard promoting the May 31st concert and made a commitment to attend. Across the street from Fred Meyer's, Baptists have perched their church high on a sand dune and its design includes a community room. The Florence Community Chorus has used it before and the acoustics are good. They have several ceiling fans that spin their blades through the evening of delightful music, performed by forty talented community members and directed by Judy, who has been the heartthrob of many musical adventures in our community.

The Chorus, which is handsomely peppered with gray heads, is an amazing blend of retired and talent performers surrounded by a bunch of locals who love to sing and are looking for a good time. Friday's concert began with New Ashmolean Marching Society and ended with a sing-a-long which included "God Bless America" and "America."

Standing with my hand across my heart and drum rolls keeping rhythm, I sang as loud as I could, and was delighted, if only for the evening, to be a part of the Florence Community Chorus.

FIRESIDE 2000

Monday nights we have Baha'i Firesides in our home. We made a commitment to host these gatherings when we first moved to Florence and have been very faithful. During one of our gatherings, one of our guests shared a story that impressed me. "There was a guitar that desperately wanted to be played by the greatest musician. It did everything in its power to be noticed by the musician and one day, to his delight, the musician picked him up. The musician had known of the guitar's desire, and was pleased to play him. When he stroked the strings, he discovered that it was out of tune because it had not been played for so long. Again, appreciating the guitar's desire to be played, the musician decided it was worth his effort to tune the guitar. He began with one string and as he tightened the key, the string broke. The strings were all out of tune and the musician decided, because of the guitar's desire to be played by him that he would play it with only five strings. When he began to tune the fifth string it also broke. Again the musician decided that because of the guitar's desire, he would play the guitar with only four strings. When he began to tune the forth string it also broke as did the third, second, and first. The musician then laid the guitar to the side and looked for another." This story reminded me that a life filled with flexibility is the means to fulfillment and joy. Without it making music is difficult, and with out music, our lives will lack the joy that God has willed for us.

PAPER, SCISSOR, ROCK 2000

"It looks a little funny, doesn't it?" When I finished my afternoon carpentry project, I found myself a little amazed as I realized I had taken a major step towards aging. A few years ago Suzanne's mother gave us her sectional. It was big, in good shape, and offered lots of comfortable seating. What we observed was that older folks who visited would often shy away from sitting on it. We didn't think much about it until we noticed that we had both developed little leverage tricks to get up. Sitting down was easy. You would just get yourself in the approximate area you wanted to sit and drop. It was really comfortable once you settled in. The problem was getting up. It appears that with age, and the addition of a few pounds, the body didn't have the power to lift itself. I found myself rolling to the side and grabbing the decorative balls on the surface of our Persian coffee table to help myself up. Suzanne, being shorter, would stick her foot under the table's thick glass top and leverage with her legs. We both would be groaning by the time we stood.

"I should see if I can get some longer legs for this sofa" was my statement, as I almost lost my balance when I tried to stand. "Wouldn't that look kind of funny?" Suzanne asked, as she joined me in the struggle to stand. "Maybe, but if we don't do something soon, we will have to buy some new furniture or hook cables in the ceiling."

The project only took a few hours and is a delightful improvement. I didn't replace the legs but instead I made a frame of one by sixes, stained it a color similar to the floor and sat the sectional on top of it. I know that it sounds ugly and it is not. It might be a little strange, but we now have easy sitting, and tons of extra storage space. We smiled at each other last night as we curled up to watch a DVD and knew that if we wanted anything else out of the kitchen, or if the phone rang, we wouldn't have to play "paper, scissor, rock."

APRIL FIRST 2000

Life for me was spent in a large and fertile meadow. In that meadow there stood an oak tree. It was the only tree and it was well rooted and hearty. I had known for years that my father was this mighty tree, and that he would not live forever. In his aging he had grown knots. His branches had lost their youthful flex, and he continued to stand tall, grow leaves, and withstand the storms of life. Today, I am a grown man and when I look across the meadow, I see that the tree has fallen. I rub my eyes to clear away this unwanted vision, yet have no success. Today I find myself alone crossing the meadow he had shaded and protected for all my life. Today is the day of my father's death.

LIVING A GOOD LIFE 2000

Our life in Florence has presented us with many more blessings than Suzanne or I expected. The wonderful location of this oceanside community, which has a population of less than 7,000 citizens, is just a few miles from the mouth of the Sisulaw River. Being small is Florence's greatest asset.

Daily I work for friends or people who will soon be friends. I value these friendships and work to nurture and develop them. My friends are very diverse, yet we seldom find our selves in conflict with each other.

A reporter with the Siuslaw News was visiting us last night. He's doing an article on the Baha'i Faith and had many questions to ask. During his sharing he said, "My wife and I are here in Florence to live a good live... not make a lot of money." I think that is what most of us are doing...living a good live and satisfied with our lot.

We have taken to crabbing. Our aluminum boat with its little Honda motor runs us out and over the tops of the incoming waves to the sides of the river where the sand dunes drop off into the water. There, twenty or thirty feet from the beach, we drop our fish baited crab-pots. For fifteen or twenty minutes we enjoy the view as we putt about. When we return to our pot's float, we pull it quickly into the boat and harvest our catch. Suzanne is the pot puller, and I keep the boat into the waves. We don't have much knowledge or experience with boating, crabbing or fishing. It doesn't matter. We love the playing.

At the very end of Rhododendron Street you can take a left on Joshua, another left on Third and then a right down Ocean Way. There you will find easy parking and you will be only twenty feet from the beach. It's our favorite place, and both our dogs love it. Lately we have taken to leashing our Sheltie to our German Shepherd. Elway, the Shepherd, loves to run and the Sheltie, left to her natural instincts, would never stray from our heels. We decided that she would benefit from more exercise, so we loop her leash around Elway's neck and off they go. At first she would look back to see if this was what we really wanted her to experience. Once she realized it was, even though she didn't understand, she took to his lead. They drew lots of smiles from other beach walkers as they, a 100 lbs male Sheppard and a 25 lbs female Sheltie, flew by in perfect stride. Well...she may have been taking a few more steps than him.

My good friend, John Flaherty, meets me every few days at the coffee house on Bay Street. We often sit for an hour drinking our coffee and sharing recent news. We find ourselves solving the problems of the world and worrying about kids and people who are confused or unkind.

Many an hour has been spent attempting to develop plans that would improve life for folks and maybe to help us understand ourselves. John's a good friend.

AFTER THE GAME 2000

They both stood with one leg on a chair and the other in the center of a table and played their saxophones recklessly to the delight of all who were packed in the small bar. We started our Florence evening attending the local high school football game. They had colorful gold and blue uniforms, and very little talent. The parents sitting around us made gracious comments about the team like "My, that visiting team is good" or "He is pretty quick for a 110 pound half back." None of it mattered much. It was a warm summer night, the bleachers were alive with teenage kids, and the smell of fresh coffee filled the night air. We, my sweet Suzanne and I, also felt alive. After the game we took a new friend up on an invitation to hear the voice of a great keyboard buddy of his from California. When we entered The Whistler, the small bar was jammed with a few tired drinkers who didn't move from their corner stools and forty seven jiving' folks, all older than me and my child-like bride. The place was hopping, and the spirit was innocent and accepting. People in our age group are happy to still have the energy to swing at 11:00pm, thus, forgive all indiscretions that are attached to dancing styles. We loved the spirit of the band, which knew well the sound of being called "grandpa." Their talent was well beyond other groups that would normally be attracted to a town of six thousand. We shared a table with a couple from Roseburg, who were visiting the coast, and talked with several other folks we had met around town. There were lots of smiles tonight. Living in Florence and smiling a lot go together. Tomorrow we fish. We have our boat hooked to the truck, bait in the freezer, hooks, and other important fishing things are in the tackle box. All salmon be warned. I do believe we will be smiling again.

RHODODENDRON FESTIVAL 2000

The third weekend of May we celebrate the Florence Rhododendron Festival. Last year my daughter decided to spend the weekend with Suzanne and me. She and her friend arrived midday Saturday and following hugs, showing off the house, drinking a pop and unloading stuff, we walked to Old Town. Bay Street was filling with Harley Davidson's of every size, age, condition and color. Climbing over and around the three-block rack of diverse metal were people of every size, age, condition and color. The Harley people were mostly dressed in black leather with various parts of their skin exposed to display biceps, tattoos, breasts, midriffs, and an impressive number of beer bellies. With their tires backed to the curb, the bikes spewed hot exhaust fumes and pushed deep rumbles into the crowd that was solidly packed from curb to tavern. The crowd would grow to fill all of Bay Street from Mo's restaurant down to the Siuslaw River Coffee Roasters. They would be stacked on their bikes sun bathing, drinking, and admiring each other and their motorcycles, while brightly colored tourists wandered through their party.

A beach party was also a part of our day's plan. We loaded the picnic basket with weenies, buns, pop, condiments, and a little fire starting fluid. Years ago I had set aside my Boy Scout training and since have been successful starting beach fires. Add a dozen pieces of driftwood beside an old beached log, several good squirts of Firequick and "voila" fire.

Jamie, her friend, Suzanne, and my dogs, Elway and Jenny, walked the beach while I heated the can of Beanie Weenies and set out the plates and stuff. By the time the five-some returned, the smell of the starting fluid had burned away, and the logs were ablaze. We cooked our weenies and were amazed at the smoke's ability to waft in all our faces simultaneously. With burned weenies in buns, topped with mustard and catsup, we gobbled up our creations and enjoyed watching the surf and the yet unset sun. After another short walk with the dogs, they both shared in our cooked delights, we packed up and headed for the video store.

We were four pretty tired folks and had decided over our fire that watching a good Jackie Chan movie would be as much effort as we were willing to expend. We got the movie, ate the popcorn, drank the pop, and celebrated another day in Florence.

COWBOY 2000

Crossing Bay Street is the sound of homegrown music blended with that of the wind and river. There weren't many of us out tonight, and the warm light of the coffee house shining across the day-old puddles was inviting. Much of Old Town had returned to clap board siding and white enamel paints, while this coffee house remained stuck in the 60's. Its face was patched with shingles, weathered by forty years of wind and rain. An old flat awning protected the smokers on rainy days, where they sat on hand carved benches that were held together with pieces of lumber stuck here and there.

Passing through the entrance, the strong smell of coffee beans releasing their flavors blended with the music the young cowboy was making. The old wooden walls were in competition with the cedar shakes outside. Both had seen too many years of hard service, and yet they refused to relinquish their roles. The tables and chairs were maple and butcher block, with black aging creeping up their legs.

It's easy in a small town to take pleasure in simple efforts. Our cowboy singer could never sing out loud in a city of size, but tonight the stage was his, and he was singing us every song he had written in his spiral binder. He had a look with his black George Strait hat, a quarter sized hole in the front of the rim, low-heeled boots with silver duct tape around both toes, and the traditional dinner plate sized belt buckle. He was a sweet young man who had a song to sing. Half of the folks sitting around, maybe twelve of us, tried to softly sing along as if our voices would draw him a little closer to key.

One would think that moving on would be the plan, yet there was something happening in that place. None of us were expecting much of the night and were content to enjoy each other, as we raised our voices in requests or silly jokes, easily laughed at. An hour or so passed with us and the other folks. One table of women, who had already enjoyed most of their lives, was playing cards between teasing the cowboy about the songs he was singing. He would laugh with them and with us, while turning the page to his next song. Maybe one of them was his grandma. Getting home was gaining in its appeal and we dropped a couple of bucks in the jar as we left and waved goodbye to every one. I like the living in a small costal town.

Andy's Bridge 2000

His name was Andrew Joseph Petry and he died almost seven years ago to the day. His daughter, Agnes, felt his presence in his ashes. For this reason, it was never the right time to carry out his wishes and cast his ashes to the sea. Last week Agnes died. Today, Suzanne, Agnes's daughter, and I carried out the wishes of Andrew.

I didn't know him, but was told, by Suzanne, that he was tall for her family, close to six foot. His body was rich with muscle to match his labor as a river man and railroad blacksmith. Blue eyed, strong chinned and topped with black curly hair, he was a ladies' man, which was his greatest blessing and life long test.

Last night, over our dinner, I shared with Suzanne my discomfort with Andy's ashes in our home. I had been told of his last wish for his body, and hoped that she would feel comfort in fulfilling his wish.... soon.

We left our home and began our drive south to Coos Bay to attend a two-man theater show of a friend of ours. Suzanne and I talked of how extraordinary the sunset was. When I realized that I had forgotten my coat and we needed to return to the house, Suzanne asked me to bring Andy along. "We will dump his ashes tonight."

I stopped the car on the southwest corner of the Siuslaw Bridge. It is considered one of the ten most beautiful bridges in the country, and with tonight's sunset, it was fabulous. I expected this to be a quick dumping of ashes, and then back on the road, so I didn't turn the car off ... only set the emergency flashers. I was emotionally very detached from the event. I took the clear plastic bag from the golden cardboard box that reminded me of a larger version of the orchard boxes I delivered to my high school dates on prom night. I was surprised at the complexity of the ashes. I expected black powder or maybe a gray sand like substance. What I saw was white shards of bone and varying sized chips of gray gravel. "My, this stuff was Suzanne's grandfather's body, and I am about to fulfill his death wish." I was touched and as we walked up the rising span of the bridge. I began to pray for the man, and wanted to make this moment a bit special.

Three quarters of the way up the span I stopped and set the bag of ashes on the carved stone rail. The river below was flowing out towards the ocean with a quickness that indicated an out-flowing tide. Suzanne came by my side and I asked "Are you ready?" "Yes," and with her word I dumped the bag. The lighter ash quickly separated itself from the heavier and formed a comet like tail as it dropped to the river's surface. The sound of a thousand splashing pebbles reached our ears as we leaned over the rail and watched a moment of magic. The river grasped Andy's ashes and swirled them so that for a moment the whiteness of it on the dark river surface looked like an Indian spirit stretching his arms and legs after a long confinement. Quickly, a whirlpool formed and caught the head and arms. It continued its spin, like rich cream mixing into a cup of coffee, until all the body had disappeared deep into the vortex of the pool. The river then, as we watched in amazement, closed its flowing surface. It had accepted the body of a man who spent the best years of his life loving and working on it. "Did you see that?" I asked Suzanne. "Yes.... yes I did."

JUNCTION CITY 2000

The car was rolling down the highway that laced itself beside the Siuslaw River. It was early and we needed to be in Springfield by 8:00 am. Suzanne was teaching her adult class on child abuse recognition and reporting, and she needed to be set-up before the students arrived.

The drive, which was filled with much of the coastal magic that attracted us to Florence, took only an hour and a half. We wound through the gray of early morning haze, knowing that the sun wouldn't come into view until 7:00 am. Our coffee was rich and the breakfast snacks filled our stomachs. We listened to PBS radio and talked a little between Suzanne's "it's too early to be up" naps.

The Goodwill building was open when we arrived, and after I set up the correct number of chairs and arranged the tables, I left Suzanne alone with the balance of her task. I had eight hours to kill and was unsure how they would be spent. I drove past my favorite coffee house and found that it wouldn't open until 9:00 am, which was an hour away. I found myself thinking about my old coffee house in Junction City, and decided to take the twelve-mile drive.

The sun was up, and the route I took was Aubrey Lane. I had owned an old farmhouse on Aubrey, and I was disappointed to see that there was no livestock in the pasture and the buildings were in poor maintenance. When I sold it four years ago, it had been crisp and white with dark green shutters. The pasture was bordered with white washed fencing. During my years there, the grass was kept short first by sheep and later by a few steers. Today I saw peeled paint, torn screens, and tall grass, with eight old rigs and a motor home jammed together around the house. I would have kept the place, but with the work demands of the coffee house, I couldn't keep the farm up. Regret welled in me as I drove on.

The sight of the mural on the side of the old theater building always pleased me when I drove into town. It had been a massive wall of peeling paint until I stripped, primed and painted it. That in itself was an immense improvement, and when the airbrush artist painted his mural, with its massive theater arches, vintage cars and patrons of the 40's, it became the pride of Junction City.

I remembered the feelings of loss and disappointment I had experienced on past visits. Today my feelings changed a bit. I felt a little pride and a lot of curiosity. I drove past the city block that held the theater, coffee house, and the commercial office building I had owned. I turned at the corner and parked in the lot beside Dr. Albert's office and got out of my car. I walked across the alley gravel to the custom doors I had installed on the back of the theater building. After pushing the window dust aside, I was able to see the interior. The massive paintings of Tamara De Limpika were still on the walls. They appeared to be in good condition. I was fearful that with two winters and no heat the walls would warp and damage the artwork. There were still case refrigerators and left over restaurant equipment sitting about. I could see that the ice cream parlor was still in place, although the spin stools had been removed. I gave the doors a shake to see if maybe a mistake had been made and a closer look could be mine. They were secure. I walked around to the front and saw that the wallpaper was peeling off the walls in the private dining area and that someone had removed the French doors. The water damage on the ceiling in the lobby had not worsened, and seeing the powder white clouds I had painted on the ceiling above the theater chandelier pleased me. There were tables and chairs stacked against the walls and the ticket machine in the booth was gone. The trim work and paint around the fancy glass entrance doors I had made were holding up well. I walked a few feet further down the block and looked into the coffeehouse. It was filled with new tile-covered tables and metal restaurant chairs. There were Mexican blankets and sombreros hanging on the walls. Every table was set with napkins and silverware. The décor was not what I had created and loved, but it was good looking. The walls, counters, carpet, tile, mirrors, lights, shelves and most important of all the neon light on the ceiling were the same. The color of the walls had changed and the patio wall I had built by the door had been moved to the edge of the sidewalk. The large garden area around the courtyard tree had been filled in and the shrubs beside the building had been pulled and concrete poured. Molly's mural, that I had loved, had been painted over with a design of red bricks, arches and a Mexican countryside. It didn't have the class of my stuff and was great for a Mexican restaurant.

As I walked by the office building and noted that it was fully occupied, I realized that I had looped the buildings and was standing beside my car. I was pleased that I had made the trip and pleased that I had taken the time to refresh my memories. I had loved much about this city block and had suffered here also.

GORE 2000

Al Gore lost his bid for the presidency today. He will concede to George Bush before the day is over.

I just got off my bicycle where I experienced my first early morning ride in hard rain. The PBS radio played in my ears and in my freshly water-proofed gear. I enjoyed the cocoon-like feeling my protection provided.

My days start well when I attend to my morning task of making Suzanne's breakfast and lunch. I fill her stainless steel cup with creamed coffee and walk her to her car. We kiss and I wish her a safe drive. As I stand by the curb I wave, grab the morning paper out of its plastic box, and return to the house.

My breakfast is simple with cold cereal, a bit of banana on top, good toast and black coffee. I glance through the paper and, with food eaten and news ingested; I set the world aside for a few minutes and say my prayers. It is nice to talk with God while looking over the beauty of our yard. The birds are in the feeder and Elway is lying under the fir tree which protects him from the rain. There he can watch the squirrels chase the birds away while they have their turn at the seeds and nuts. With all the important parts of my morning in order I go to my office, look over my projects for the day and complete my paper work. I usually find myself out the door by 9:00am.

Last night I asked Suzanne how she felt about my role as househusband and handyman. She said that she is jealous of the way that I get to start my day. I said, "I understand." And I do.

DREAM 2000

I dreamt last night that I was with Dad. He was dressed in white cotton. I felt that he, possibly we, were in danger. I had a large case, which I had Dad climb in to hide. I lifted the box on my shoulders and walked and walked until I felt that the danger had passed. It took a very long time and I was fearful at the end that Dad could have died. When I opened the box up, he was alive, exhausted and limp. I lifted him and placed him on a white sheet. He had dry leaves on his lap and legs. He kept his eyes closed and softly breathed. I sat back and felt I could do no more.

WRITING CLASS 2001

Taking a writing class wasn't high on my desires list and it would probably be far more interesting than TV. Suzanne had signed us both up for the class and tonight she had to teach a class in Eugene and wouldn't be able to join me. We had missed the first two meetings due to my father's death in Yakima, Washington.

I arrived twenty minutes early to talk with the instructor and to see if a late start would cause problems. She was a tall woman with bright clothes and cheerful makeup. "Sure, you can join us. There aren't too many men in the class and you are very welcome." She went on to say that I needed to pick up the class text at the front counter. I thanked her, and, with her directions, went down the hall. The book was only $16.95 and had a most interesting title. "Writing from Life, telling your soul's story" by Susan Wittig Albert, PH.D. Across the top of the cover it said, "A Journey of Self-discover for Women." "Are you sure this is the correct book?" was my question to the receptionist. "Yes sir. It's the book." I have spent a lot of years attempting to figure out the guy/gal thing and have settled with they are OK and I am OK. Sometimes I will go even further and say, "If you can find things to love about the opposite, sex you are on the right track." I had a feeling that this class was going to be another opportunity for me to enter the unknown world of women.

Upon my return to the room I interrupted the instructor's writing on the board with a "from the title of the text it looks like I am going to be working on my feminine side." She turned and sat in a chair across from me and said, "I am a feminist. The purpose of this class is to give voice to the female body and tonight the vagina will speak." I am often quick with wit, but at this moment I was unsure if I had just been swung into the sight of a feminist insurgent or someone who had escaped from a special ward of the local hospital. I was quiet. I sat back and listened to her explain that the class was giving voice to all of the female body and that those voices, once released would allow women to understand themselves and thus tell their soul's story.

The class was soon filled with wonderful old women, most over the age of sixty and a few twenty years beyond that. Great stories were told and not once did I hear a vagina speak. Not having heard a speaking vagina before, I may have heard it and not realized the experience. I have found that we men sometimes do that.

As the class drew to an end, I watched our instructor delight in women sharing their pride in divorce, breaking away from their rotten husbands and discovering themselves as individual women apart from the influence of males. Words, against my better judgment, began to come from my mouth, as I thanked these women for allowing me to be a part of their writing class. I shared that being the only man in the group it was important to me that I relate to their issues and attitudes. I went on to say, "I am a member of an exclusive group of men who identify themselves, with pride, men who have breasts." It was quiet for a few moments, and then I felt welcomed as one of them gave a short titter that was followed by the others with warm-hearted laughter.

FORTUNE TELLER 2001

Stepping from the fortuneteller's home I am delighted to catch my wife leaving me a note. "Baby, what are you doing here?" She pops her head up from the back of my truck's toolbox and splashes a big smile across her face. "I thought I would stick a note in the back of your truck to see if you would want a date tonight. I want to see "Anna and the King" at four. Do you think you can make it?"

Having made several attempts during the week to see the movie I found myself delighted with the thought of an early afternoon escape from the realities of the working world. "You bet ya, Baby." We kissed a couple of those midday pecks that seem like nothing and are one of the foundation stones of our marriage. I waved her away and returned to the plumbing project in Madam Falala's bathroom.

The madam looked like a fortuneteller should. She was dark with a massive, let me suck the pit out of a plum, mouth. Her hair was black and long. The eyes were clear, mouse brown and extra glazed with a penetrating look I knew. She lay on the end of her bed watching the end of a video movie while her small children crawled over her like otters' pups in a pool. She snapped at them from time to time, like her grandma had done when her dad ran around their gypsy wagon. She told me that she could read one of my hands and tell me all about myself for only twenty-five dollars, but if I was willing to spend another ten I would get it all. My whole future would be laid open to me for a mere thirty-five dollars.

PHOTOGRAPH 2001

The photograph was on their Christmas card. She is holding up the hem of her wedding dress. He is standing close to her. They are beside each other and not engaged. She seems occupied in kicking the bubbles that are blown in their direction and dancing about her exposed feet. He is standing in the most relaxed position with his arms limp and at his side. His head is tilted back, little to the right and his smile is overwhelmed delight.

This picture has captured these two lovers, Erica and my son Jordan. The way they are and how they chose to live their life is frozen for us all to appreciate.

Life can be hard on romance, so it's good that photographs capture love, kidnap us, lift us closer to God, and fill our chests with hope and optimism.

NATIONAL PUBLIC RADIO 2001

The keys on the laptop moved slowly as the sluggish thoughts in my mind attempted to drain from head to hands. I am working today in my real estate office and all the tasks I expected to complete are done. The hands on my watch are close to 4:00 p.m. and the bright light of the sun is heavily filtered as it pushes through the gray layer of overcast. National Public Radio fills my office with the world's problems and I am disheartened.

Today is a half empty day. All efforts to view it in a more positive light have failed. Our country is perched to commit war and much of the world feels browbeat or deceived. I am ashamed and feel powerless to redirect the blow America's leaders are about to hurl into the body of Iraq. I understand that God has a greater plan and like a mourner in a funeral procession, I find little joy in my heart.

TOOLBOX 2001

I dragged the last of my toolboxes into her shop and set them to the side of the work area. It was a Sunday night project, and my energy level was low. My body was saying "It's time for a good movie and popcorn" not "Let's get this project on a roll."

Diane was a dear friend who had several projects that needed my attention. She had been patient with me finding available time and needed to keep her shop open until 6: 00 pm seven days a week. We weren't going to do much tonight, just hang several shelves and maybe do a little trim work around her large arched window that looked out on the Florence Bay.

Diane quickly told me what she had in mind, and then attended to her own day's paper work. Twenty minutes or so later she sat down her pen and looked up at me working on my ladder. "James, I had a very interesting experience today. A couple came into the store today who were representing a church organization and wanted to ask me some questions about my beliefs."

Diane had been attending Firesides at our home for months, read several books about the Baha'i Faith, and had been invited to join the Cause. She had reported to us that she was comfortable with all of the Teachings of the Faith, but wanted to be sure of her decision and she would know the time.

She went on to say that these people asked her what church she belonged to and she responded, "I am a Baha'i." In that moment, as a result of that question, she knew that the time had come. "So, James, I guess I am letting you know that I now consider myself to be Baha'i."

I sat for a moment on the top of the ladder and basked in the beauty of the moment. I stepped down and walked to her, "Wonderful…I am so happy for you." I held her hand and told her that when a Seeker discovers Baha'u'llah the Concourse on High gathers around to celebrate the moment and that she would probably find me standing close by basking in her glory." She laughed at me and said, "Well James…that will be just fine."

HARBOR THEATER 2001

I promised that I would be back soon and I meant it. Four minutes south on 101, right for several blocks on 7th Street and home. Suzanne isn't there and the movie starts in fifteen minutes. I call. Her cell phone is on the table beside me. I have to trust that she will come through. Quickly I remove my work clothes, hanging my red suspenders across the saddle. I tossed the rest into the green laundry basket that sits by the saddle's stirrup. I wander into the kitchen in my flannel boxer shorts knowing that the neighbors have probably seen far too much of me over the months that we have lived here.

Lava soap is the best for cleaning hands and in a bottle it spits like a camel with attitude. I scrub my hands clean and wipe the excess spiting off my belly. I hate that pumper soap. I wash my face and comb my hair back off my face like Jack Nickelson. I like that slick look and head to my closet for fresh cloths.

The sound of Suzanne opening the door pleases me. "Hey, Fella, are ya cleaned up for the movie?" she yells. We are quickly out the door and driving down to Florence's Old Town area.

In the middle of the block facing the Siuslaw River is the Harbor Theater. Although the screen, projection and sound system are modern the rest of the building is 1930s. Few attempts have been made to update it and that is where the charm of the place lays. The seating is old loge's which are in need of repair and more comfortable and wider than anything in the new theaters.

It was an adventure movie filled with excitement and love. We left with tears and smiles. It was then a quick dash to the bathroom, which is built under the staircase to the projection room. If you use the urinal and are over five feet tall you have to lean back and are denied a view of the task at hand. Locals have developed the skills for this motion. I find myself a novice.

The weather outside was thick with cold costal fog. Both of us were dressed lightly and the dash across the street to Mo's was not easy. My chin was shaking as we entered the restaurant's reception area. "Baby, look at me. I am freezing to death," I whined. She responded with the expected, "Poor Baby." We enjoyed the best clam chowder in the world and drove home to our hot tub and bed.

TAROT CARDS 2001

The reading of the Tarot cards said that great success was at hand in my business and creative adventures. Saturday afternoon I found myself in the meeting room of the local library reading for a mid-April performance of "On Golden Pond." What the hell was that all about? I wanted and feared theater in high school. My fears won out until I have found myself socializing with friends who have loved and participated in Florence's community theater. They said, "Once you start, you won't be able to stop. It's like an addiction." I have heard those two lines a dozen times and am still unsure if it's true.

All the feelings that were so powerful in high school have not dissolved with the years. My new determination to experience what my fears have protected me from has proven, in this and other recent situations, rewarding. With both feet firmly placed on the carpeted floor I heard my voice respond to a line read by another. "Hello, you must be Norman?" The boom of my father's voice filled the room and faces turned to watch the baby thespian dip his toe into the addictive waters.

Re/Max Rising Star is the name on the sign that remains illuminated every moment of every day. The sign faces south towards the Siuslaw Bridge, and north in the direction of the intersection with Hwy 126. The blue building has a face of large square windows that have been set on end in white wooden frames. It's a funky look and blends well with the design of many of the buildings on this highly traveled and beautiful road. Behind the double wooden doors and up the flight of open steps is my office. I'm a Sales Associate and like sitting behind my new computer center that Suzanne and I constructed three weeks ago when I joined this sales team.

I began working in real estate in 1985 and have found that financial responsibilities denied me the opportunity to develop a full time career. Today I can afford this business adventure and feel unencumbered by the financial demands I once had.

Tarot cards and other future telling games entertain me. Today I find myself hopeful that the cards do see my today and the days to come. I believe I am blessed, and am exhilarated with my hopes for tomorrow.

CANARY ROAD 2001

For three weeks the drive down Canary Road has been interrupted by a road construction crew carving away the side of a massive, shrub covered dune. The workers had the look of children playing on the beach with Tonka trucks and toy earthmovers. It was the end of my workday and doing another estimate on a low profit repair job was low on my "what I want to be doing" list.

When I called June & Jerry, a couple who acted like performers who had been raised by vaudeville parents, they were yelling at each other. "Get him over here as quickly as his truck can drive him," shouted June in the background, as Jerry barked back, "OK! OK!"

One of the numbers in their address had fallen to the ground years ago and had been devoured by the shrubs and undergrowth, resulting in my doing several drive-bys. Jerry was at the gate and flagged me down. Once inside the yard and behind the chain link fencing I discovered dogs the size of horses, and cats fatter than blowfish. The dogs' barks were threatening. It required courage to step from my truck and approach the house.

Jerry…a mighty mite of a man with his thick belt tightly hitched around his full belly, strutted towards my truck. He reminded me of a Russian nesting doll. "Hi James…welcome to my home." His Liberace hair was brown except for the week's growth next to his scalp which was white and proclaimed his aging. Above his sparkling eyes were wild and overgrown brows. They were the type one sees on the mad scientist in late night monster movies.

June walked out of the house and joined the dogs and cats, which were jubilant to have her join us. She kissed them all as she packed three of her smaller eighteen-pound cats in her arms. "They just love her," chanted Jerry as he elevated her chin with his hand and kissed her lips.

The next hour was filled with little talk of the project they wanted me to do and lots of personal disclosures that bordered on illegal, if not crazy. We drank tea and they praised God numerous times for his protection in their chaotic world. With our visit completed I left their home with a job, an hour of memorable entertainment, and the knowledge that there was more to come.

REAL ESTATE 2001

My office is small and very male. The computer work center is rosewood and fills most of the room leaving enough space for two black client chairs. Suzanne and I spent three hours assembling the center and are pleased with its look. The walls are butternut yellow and on them hang three of Jamie's best rodeo photographs. They are all well matted and framed. The top of the bookcase serves as the parking place for my old 20's racing car. All together, with pictures of loved ones, computers, printers, multi-media speakers, phone, a few books and a vintage floor lamp, the office is very attractive.

I am now a Realtor with Re/Max. I have tried to work in this profession for sixteen years. I held my first real estate license in 1985 and worked with a broker named Charles Ellis in Springfield, Oregon. I also worked with Re/Max of Eugene, Dick Sage, back in Springfield, and Coldwell Banker in my old hometown...Yakima, Washington. I have never before had the opportunity to give real estate my undivided attention, and am hopeful that I will be successful and happy in the profession.

ELKS LODGE 2001

"Good God!!!! What did you think about that?" Suzanne and I had just attended a memorial service for the husband of a friend. It was held in an Elks Lodge. We were looking at each other with wide eyes and a snicker close behind our lips. The service wasn't funny but rather disquieting. We both had new emotions and were unsure which hook to hang them on.

The lodge building, like so many buildings from the late sixties and early seventies, had low ceilings stained with years of nicotine, wooden trim and walls of dark paneling. The floors and the bottom eight inches of the walls were covered with carpet that was a mix of red, orange and aged yellow blended with patterns lost in a swirl of stains and paisley.

We followed the gathering through the dining area into what we guessed was the lodge's meeting room. The colors and patterns of the dining area had continued uninterrupted into this smaller space. The center of the floor was light hardwood and was boxed by cubical desks on each side and in the center. On the desks were carved words like Justice, Charity, and Honor & Loyalty. Behind each desk there was an old man in a black tuxedo that sat looking towards the center of the room like the Sphinx guarding the pyramids. Draped over their shoulders were massive golden necklaces that were linked squares of metal with massive medallions holding them together in the middle of their chests. All these Elks officers had white hair except for the chaplain who kept his dyed cobalt black.

Elk horns were everywhere. The desk in the center of the room had a massive pair with their base wrapped in purple felt and golden upholstery brads. Many more were on the walls with mixed tapestries and other objects in the shape of elks or representing them in nature. The stage, which filled the west wall, was framed with trophy horns.

One of the old Officers mounted the stage. His white hair was abundant and seemed to bring balance to the hammered gray cowboy boots he wore. He had a cane and used it slowly and skillfully with each step until he stood behind a podium. With a deep and rich voice that was only slightly shaking with his age, he talked about Elk things. He, much like an ancient forest king, waved about strands of ivy and laurel, and talked about the words carved into the desks. The others, upon his command, also talked about the words, opening ledgers to read the successful efforts the passed away Elk had made in these areas. An electrified clock with colored lights and hands of horns chimed out eleven hours and then flashed red as all stood silently. Again, responding to the cowboy booted officer, each tuxedoed Elk approached the center table. They walked with their bad hips, wooden legs, and fused ankles, and placed sprigs of ivy on the binding of some great book. They each made a formal statement in the direction of the stage, then, with all the dignity they could, returned to their chairs and their sphinx like positions.

When all four Elks had their time at the room's center, the lead Elk descended the steps and walked to the center desk. He picked up a small flag, folded it four times over, then, with his cane hanging on his arm and the flag held between his hands, he limped to the widow and presented it to her. Then he, with his fellow Elks, left the room.

"Well, Baby," I said, as the lodge door closed behind us, "between the room, rituals & Elks, I found an amazing parallel with pagan rites of old and the ceremonies that were held in the woods behind the churches when wizards and witches spun their magic. Kind of disquieting isn't it?"

HAPPINESS IS SINGING 2001

I remembered last year standing on the third row of risers and singing great old show tunes for appreciative spectators. This year I was part of a charmed audience and wondered how I happened to be sitting and not standing there in my black slacks, starched white shirt with a green and yellow scarf draped around my neck.

My wife and I saw the signboard promoting the May 31st concert and made a commitment to attend. Across the street from Fred Meyers, the Baptists have perched their church high on a sand dune and its design includes a community room. The Florence Community Chorus has used it before. The acoustics are good. They have several ceiling fans that spin their blades through the evening of delightful music performed by forty talented community members, and directed by Judy Wales. This year Judy concentrated on her keyboard accompaniment and delegated the conducting to Joan McCrary, Jan Kinslow, Dorian Carter, Beth Johnston, and Marti Sautter. Rich Reich sat beside Judy to enrich the accompaniment with his patriotic drum work.

The Chorus, which is handsomely peppered with gray heads, is an amazing blend of retired and talented performers, surrounded by a bunch of locals who love to sing, occasionally dance, and want to have a good time. Friday's good time started with New Ashmolean Marching Society and ended with a sing along which included "God Bless America" and "America."

Standing with my hand across my heart and Reich's drum rolls keeping rhythm, I sing as loud as I can and am delighted, if only for the evening, to be a part of the Florence Community Chorus.

ON GOLDEN POND 2001

Two performances are behind me and this afternoon's matinee will bring to a close my adventure into the world of stage acting. Several months ago I was approached by David Lauria, who asked if I would have an interest in performing in the Florence Repertory Theater's presentation of "On Golden Pond."

My dear friend, John Flaherty, who has been acting professionally most of his life, encouraged me to give the theater a try. The adventure began with an audition, which was held in a meeting room of the local library. I had expected a large turn out for the five parts, was surprised when I discovered that there were only two of us interested in the roll of Bill Ray.

I read my lines as well as I could and used my deep voice, which I had inherited from my dad. When I drove away from the audition, I was excited, feeling like a dog sticking his head out a fast car's window.

There are so many aspects of myself that I continue to find interesting. One internal rule I seem to have deeply molded into the folds of my being is, "Ask me to do anything, and we will probably be able to work something out. Tell me, or order me to perform, and strap on your armor. We are at war." The reason I talk of this little character blemish is my being directed and spending so much time over the past weeks listening to the buckles of my breastplate snapping into place.

When I first began practice, they want me to call it "rehearsal," I was tickled by the theater protocol. The Director is God, and his stage manager is his pit bull. I remembered smiling and thinking that in the New York Theater, this system probably worked. I was shocked when I began to realize that our Director and our Stage Manager wanted us, a bunch of first time actors or amateurs, to play by the big boys' rules. "Who in the hell gave you the right to ask me to practice this much? What do you mean I had better know my lines by tomorrow? Don't you think it is a bit overboard telling us that we need to keep our bodies clean and not wear after-shave or perfume? You want me to take off my wedding band? I never take off my wedding band! I can't get my haircut? Why in the hell can't I get my haircut? You will do what if I miss an entrance? So, what I hear you say is…my life is on hold until this play is over? My previous commitments to God, family, and job are now all second to the preparation for this play, and you are the boss of my life?" They said, "YES!" Had I known, I would have smiled at my friend David and said, "No thanks, I don't have what it takes to be an actor!"

With all the weeks, days, and hours of theater work behind myself, I have found the experience full of opportunities for personal growth… most of which I don't want.

My dear friend, John, has said again and again, "Once you have performed on a stage, all the hard work and discipline will be worth it. Once you have performed, you will be HOOKED!"

With two performances behind me, and only one left, I have many feelings, and hooked is one of the weaker ones. My love of service to God, family and the responsibilities of my work are greater than the rewards I experienced on the stage. I am proud of my accomplishments. It is a thrill to perform in front of hundreds of people and to feel that I performed well.

BOY'S EYES 2001

Sitting on the music board of our old organ are two black and white photographs of my four-month-old grandson, Skylar. The organ is by the front door, so when I leave for my day's work, I can pause and look at him. Sometimes it is a long pause. I have always thought that I loved my children more than most parents, and yet this little grandson has found a spot in me that no one else has ever touched. I feel a responsibility to bring joy into this child's life and don't seem concerned with teaching him about the difficulties that life offers. I felt I needed to teach difficulties to my kids, but not this grandchild. I want this boy's eyes to sparkle when he sees me, and I want to hear him squeal "Grandpa, Grandpa, come play with me." As I approach my fifty-seventh birthday, I find that I have a heightened appreciation for all the trite sayings we have heard all our lives. The one that rises to the top of my aging brain today is "Grandparents always spoil their grandchildren."

DYSLEXIC 2001

The type size is #16. I use this large print so I can read my computer screen. I can, if I feel like abusing myself, read the smaller letters yet haven't disliked myself that much in a long time. I am not sure that I have ever disliked myself that much. Bette, a woman I sold a house to last year, called the other day and offered to proof-read my monthly newsletter. She said, "You could benefit from my looking over your articles before publication." She didn't want to hurt my feelings, and she didn't. I did feel a bit off center with the offer, because I have always used my spell checker. Hummmmm! I wonder if my sentence structure is a little dyslexic.

I am unsure what all I can or cannot blame on my wonderful, cover-all dysfunction. I have found that dyslexia catches the brunt of most all of my shortcomings, and I get away with it. "Oh, I am sorry! I'm dyslexic and can't spell, find my way out of a parking lot, turn a knob the correct direction, remember my left hand from my right, my phone number, social security number, your name, the birthdays of all the people I love, my anniversary, when I did all the things I have done, what you said, and millions of other things most folks do easily."

I was, at one time, a huge test for myself. Anymore, I am as I am, and am not bothered by much. I am troubled, though, by my being wrong more often than right. It seems that it should be at least 50/50.

TUNA FOR SALE 2001

We were driving through Old Town and saw the TUNA FOR SALE signs posted on the sides of the boats. Suzanne had heard that this year's tuna run was only thirty miles off shore and many of the smaller fishing boats were doing well. We had never purchased fresh fish from the boats and thought it would be fun. I parked the car and we walked down the ramp to the waterfront where they were moored.

It was an exceptional day. The sun was out and we had the car's top down. We had enjoyed a short run up to Yachats, finishing our outing with a drive through Old Town, where we grabbed a cup of coffee at our favorite shop. The river was like glass as we walked the docks and watched the fishermen sell, clean and wrap their catch. We found a boat we liked, but were told that he had sold all his catch. We soon discovered that the other fishermen had sold or committed their catches also. It was then that we spotted a boat powering under the bridge. "Do you have any tuna?" I yelled as he motored into range. He smiled, waved, and didn't say a word until he had tied off. "Ya, I do. How much do you want?"

Not knowing how to buy the fish I pointed to the one on the top of the pile and said that it would do just fine. Fearful that another buyer would grab my fish I didn't ask to have it cleaned and took it the way it came from the ocean. "Watch out for the blood" the fisherman warned as I lugged my fifteen-pound tuna up to the street. Standing by our Mercedes convertible, with fish blood dripping on my shoes, I decided there was no place in the car I was willing to stink up with our fresh purchase, so decided to transport the fish on the outside. We were only a couple of miles from home so Suzanne held the fish while I settled myself in the passenger seat. Once I closed the car door she handed me the fish by the gills and I held it as high as I could. The fish was long and the car was low. Stretching my arm as high as I could the ridged tail still touched the street. Suzanne drove our aqua colored roadster slowly down the main street, as delighted onlookers laughed and waved to us.

Fresh albacore tuna is a delight to eat and worth whatever efforts are required to get one.

MERCEDES SLK230 2001

People have the wrong idea about winter. Many folk, who live out of the area, believe Florence is under water for six months of the year. When I moved here three years ago, I had a bunch of prejudices about the coast. Some were true, and most were not. I knew there was lots of rain in the winter, yet was very surprised to discover that, with the rain, there were hours each week when the clouds would, part and the blue sky and bright sun would make an appearance. Sometimes the sun's visits were short, but even an hour of sunshine can lift the spirits and improve the day. In Eugene they aren't so lucky. A blanket of something thick and gray settles in between the mountains from November to March. My daughter, who still lives in Eugene, is often surprised when we talk on the phone and I am looking at blue sky and she isn't.

A couple of weeks ago, on a cold winter day, Suzanne and I took a little drive to Reedsport. We spoiled ourselves last year and purchased a little Mercedes SLK230. It's aqua and the hard top folds down into its trunk. Our top was down that day, and we were delighted with a four-hour drive under blue skies with puffy white clouds. Two nights later we took an evening cruse up to Walport to see friends. The top was down again and the sights were magical. The star-speckled sky was mixed with a gray metallic color that covered everything in sight. The edges of the clouds and the white of the surf sparkled and seemed to belong to another gray-toned and enchanted world. The moon sat on a thick cloud and rolled from side to side as we wound our car down the twists and turns of the costal highway.

We have found that one of our real pleasures in life is our nightly hot tub. Not being kids anymore we have many aches and pains that disappear with twenty minutes of tub time. Our tub is open to the weather, so some nights we a bring umbrella into the tub with us. Many nights we get to watch the clear Florence sky and count shooting stars.

I would never want to imply that it doesn't rain in Florence. The monthly rainfall statistics can register in the high teens during the winter months. That is a big part of why everything under our blue summer sky is green, except for the blue lakes and ocean. Rain or shine, living in Florence is wonderful.

DOMINICA & HAITI 2001

Before the days wash away the freshness of our experiences, I need to capture them on paper. This is the first day of the year 2001 and we returned late, on the eve of this New Year, to our home. My sweetheart, Suzanne, and I traveled across our country and out over the southern Atlantic Ocean to visit the Caribbean Republics of Dominica and Haiti.

We began and ended our adventure with the disappointments that can accompany flying. Our holiday days were few, and American Airlines demanded far more than their due. We spent ten hours in airports on our way to the Caribbean and twenty-one hours on our way back.

My first observation of Dominica was the population. Dominican's are diverse in shade, size and presentation. The most common attributes were open-faced kindness and cleanliness. The cleanliness did not extend to the roadsides that were blanketed with paper products between the sparkling clean airport and our immaculate resort. All roads in Haiti and Dominica share the same problem.

The trash-strewn roads operate by a primal rule of order that is common in the animal kingdom, "the biggest rules." Massive tour buses drive where they will. The oncoming lane is theirs to occupy, if they will, and most often they do. Smaller buses can run cars off into ditches, and cars can do the same to the thousands of small motor bikes that attempt to occupy the unused portions of the roadways, much like bumblebees flying through grapevines. The pedestrians, who are low on this highway scale of importance rate, seem less important than the flies we nonchalantly smash on our summer windshields. To fully display their determination to carry out their primal rule, all vehicles larger than motorcycles are wrapped front and back with steel pipes much like bumper cars. We had fanaticized putting about Puerto Plata in little brightly colored scooters, but allowed that thought to dissolve following our first taxi drive from the airport to our resort.

Our accommodations were perfect. We stayed at the Playa Naco, and were on the ground floor of a three-story complex that was surrounded by grass, and only two hundred feet from the surf's edge. Behind us were many similar buildings, all surrounding a large central complex which sported several massive pools, hot tubs, restaurants, outside stages with live Latin music, and many tennis courts. Large wicker chairs and wildly painted tables filled every corner, and intricate tile designs climbed the columns and walls. There were gaming rooms, and a world-class golf course.

The beach was long and wide. The sand was light, and the warm Caribbean waters were extremely inviting. The beach wrapped around a distant point and went on to places we didn't have time to explore.

Clustered on a wide section of sand were a dozen shacks filled with all the items that tourists buy for their friends and themselves. The young men operating the shops would greet you with, "My prices are so low that I am almost giving my things away." They weren't, and great pleasure was taken in haggling. Or at least I enjoyed haggling. Suzanne believes that if someone is overcharging you, they must need the money.

The surf was different every day. Our first night we were welcomed by surf so mild it could have been lake. The next day the Boogie Boards were out and the water would crash you to your knees if you didn't dive under the waves. Suzanne could stay out of the water only long enough to read me a chapter of Harry Potter before she had to return. We spent several days wandering from our quarters to the beach, to lunch, to the beach, to dinner, to the evening's entertainment and then to our quarters. They were restful days of simple bliss.

On Christmas Eve we attended midnight mass at the Cathedral de San Felipe. It was delightful. The choir sang in Spanish, and was wonderful with its mix of formal Catholic songs and local rhythm. There were bells, incense, fancy robes, and a beautiful building filled with local believers.

On our third day in we traveled to Haiti. A book could be written about that day's adventure. I found it to be shocking, sad and scary. We saw smiling children dressed in rags with scars and skin disorders, women with bare feet wearing fancy dresses given to them in the UNICEF boxes. They were moving large baskets of stuff on their heads from one shack to another. There were puddles of mud and water that were impossible to avoid. Thousands of women and children were squeezed into small work places cooking and working, with the men and donkeys passing through. Everyone was middle aged or young. People don't live to be old in Haiti. We saw the countryside and mud huts with many naked children and waving mothers who smiled. There was the Voodoo priest, the glass he ate, and the fire he washed himself with and stuck in his mouth, the flapping chicken whose head he ripped off with his teeth, looking at us with evil white eyes as the blood ran down his neck. We saw no electricity, no refrigeration, and no sanitation. We left Haiti with a small amount of knowing about what living in the third poorest nation in the world was like.

We visited a school owned and managed by the Baha'is in Puerto Plata. There were Baha'i pictures on the walls and prayers written in Spanish. A student named Danny who fed us delightful fruit from a tree in his yard gave us a tour. We plan to help this school and the efforts they are making.

There were snow storms in New York and our scheduled flight home was canceled. In our attempt to get home, we traveled from Puerto Plata to Santa Domingo. We had a choice of taxi, bus, or fly. We took a small six-place plane and flew across Dominica. The flight was low, so we were able to see the inland and mountains. This travel by air ended up being a great treat, even though it landed at the wrong airport in Santa Dominica. We didn't even consider there being more than one airport. We did all the things stranded travelers do to get home and failed. We ended up sleeping on the airport's marble floor with our bags as pillows, and our beach towels as blankets. When we arrived in the States we were tired and road weary. It was a fantastic trip.

DAUGHTER 2002

"Oh Papa, you are so important to me." We were walking by the river again. We have spent some of our best times walking and watching the white water of the Willamette dance on the river rocks as it rushes past the park. It has been a difficult path for my daughter. She is extremely intuitive, yet does not fully trust what she knows to be true. Sometimes reality doesn't fit into the fantasies we have around our lives.

"You are doing great, Daughter. I am so proud of you and all the hard work you have done." She smiles and drops her head in an appreciative nod. Her hair, a sun streaked blonde, swings out over her shoulder and backs away from her cheek. "I love you, Daddy."

Next week Jamie will be thirty-four. She has a nine-month-old son who captured my heart and with his first dimpled smile, assuring himself of my love and support for the remaining days of my life.

Watching Jamie grow has been a delightful and emotional experience. She, much like a springtime tulip, has had to push and stretch to find her place in the garden. Other flowers have found growing easy and seem to lack the strength and resilience Jamie wears so naturally. You can see the difference in the way she carries herself, holds her head, her style of communication and her unbreakable eye contact. "Hi! I'm Jamie and I have something interesting I want to share with you." Immediately all respond to the strength of her voice and the warmth of her presentation. She is an undeniable presence.

A thousand times I have held my curved and empty arm in front of me and said, "I could hold her little head in the palm of my hand and her bottom would be snuggled against the bend of my elbow." Remembering my life with Jamie is like spinning a Rolodex and watching hundreds of precious moments eclipse one another.

I remember her giggling as she road on my shoulders, with her little hands pulling my hair. She was on my back in a pack squealing as we drove the motorcycle over all the bumps in the neighbor's lot. I would pack her on my hip and in my arms and swing her high in the air, and always, she would laugh at every moment of excitement I could offer. She was so ready to play and be entertained.

She cried when I dropped her off at school. There were too many schools for Jamie and too many moves. She would have thrived if she had lived in the same house with the same neighbors, but that was not her story. Friendship was something she deeply wanted and rarely found. The children that mattered to her when she was little are still important to her today.

Jamie was a beautiful little girl. I would pose her for a photograph and she would always have the greatest smile, and would sit just so. She knew how she wanted to look and she made you wait until everything was perfect. Curls in her hair, a new dress, pretty shoes and a camera, were close to heaven for my little daughter.

I can summon up a highly charged moment when everyone was silent and the lights around the perimeter of the floor were dark. In the center of the room, frozen in a graceful pose, was my daughter... the skater. Her dance dress was beautiful, her hair was up, and as the music began, she spun into motion and glided across the hardwood floor. I had watched her routine a hundred times, yet I held my breath as she executed one difficult move after another. As the music ended I was delighted and I marveled at her ability and courage. She ended this memory with a smile on her face, her hands in the air with her head tossed back. Yeah, Jamie!!

It was her fifteenth birthday and she wanted to declare her belief in Baha'u'llah. The patio was covered with her friends and most of the Baha'i adults in the community. It was a beautiful day. We all stood quietly as she filled out her card. Then, with a unified voice, we yelled "Greater is God than every Great One." It's special when folks think your kid looks a bit like you and miraculous when your child chooses to share your spiritual path.

She is an artist. Finding a good tool for her to express herself was difficult. I remember when I gave her my camera and told her to "go for it." She did, and my walls are covered with her creations. She sees beauty and balance in the world and captures it on film.

I remember the greatest pain of separation when Jamie flew away to Haifa. Jamie had decided to do a year of service at the Baha'i World Center in Haifa, Israel. We went to the Portland Rose Garden to take goodbye pictures. She was eighteen and would be out of my sight and touch for a whole year. I felt so good about her decision to serve, and truly suffered being apart from her. Daddy couldn't protect her anymore. Despite the pain of it all, to watch your child make a major step in service filled me with gratitude.

"Look at that! Isn't she amazing?" She had invited us to come by the hall on the university campus where she danced with her swing club. We were a little late, and when we entered she was dancing with some man who seemed delighted to be her partner. There were several other couples dancing, but Jamie was exceptional. She had on black dance shoes with tight black slacks that were flared at the ankles. Her midriff was bare and her sleeveless top sparkled in the softly lit room. He moved around her like a director leading an orchestra, and she moved like music. Each motion was swan like, and every finger found a graceful position in every movement. His smile matched mine as he marveled at her ability to respond to every direction with elegance and skill. In a dramatic spin she caught my eye and left her partner to welcome us. I was so proud to have this Diva call me Papa.

She had said that is was a private time for a woman and she wanted only her mother and husband at her side as she labored to birth her child. Circumstances allowed me, for just a while, to watch her. She was covered with sweat and her bed wear was loosely draped across her body. She was sitting on the bed and there were women all around her.

"Hi, Daddy." "Hi, Baby Girl! How are you doing?" She replied with a, "It's hard, Dad." It was at that moment when another contraction hit, and she, like a samurai wrestler stretching before a fight, spread her fingers and arms as she prepared to grab the bars. Her eyes closed and she moved into a state of concentration and labor that isolated her from everyone present. I was so proud to be in this birthing room with my child who was gifting me with a grandson.

She can sit on the floor with him for hours. He is wild about her, and she seems to have an insatiable appetite to be with him. As we walked the other day, she asked if I thought she was a good mom. I replied with, "I would have loved to have you as my mom." She liked my answer.

Spinning life's Rolodex does not begin to capture all the joy and pride I have experienced being Jamie's father. There have been all the normal days that have been punctuated with special moments like graduations, accomplishments, acknowledgements and the other occurrences that pause one long enough to feel the pride and pleasure of parenthood. Jamie has filled my life with many exceptional pauses and my gratitude to God for such a gift is endless. "Oh, Jamie, you are so important to me."

THE ALMOST PRIVATE SHOWING 2002

Suzanne, my wife, was out of town for the evening, and I wanted to watch a movie I knew she wouldn't attend with me. She seems to have a protective filter around violence that I never developed and is selective about what she exposes herself too. After work I had a quick bite to eat and found myself standing in front of the ticket person asking to see "Black Hawk Down." "Just one sir?" she asked. "Yes…just me tonight. My wife's out of town," was my reply. I ordered my popcorn, light on the butter, diet coke and entered theater three at the Florence Cinema.

Several times I have gone to mid-week movies and found myself alone. Last summer it was in the Harbor Theater, a big old single screen movie house I love. The movie was "From Hell" and was about Jack the Ripper. It was another movie Suzanne's filter protected her from. As I sat alone in one of the big loge seats and realized that I was watching a really scary movie, I stood. I walked out to the concession counter and asked the gal there if she would join me. It was good for a laugh and I, alone, walked back to my seat. I tried to have the appearance of being comfortable.

Tonight, as my eyes adjusted to the dark, I found that I was almost alone. Across the aisle and down a row or two was a couple. I slid down in my seat and began my ritual of popping popcorn into my mouth. "You going to eat all that popcorn, or are you going to share?" were the strong male words I heard over the previews. I glanced over to the couple and was delighted to see Jackie and Al. I had helped them buy a home last year and couldn't have asked for a better pair to watch a good war movie with.

When the movie action reached an extremely high level of viewing anxiety, I yelled to Al, "Damn…what are those poor guys going to do?" From time to time he would yell back, and together the three of us experienced a piece of war that was unbearable for the kids that lived it, and not that easy for us to watch.

With the movie's credits rolling, we stood and walked out together. "How are you guys doing?" I asked as we entered the light of the lobby. We took a moment to visit before we walked out into the cool night air. I love living in Florence and the friends I find at every corner and theater.

A LITTLE COSTAL STORM 2002

The power of nature and Florence can stand hand in hand when the storms of winter visit our coastal town. In the middle of December I stood in the front room of my friend's home. I sold Paul and his wife their piece of paradise this past spring, and this is their first winter. The gusts of wind were over eighty-five mph. I was impressed with nature's display as I watch the wind grab at the tips of the massive sea waves and toss them across the South Jetty and against Paul's glass windows. The white caps on the Siuslaw River were packed tightly together, giving the river the appearance of whipped milk. The lean and artful shapes of the coast pines press themselves closer to the ground, only to spring back up when the gusts relax their force.

"Would you like a bowl of chicken soup?" Fran asked as I pulled my stool up beside the kitchen island. Despite the charm of my hosts, I could not take my eyes away from the unbelievable display I was viewing. "The past owner did say these windows were good up to 120 mph, didn't he?" I asked. "Ya, he did, James. Don't worry they can take a lot more than we will see today," was Paul's reply to my anxious question.

We sat there together for an hour or two and enjoyed our coffees and each other's company. At times the windows had the look of glass blocks tumbling in a washing machine, and then in the next moment they had an eerier calm and clarity.

Some folks are uncomfortable when our storms roll in from the ocean. I love them. They open my eyes and take my breath away. What a wonderful way to remind us that we are alive.

OLYMPIC CROQUET 2002

I am unsure if there is or isn't a croquet god in California. If there is one, he would have been disgusted with the game I experienced last Sunday. My son, Jordan, and his best friend Max invited me to participate in a friendly game. They called it "Olympic" croquet. I had never played this hybrid of the game and was anxious to have the experience.

The park was several blocks from Jordan's apartment. It was pie shaped and filled with large trees. The trees had massive root systems that had pushed themselves far above ground and provided an additional challenge. Max drove the first stake into the grass on the far end of the park as Jordan did the same a full city block away. The wickets were placed in the traditional pattern but were placed behind trees, in sinkholes or between roots.

I should have known I was in trouble when they both returned to the center of the field and spread out their arms towards the playing field as if they were showing off their new car.

We began the game at the east end of the field. I led off and was half way to the third wicket when Jordan followed me. After passing the paired wickets, he faced in the opposite direction and whacked his ball with the side of his mallet. "What the hell was that, Jordan?" I yelled in disbelief. He smiled as his ball with one swack passed mine and rolled up to the mouth of the third wicket. With his next move he swacked his ball passed the wicket and was on his way to the next one. Max, with the same smile I had seen on Jordan's face, whacked his ball past me and close to where Jordan was standing. "What kind of game are you two playing?" I moaned. "I thought the rules taught us to hit the ball with the end of the mallet and between your legs in the direction you wanted to go." They both smiled and said together, "It's your turn, Dad."

The game was an abomination. They would push their balls through wickets when I wasn't looking, take extra shots, and if they could hit the tire of a passing car they claim they had the right to place their ball anywhere on the field. Jordan further violated the rules of everything that is right by knocking my ball the full length of the park if I came within one mallet width of his ball. When I protested and said, "That's against the rules." they both smiled and continued the unorthodox practice.

I lost the three games we played. They didn't play fair. I loved the time we shared together.

PIT FIRE 2002

I seem to be up. They seem to be down. Maybe I go to bed too earlier, or maybe I need less sleep. It's Monday morning in Long Beach and I have just returned from a delightful breakfast of a bagel with cream cheese and an excellent cup of coffee. I read the Los Angeles Times from front to back and slowly walked home taking time to look at the flowers and the occasional cat invisibly crouched behind some tropical yard plant.

Last night we had a pit fire in Jordan's back yard. Most folks love such fires out in the woods, and rarely feel comfortable having them in town. I like city style fire pits and so does Jordan. He didn't have one, but we decided that we wanted to sit around one that night, so made up a list of building materials we would need. Following our mid-town adventure to the Tar Pits and an excellent Mexican dinner of green tamales, we found ourselves in the brick department of Lowe's Hardware and Building Supplies. With minor discussion as to the color of the pit's bordering stones, the purchase was made and loaded into the trunk of Jordan's Saturn.

We found a parking spot fairly close to the house and packed the bricks up the street to the back yard. We were creative in the design of the pit and were pleased when we finished. Jordan refused to allow a fire until the sun had set and the full beauty of the first Heintz-built fire pit in Long Beach could be appreciated. He walked to a nearby store where he hoped to find firewood…they didn't have any. We went back to the house, drove to another store, and bought a small bundle wrapped in handy wrap with an easy carrying handle included. We also purchased crackers, chocolate and marshmallows. This new fire would be christened with S'mores.

I wadded up the paper while Jordan unwrapped the wood. It was our plan to have the fire burning nicely by the time Jason, Suzanne, and Erica came down to enjoy the evening's ambiance. It was dry wood and within moments the smoke was curling above us and the crackle of the freshly ignited wood charmed our ears. We leaned back in our white, plastic lawn chairs and smiled at each other, a father and son sharing a family tradition.

We had talked earlier about fire regulations and such and were unconcerned. By the time Erica, Jason, and Suzanne arrived, the fire had leapt into full maturity. There was also lots of smoke. "Why do you think there is so much smoke Dad?" was Jordan's question as he pushed the logs around and scorched his fingertips. At this juncture, the folks in the lower apartment turned on their lights and closed their windows. "Damn, I think I smoked them out," were Jordan's words as he began placing blame for the excessive fire smoke on my paper logs.

Lots could be said about the next twenty minutes. We could talk about the truck in the alley that scared us and sounded like a fire engine about to engage its water pumps, or how the wind pushed all the smoke against the neighbor's building where small fingers of smoke could be seen slipping through their window cracks. Or we could talk about Jordan's anxiety as he worried about being a responsible neighbor or keeping his fantasy backyard fire. Finally…with a garden hose in hand he stood in the path of the swirling smoke and flooded the fire. He sadly said, "We will do this another time, but not tonight. Too much smoke."

The best part of our evening began after the fire was out and we… in the flame of our bug candles toasted our marshmallows. The smile on Jordan's face as he bit his S'more gave hope to another pit fire on a less windy evening.

KAUAI 2002

With one of the Cheerios eaten, the rooster flapped his wings and released his morning call. I had been tossing morning cereal into the yard below my lanai where half a dozen chickens were scratching for their first meal. They were the reason I was up, and I felt thankful.

I sat with Suzanne around a small glass table and admired the exotic trees, listened to the sound of the ocean surf and smelled paradise. It was the twenty-second day of December 2002, and I was drinking coffee on the north end of the island of Kauai.

We were in the early days of a year-old dream that stumbled, and then regained its balance to provide us all with the promise of a fantasy we share. Yesterday, Jamie, Skylar, Suzanne and I climbed aboard our airplane and flew to San Francisco where we would join Jason, Jordan & Erica. The kids flying out of Los Angeles had started earlier than us Eugene folks, and we were very anxious to see them at United gate eighty-eight. When we stepped off the moving walk, we didn't see them. We felt a wave of disappointment as our fantasy holiday slipped and dropped to one knee. Their plane had mechanical problems and was delayed. It gobbled up time and make connections with us in San Francisco impossible. They were told that the week was booked tight and seats would not be available to them until after Christmas. After twisting and turning the system every way they could, we received a phone message informing us that they would be twenty-four hours late. We made sad plans for our first day that would be a bit hollow, but we knew we could make the best of our circumstances.

That evening I fell asleep early while Jamie and Suzanne dealt with Christmas cards and Skylar. A few minutes after 9:00 p.m. the kids called. They had made magic happen and were at the airport. Suzanne and I were in the cars and down the street in a flash, and forty-five minutes later we were hugging and kissing our late children.

Today we spent the day on the beach. Well, some of us spent the day on the beach. We cooked up eggs and pancakes together, then cranked up both cars and drove down to Hanalei, where we went to the Saturday Farmers' Market. It was filled with local folks selling fruits, vegetables, and a variety of island crafts. We stocked up with a bunch and drove to the beach.

The Hanalei Bay has a long pier that runs into the pounding surf and is a halfway jump off for some of the big wave surfers. The end of the concrete pier has a roof of tired corrugated steel. It has a weathered look that adds to the undeveloped charm, that makes Kauai, Kauai.

We packed up in the late afternoon and dropped by the market for fish and other dinner items. The fish we chose were Opah (moon fish), Ahi, and tiger prawns. We were slow getting dinner together. Jordan and I played with his computer, making our movie, and the rest of the tribe seemed slow to do much of anything but visit and lay about.

Long after dark Suzanne began making a salad, and Jason sautéed garlic and onion with salsa to flavor the fish. Together we packed the seafood down to the pool where we fired up the B-B-Q and deveined the prawns. We sat together in plastic chairs watching the fish cook until we were all satisfied.

We all sat around the round glass table and filled ourselves. We didn't eat it all and were slow to stop our nibbling and chatter to clean up. It wasn't long before we slipped off to our beds and an early night's sleep. Jason watched us melt away with an "It's only eight thirty, what's going on?"

Seven-thirty found all of us kind of up. We all do "up" a little differently. We had agreed that going to a free breakfast that would promote a variety of tourist activities would be OK. Shortly after eating, Skylar and I escaped and the others took notes. We didn't commit too much, deciding that a Luau on Christmas Eve will be perfect.

After a quick return to Makai Club to change clothes, we headed back to, Hanalei Beach. This time we had surf and boogie boards. For five plus hours we played in the tropical bay, built sand castles, watched very casual beach people, and admired the prehistoric mountains that surround the bay and keep their tops dipped in ocean crossing clouds.

Tonight we have split up. Jamie, Jordan, and Erica are off to a Walmart and Jason is on a drive. Suzanne and I will take Skylar for a little walk and later we will do our dinner.

Kauai's beaches and hidden coves consumed our days, and far sooner than expected we left the island with suntans and memories. How wise Suzanne and I have been to spend our dollars on memories and family.

BEST TEARS 2002

Today over a Wendy's taco salad I watched a man reach way down and pick up his little daughter. He swung her up into his arms and buried his nose in the soft part of her neck. I knew he was taking a deep breath, inhaling the sweet smell of her body. I knew because I did the same thing thirty years ago. I looked into Suzanne's eyes and said, "That is the best.......... (tears rushed through my eyes and closed my throat).............."load a man can carry."

BIKE RIDE 2002

I ride my bike most every morning. It's not a big deal. My home is in the 700 block of 7th street, which is a twenty-five year old residential area close to the center of town. We love living here, and this time of year, around 6:30 a.m., I bundle myself up in cold weather gear and mount the old Diamondback bike I inherited from my son.

The route I take does not vary. I peddle down 7th to Kingwood turn north and ride to 35th Street, where I turn around and head back. There are a few steep hills, so twenty minutes later, when I return to my garage, I have usually worked up a sweat. It is just enough morning exercise to give me hope for a longer life.

Most every morning I plug my earphones in, turn the radio to KLCC at 88.1 and listen to the news. It puts me in my own little world, which I enjoy in the rain or shine. This morning the battery is dead and riding without the news is an uncomfortable option. The weather is cold and bright, and I am surprised to hear my chain drag in its shifter. I make a mental note to adjust it when I get back to the garage. "Gosh! Where did all these birds come from?" I wasn't sure if the birds had been there all the time or not. I did know that I hadn't been listening to them. As I ride along, I become aware of many delightful sounds I had left outside my little radio cocoon.

The sounds of my bike tires change as I roll from the pavement to the small sand drifts that reach across the road like skinny coastal fingers. The brush rustles and a small brown rabbit with black stripes pauses to watch me pass. He probably watches me every morning. Seagulls and hawks fly over my head and I can hear the distant sound of the surf as it rolls across the miles of open sandy beach.

At the top of the hill where Kingwood intersects with Pacific View Drive I always stop for a moment to look at the ocean. Some days it is a rolling black sea with deep choppy surf. From this distance the winter surf often has the look of thick ribbons of layered lace. Today, the Pacific is rich and blue with thin threads of surf that are backed with small green walls of salt seawater.

With a quick turnaround I am southbound, and the ocean air pushes against my face as I speed down the backside of the steep hill. Fresh air in my lungs and wind whistling past my ears heighten the pleasure of this "out of my cocoon" bike ride.

I watch and listen to a small plane land at our little airport and wonder what businesses would occupy the numerous commercial lots that line this section of Kingwood.

The only busy street I cross is Ninth, but there is almost never traffic on it this time of day. I should stop, but I can hear that there aren't any cars coming, so I don't. Breaking the little rules seems like a reward for this early morning commitment. The last little hill is up to my home. I pull into the garage, lean my bike against the toolbox, turn off the taillight, and walk to the newspaper box. With paper under my arm and my exercise behind me, I make a mental note to pick up a couple of triple AAA batteries for the radio. It is hard to change old habits.

THE KIDS 2002

My children, Jamie thirty-two and Jordan twenty-five, stood on the sidewalk in front of the Old City Hall. I had returned to the restaurant to exchange dollars for parking quarters. We wanted to walk and needed more time. While dropping coins into the meter I looked down the block and watched them. They were dancing. Hands were above their heads in full flamenco as they wrapped around each other swinging and laughing. He stood tall and haughty with the sun glinting off his California bleached hair. He had a day's growth of black beard, big shoes and pants with cargo pockets, topped with a bulky knitted shirt, open necked and collarless. She was tossing legs, arms, and head about like Tina Turner. She wore flat velvet shoes with lots of thigh behind a short black skirt. Like her brother, her collar is open and the top fits tight. Her neck is wrapped in a brightly colored scarf and her blond hair is rich in color and full. They laugh and hold and spin around again. What a delicious sight. My son…my daughter caught up in their love and appreciation of each other and delighting in a shared moment.

OLD PEOPLE 2002

I am surrounded by old people, and I am fearful that I am one. Suzanne and I celebrated Valentines' Day with an excellent dinner at the Pier Point Inn. She had duck, and I, a peppered steak. We saw and were waited on by friends who care for us, and we for them. Florence is like that…friends most everywhere.

The piano player is the father of friends who own a little fish and chip restaurant in town. His name is Fred and his piano skills far exceed his memory of recent events. Fred joined us for a coffee on his break, sharing several stories of his days in real estate and the people he had worked with. He apologized for boring us to death as he returned to his piano. We laughed and left our table to pay our bill. We needed to rush if we were going to be seated before the performance. We didn't have time to wait for the server's ticket.

Steve Stone & the Emerald City Jazz Kings were performing the Fabulous Dorsey's. What a delightful evening! The music was excellent.

As one would expect, the Jazz Kings performed the big band music of the early 40's. The female singer was dressed in a rich, red dress, off the shoulder, and completed with matching platform heals. Her long blond hair was in 1940's rolls and was perfect. For me she could have been one of my mother's friends when she and Dad were only thinking of having kids. The male vocalist, who was also excellent, reminded me of Pee Wee Herman attempting to behave. As the evening progressed and he released himself to the music, the similarities did not diminish but intensified.

A few seats down and a row or two in front of us, there was an old guy with glasses and a red flannel shirt. I guessed him to be a retired mill worker and noticed that a section on the top of his head had been shaved and something was stuck there on the bare skin that reminded me of the head of a railroad spike. I watched it for a long time and noting that his behavior was normal and presumed that it must be something other than a spike. Suzanne guessed it to be a wad of duck tape. Why would a guy shave the back of his head and stick a chunk of tape on it?

There was a pair of gray headed women in row ahead of us. It was easy to see over them, but very difficult to breathe. One, I was not sure which for a while, smelled like a bottle of old lady perfume. I found that my lungs were unable to fully inflate. When she began waving her Japanese fan and drove the bulk of the fragrance in my direction, I reminded Suzanne that I was sensitive to some odors, and if I passed out to just leave me there until the performance was over. As time passed, I seemed to acclimate to the fragrance until she opened her purse, pulled out a little bottle and redouced herself in the pungent odor. She also seemed to have difficulty with her ears. When the trumpets were hitting the higher notes she pushed her long nailed fingers, which suffered from a bit of arthritis, deeper in her ears than I thought possible and would then roll her head slightly from side to side. She and her girlfriend did not return following the intermission. I considered it a reprieve.

When the performance ended, we stood and gave them a standing ovation. Florence audiences always give standing ovations. I did notice that many of us rose slowly and there were audible grunts over the sound of the clapping hands.

STARS 2002

Early morning often finds me walking my dogs. This morning was exceptionally crisp and clear. The dogs dragged me from one side of the street to the other, until I stopped to appreciate the blanket of stars that were stretched across sky. Soon the sun would push the darkness away, but for the moment I stood dazzled. Last night I watched the same sky as I settled back in the hot tub. We get to watch the stars a lot in Florence. I think that the ocean works hard to keep the skies clear. When the lights of the town are soft and the clouds are few, the powder like stars that hang around the brilliant ones show off their stuff.

When I lived in bigger cities it was hard to appreciate the stars. City lights seem to fade the sky. As a boy in my little farming community, we would lie on our backs and watch the sky. We didn't talk much then. Star watching seems to require quietness, except for the occasional "Did you see that shooting star?"

HAIFA 2002

We were exhausted when I sat at the desk in our room on the nineteenth floor of the Dan Panorama hotel. It took us twenty-five hours to transport ourselves from the comfort of our seaside home in Florence, Oregon to Haifa, Israel.

Our adventure began several days before on Thursday, November twenty-first. Our sweet Baha'i sister, Elizabeth Alway, watched our home and our dogs. We spent the morning attending to small household chores before we left town for Springfield, where we visited with Jamie, Skyboy and Gregg for an hour or so. We couldn't bring ourselves to start our voyage without seeing our daughter and getting a sugary kiss from our grandson.

After gobbling down a Carl's Junior burger together, we drove north to Portland. We had made arrangements to stay at the Quality Inn, where we could spend the night and park our car free while we were out of country for only eighty dollars. What a deal! We did hang a Club on our steering wheel to give us a greater feeling of comfort.

Moments after we entered our motel room the phone rang. Paul Klippel, a Baha'i friend from Florence, was on his way to pick us up for a tour of his ship before we rode with him to the airport to collect his wife, Fran.

His ship was moored by Swan Island and was an impressive vessel to visit. His ship lays fiber optic cable along the bottom of the sea. I delighted in following Paul from one end of his ship to the other, as he, with great professionalism, showed us the workings of his very technical vessel. We began with a quick glance at his room, and then dinner. We went up, down, fore, and aft, and felt exercised when the tour ended. We gathered up Fran and visited as we drove back to our motel. Both the Klippels had prayer requests that we packed in our hearts for sharing at the Holy Thresholds. We deeply value Fran and Paul's friendships.

We were afraid that sleep would be elusive that night and were surprised when the phone rang with our wakeup call. We took thirty minutes to dress, repack and board the motel shuttle to the airport. Our driver was a young man from Croatia, who had been in the states for seven years, and was happy to have his entire family, less his grandmother, living in Portland.

The airport went well. We passed through several long security lines and ended up sitting by a Coffee People kiosk visiting with a young couple who were flying to the east coast for the holidays. They had a baby girl named Hanna and were anxious to present her to their family. They had never heard of the Baha'i Faith, so we were delighted to tell them about it.

The flight from Portland to Chicago went well and we felt rushed as we dashed from one Chicago terminal to another to catch our flight to Frankfort, Germany. We smiled at each other when we immediately joined the boarding line and were seated. Our timing was perfect. We flew up and over Toronto, across the Atlantic, over London and landed in Frankfort. The night view of London was beautiful. The city lights looked like an intricately fashioned necklace.

We had three hours to kill in Germany. Our shuttle from an open port landing to the terminal used an hour of it. We packed our carry on bags from one end of the airport to the other, and were delighted that we had the time. We missed the speed-walk passages Portland has between the different areas of their airport.

We had eaten too many airline meals, so decided to have a good cup of German coffee and a bit of their food. We didn't really know what meal we should be eating, but did know that it was early Saturday morning and we were hungry. Our breakfast was an excellent cup of coffee with bread, meats and cheese, served by a young man wrapped in a white apron that brushed the tops of his shoes. It was tasty and expensive. The airport snack cost us twenty-five dollars, and that didn't include the tip or the Tums I needed to digest the fine German meats.

The airport's marketing area was beautiful and was in the early stages of being decorated for Christmas. We began our journey down several very long tunnels that ended up in a glassed room which seemed far from the rest of the airport boarding areas. There were many languages floating in the air. German, Hebrew, and maybe a little Arabic over the few others like English and Hindi. I was surprised by the large number of travelers dressed in the fashions of India.

Suzanne and I, up to this time, had felt excited and energized. As we sat in our undecorated and isolated boarding area, we questioned our ability to spend another minute sitting. Our bodies had reached the state of "I donna wanna doa this any mora."

We did do more. As we left the terminal, we identified our bags, which had spent their time in the bellies of airplanes and were now spread out across the Frankfurt tarmac waiting to be identified. No identification, no trip to Israel.

We had been served by United Airlines from Portland to Chicago. We then, and for the balance of our flight, were in the care of Lufthansa. The service was great, and I loved the sound of the language. When we landed in Frankfurt, the Heintz in me appreciated coming home.

As our craft lifted off, I felt a little anxious appreciation about the location of our next airport...Tel Aviv. This last leg of our trip passed and we endured. Our Israel landing, like the one in Germany, was separated from the general terminal. We walked down another steep ramp and boarded a space-age bus which took us to customs. Upon our arrival I pulled out my video camera and began to record. Quickly I found myself being visited by security. I played them back my film, and with a look of tolerance, I was released to enter their country.

We delighted in standing behind Jim, Wendy, and their children, from Bend, Oregon. There were lots of smiles and pleasure in getting to know each other. They were planning to spend the night in Tel Aviv, while we were going on to Haifa. With all our bags, we left the building and rolled around a block or two looking for a van sherut to take us north. We had exchanged a little American money for shekels and discover that a shekel is worth twenty-five cents…maybe a little less. We were about to give up and take a taxi when we spotted them. There was a row of white vans set to take off for different parts of Israel. We found the Haifa sherut and climbed on board. An hour later the rig was full, less one seat, which we all shared the cost of so we could avoid waiting for the final passenger. It was a two-hour drive. One of the passengers was a seventy year-old man who had been born and raised in Haifa. He was rich with stories, which filled the two-hour ride. He told us that the citizens of Haifa were proud of the Baha'i Gardens and now, with the additional development of the terraces, their pride was even greater.

We were lucky when the driver dropped us off first. Our cost for two-hour drive was one hundred shekels. The history lessons were free. Our hotel was in the center of much street life and was beautiful. It had two very tall towers housing almost 300 rooms. There were only one hundred people staying during the week days, but on the weekends it was full. Many Jewish families love coming to Haifa for weekend visits.

After we checked in, we went to our room on the nineteenth floor. Our room number was 1909 and it had one large corner window that opened to a view of the Baha'i gardens. For the longest time we stood and watched the Haifa nightlife drive on the roads that circle around and through the gardens. Powerful feelings rushed through us. We thought we were too numb from travel to appreciate our view and where we stood. When every waking fiber was screaming to sleep, we discovered we needed to have the hotel find us power converters for Suzanne's sleeping equipment and my computer. After several attempts we were successful, and with most everything in place, we slept.

SUNDAY NOVEMBER 24, 2002

"What time is it, Baby?" I asked as I heard her rustle in her blankets. I had been standing at the window for several minutes, not wanting to wake her. She joined me and we, during the early morning hours, looked across Haifa Bay and watched bolts of lightning spark the sky over Akka. Below us, on the side of Mt. Carmel, the Shrine of the Bab glimmered and reflected the storm's flashes off its golden leafed dome. We watched the morning light push the night's darkness out to sea and slowly reveal the details of the buildings on the Arc. We loved our view and found little need for words as we watched morning claim the city.

Time passed and I wrote while Suzanne slipped back under her covers. Five a.m. found us hungry and raiding the little storage box and refrigerator in our room. The chips and nuts disappeared and were chased down with light Cokes. Finally, two hours passed and we took advantage of the real breakfast offered by the hotel. Breakfast in Israel is different from eating at Denney's. The array of food at the breakfast buffet took our breaths away. A large section of the dining room was filled with tables displaying rows of white coated cheese in sliced blocks that were stacked beside little round cheese balls and beautifully arranged slices of others I hadn't tasted before. Another table had tuna, or a fish much like it, mixed in bowls with colorful spices. Thick filets of red and white fish were offered beside others that I had not tasted before and didn't know their names. There were eels and other fish that had been pickled or smoked. The next section had yogurts, and then there was the entire table of breads, rolls and pastries. The other side of the room offered steaming trays of pasta, eggs boiled and scrambled, hot fish, and lots and lots fruits. To one side there were plastic tubes filled with dry cereal with milk dispensers. We found a table by the window and drank good coffee, delighting in the view and wondering why there were only eight other people in this large, lovely dining room filled with food.

We wanted to shop. "Let's buy some gifts today in case we don't have time during the Pilgrimage," was our thought. We discovered that although the streets were filling with cars, the shops weren't yet open. We climbed flight after flight of white and black rock steps that were common to, and unique to, Mt. Carmel. If it weren't for the Hebrew and Arabic signs…this part of the city wouldn't feel much different than Portland, Oregon.

Finally we found a little market open, and were surprised when we received an airport-style scan as we entered the building. I bought a beautiful green fruit with leaves tipped in red. It was expensive, soft, about the size of a large artichoke. I was anxious to taste it. I tried to repeat the clerk's name for the fruit, but was unable to teach my mouth the Hebrew sounds I needed.

We returned to our hotel and took a four-hour nap from which we awoke feeling very detached from place and time. Needing exercise and a bit of food, we went back to walking the neighborhood streets. We wandered past the hotels Nof, Dan Carmel and the Beth Shalom on Hanassi Avenue, which winds down Mt. Carmel towards Haifa Bay and past the Baha'i Gardens. There were very few people on the streets, and our walk was very pleasant. Women with their children shared the evening with us and poked their heads into the same restaurants and shops we did. Our walk ended with an exceptional salad in our hotel.

It's midnight in Haifa and I'm awake. Tomorrow is the first day of our Pilgrimage.

DAY ONE, MONDAY, NOVEMBER 25, 2002

My father was born on this day. As I realize of where I am and what I am doing, I wonder what he would think of all this. We slept well, and the early morning hours found me, once again, enjoying the view from our window. I stood there and watched as the rising sun spread a golden blanket across the side of every building. For just a moment the dome on the Shrine of the Bab, with its gold leaf tiles, blindingly reflected the sunbeams. I found myself feeling a bit like a guy who was going to receive something he had wanted every day of his life.

We started with registration, followed by orientation in the Pilgrim Reception Center. It's a pair of beautiful new buildings perched on a steep slope. Like many buildings in Haifa, they are surrounded by beautiful gardens built into the large block retaining walls.

The hospitality room was filled with unknown faces that all had Allah-u-Abha (God is most glorious) on their lips, and sparkle in their eyes. We were strangers for only moments, and then we began the process of becoming lifelong friends. Canada, Ireland, Maraquesh,

Australia, England, Brazil, Russia, France, United States, Taiwan and the Philippines were all represented, as well as others I have forgotten.

The staff treated us like gold as we were informed that we were the guests of Baha'u'llah and could expect to be treated as such. I was filled with appreciation for the honor of being allowed to be on Pilgrimage, and the staff seemed even more appreciative of my being there. What a lovely balance.

Our orientation didn't take long, and then we were free to wander in the gardens until mid-afternoon. The staff asked us to allow the public visitors to complete their tour before we, as a group, would all walk through the small wrought-iron gate and up the white rock path to the Shrine of the Bab.

Suzanne and I spent our waiting time walking around and photographing the gardens. We admired the new buildings high above us on the side of Mt. Carmel and the recently completed terraces. The Seat of the Universal House of Justice, International Teaching Center Building, International Archives Building and the Center for the Study of the Texts were all perfectly placed on an Arc above the gardens we walked. Their white marble pillars and walls glowed in the bright Israeli sunshine. We were patient as we gathered in front of the Haifa Pilgrim House. Our voices lowered when the guards opened the gates and invited us forward. Slowly we walked and listened to the sounds of the rocks moving beneath our shoes, and the chirps of birds that seemed to have gathered to watch and welcome us.

All of us were allowed to stay as long as we wanted. As the sun set and the lights of Haifa city began to glow, the Shrine, paths, pools, terraces, and gardens took on a new appearance. The bright strength of the daytime sun turned soft, and its rays were replaced with the light of lanterns and garden globes. I photographed until my camera was tired and my eyes blurred. I even photographed the spot my son Jordan had stood years ago, during his months in Haifa, watching over the Shrine while the rest of the city slept.

For me the time I spent inside the Shrines of the Bab and Abdu'l-Baha' was beyond words. I loved slipping off my socks and walking barefoot on the cool marble apron that surrounded the Shrines.

Bed was a welcome place that night. We were very tired and quickly slept, knowing that our second day of Pilgrimage was only hours away.

DAY TWO, TUESDAY, NOVEMBER 26th, 2002

The day found us standing by the entrance of the Carmelit. It's Haifa's mountainside subway that has dozens of stops up and down the side of Mt. Carmel. It reminded us more of a ski lift than a Chicago style subway. The entrance and tunnels are bright with yellow tiles that have framed movie posters mounted up and down both sides. The ride costs a buck, or five and one half shekels in Israeli money. Our ride is short, and within minutes we stop at the Golomb exit, just a few short blocks from the Pilgrim Reception Center.

The Center, to my delight, had a fabulous coffee machine I used often. Within a few minutes, the Friends arrive and we all continue to make much of each other. We were scheduled to visit Bahji, and three buses have been hired to transport us across Haifa, around the bay and near Akka, where we are deposited at the new Visitor Information Center. This building, like every building purchased or built by the Faith, was spectacular, and, to my delight, had a coffee machine just like the one at the Pilgrim House. God's blessings are endless.

I experienced a Pilgrimage in the early 1980's and expected to see what I saw then, and to have similar feelings. I didn't. Although the places we visited were the same, the experiences were totally new and fresh. Our first destination was a visit to the Shrine of Baha'u'llah.

We arrived at the New Visitors Center, and then began the long walk to the Shrine. New gardens covered the old parking lot I remembered from the eighties, and acres and acres of other undeveloped lands were now covered with gardens. We were also told that in days to come these gardens would surpass those on the side of Mt. Carmel.

The path from the Center to the Shrine was long and straight. A short time into the hike, my heart jumped when I recognized the beautiful wood doors and black canopy of the Shrine. With each step I took on the crushed clay tiles, I knew that I was drawing closer and closer to one of the most sacred spots on the planet. I remembered Jamie talking about her year of service in Haifa and her washing the windows that crowned the upper section of this room.

We all gathered in the Shrine and prayed and visited the threshold of the chamber where the remains of Baha'u'llah are interred. Before I stepped through the doors, I slipped off my shoes, and with my first stride I felt thick Persian rugs under my feet. A rich brightness passed through Jamie's clean windows and flooded the room. The walls were white and several tapestries were hung in the open spaces between the lush foliage that brought the room to life and framed their beauty. In the center of the room a garden, composed of many diverse plants, reach up towards the sparkling windows, and wrap themselves around the chains that suspend the lights hanging from the ceiling. Carpets cover every walking surface and are varied in design, color and size. I found myself sitting, with my back to the wall, across the room from the threshold. In the vivid sunlight the letters on the pages of my prayer book became too bright to read. I rested my head against the white stucco wall and closed my eyes. Time passed and when I felt refreshed I rose and slowly walked to the threshold where I knelt and placed my forehead on the cool marble. I prayed for my family and friends. I asked God to assist me in serving His Cause and dealing with the tests I would endure during my life.

Slowly I backed from the Shrine, put on my shoes and walked into the gardens. Suzanne joined me and we admired the gardens that seem formal at first glance and then, upon further inspection, discovered that they weren't. Each turn in the garden had a new surprise, a new plant, vase or statue, and the trees continue to grow where they were when Baha'u'llah walked these grounds.

We could have spent days at Bahji and not have seen enough. Our return bus ride to Haifa was hushed in contemplation of our visit. When we gathered back at the Reception Center, we share feelings and spiritual experiences, as we enjoyed the lunches we had packed. After eating we rode the local bus to our hotel where we rested until the evening lecture. The presentation that night was by a member of the International Teaching Center. It was very informative and we enjoyed learning more about the Baha'i World Center works.

DAY THREE, WEDNESDAY, NOVEMBER 27th, 2002

The day began with my dragging Suzanne through all the shops on the top of Mt. Carmel in search of a special power adaptor for my computer. After several hours we found a computer shop where I learned that I only needed a simple adaptor. Suzanne gave me one of those looks that I don't want to understand, as she took my hand and, with the new adaptor in bag, walked me back to the hotel.

Today was a free day for us, so we wanted to walk down the Terraces to the Shrine. When we were young we could have walked from the bottom up and lived. Today we were content to walk from the top, half-way down to the Shrine of the Bab, where we stopped to pray. I was delighted to have lots of alone time in both Shrines, and emerged a bit late for a presentation at the Reception Center which was followed by a walk up to the International Teaching Center Building.

The Terraces are such a pride. Pictures diminish them. The citizens of Haifa are so proud of the Baha'i gardens. There are nineteen terraces, nine above and nine below the Shrine, plus the one that holds the Shrine. The terraces are bisected by a stream of crystal clear water that flows down the mountainside. The bubbling sounds drown out noises from traffic, and create immense peace. Each Terrace is different, totally symmetrical, and well worth the time to explore. We didn't rush and were thankful that God had blessed us with the opportunity to be in the gardens, and with the ability to enjoy their magnificence.

The International Teaching Center Building is striking. Like everything the Baha'is built, the design and craftsmanship are excellent. I am so proud to be a Baha'i and am happy that I have been able to contribute to the creation of the World Center.

We returned from our tour and climbed into bed for a few hours nap before the evening Observance of the Ascension of Abdu'l-Baha' at 1:00 am.

Feeling somewhat rested, we made the trip down to the Seat of the Universal House of Justice, where we gathered with the Hands of the Cause, their wives, other dignitaries and many of the World Center Staff members. We entered the Reception Concourse and observed that the first two rows were reserved for the members of the Universal House of Justice and then the Pilgrims. Around us were all the staff and others who filled the Concourse from wall to wall. I felt like a mutt among pedigrees, yet we continued to be the honored guests of Baha'u'llah.

The program was filled with prayers and readings in Arabic, English and Persian. I heard chanting that night that delighted every fiber of my being. We then stood on the front steps of the Seat and the Tablet of Visitation was read in both Arabic and English. Universal House of Justice member, Kaiser Barns, read the English prayer, and his powerful voice rang out over the city of Haifa during the first hour of the new day. His voice and presentation reminded me of James Earl Jones with a bigger smile and broader shoulders.

We then walked down the terraces, across the bridge, and followed the members of the Universal House of Justice in the circumambulation of the Shrine of the Bab. Every light was on that night and not a single bulb failed. The mountainside was aglow, and every smooth marble surface reflected the illuminations. There were so many people involved in the observance, yet there was such quietness. The Shrine was exquisite and the gold of the dome wrapped with bans of white marble above the richly colored windows had beauty that seemed unearthly. Perfection seems impossible, and yet I saw no flaw. I saw only heavenly beauty in everything from the Terraces, Buildings, Shrine and the Friends. Even the round oranges hanging on the groomed trees seemed perfect.

DAY FOUR, THURSDAY, NOVEMBER 28th, 2002

Because Wednesday was the Observance of the Ascension of Abdu'l-Baha', and Pilgrims hadn't reached their beds till the wee hours of the morning, the traditional schedule for pilgrimage was changed, and we were confused.

It was a very nice day, and I awoke in a "where am I and what time of day is it?" mode. We didn't go to bed until sunrise, but we were up a couple of hours later hungry for breakfast. We returned to our room for a little house keeping, and then caught the cab down to the Gardens. We walked the lower Terraces, from the Shrine down to the bottom of the mountain, and loved them. Our pace was slow and the view was wonderful. From time to time we would turn and look back up the mountain at the Terraces and the Shrine of the Bab. When we descended the final flight of steps, we were treated to the view of the nine-pointed fountain in the shape of a star and the waterfall that cascades down the center of the broad span of steps. We felt special as we walked around the star and were aware that there were people on the other side of the gate that wanted to walk in the gardens and couldn't until it was opened to the public later in the day. When we were ready to leave, the guards opened the gate and released us to streets of Haifa. We crossed the street filled with bustling car traffic and turned to appreciate the full view of the Terraces which the citizens of Haifa enjoy every day. This is the view the Kings and rulers of the earth will have when they walk up the Row of Kings and come to the Universal House of Justice to consult.

We found a tourist shop and purchased a DVD of the gardens and some large, poster-sized photographs. Across the street from the tourist shop we found a fabulous café to have lunch called the Aldiyar. We didn't understand the menu and thought we had ordered a salad bar. When our waiter was slow to return we became concerned. Suddenly out of the kitchen he came with arms filled with nine or ten boat like dishes filled with lots of stuff I hadn't eaten before. With a basket of pita we began dipping into everything and were delighted. I liked the Tahini, which Suzanne said was a sesame paste, and the garlic-laced hummus. The other dishes were a variety of vegetables and spices. Yum!

It was our intent to catch a bus to Bahji, but we decided that although the bus was probably full of gas…we weren't...our late night had caught up with us. Suzanne was sweet and took me back to the hotel and my bed. Three or so hours later, I was up and felt like it was early morning rather than early evening. We met up with some Friends from Bend and shared a table and falafels. Visiting has a new meaning here where even light conversation seems closer and more complete.

We caught a cab together and rode down to the Gardens where we visited the Shrine. We stopped at the Haifa Pilgrim House to use the bathroom, and discovered several friends visiting with Mr. Furitan, one of the two remaining Hands of the Cause. We joined the group and for a long time the six of us talked about little things that made us all smile and laugh. When I shook his hand our eyes held for a little longer than normal and the moment felt special in some spiritual way.

Walking on the Shrine's apron between the marble columns and the Haifa-stone wall is like a mantra. I found myself reading the Tablets of Visitation while going round and round the exterior of the building. When the Tablets were complete I stopped, and found myself in front of the doors entering the chambers where the remains of the Bab were interred. For me this practice helped me feel more prepared to enter such a holy place. When the door closed behind me, I felt complete. Every visit I had was filled with thoughts of everyone I loved, and I could feel myself gathering up the strength I would need to be the Baha'i I wanted to be.

Following our time in the Shrine, we quickly dashed down the hill to the Reception Center where Member of the Universal House of Justice, Mr. Fatheazam, talked about the power of the Faith. These men that serve as members of the Universal House of Justice have so much responsibility, and when they hold their hands across their hearts in appreciation of our being in their presence, I am so honored to be a part of this Faith.

Later we visited with Mr. Fatheazam and when we left for our hotel, we were lucky to quickly catch a sherut.

DAY FIVE, FRIDAY, NOVEMBER 29th, 2002

I dreamt that I was with Friends and we were walking a Holy street. I was in a large clear ball and floating along with them. I was unsure what they thought of my floating ball and asked them. It didn't matter to them...so it didn't matter to me. I was the man in the ball, and that was how it was.

We got up and didn't know our schedule, and wouldn't know until we called the Reception Center. Being confused has an edge of excitement to it.

We took a sherut down to the Shrine and enjoyed our morning visit. The three chambers in the Shrine are designed for visiting the burial place of His Holiness the Bab. The chambers are in a row and the two on the outside have broad arched entrances that allow the visitors, through transparent drapes, to easily view the center chamber. The threshold between the chambers is marble and several inches off the carpet-covered floor. It is covered with crisp white linen and an oriental bowl set in the middle. Rose petals are on both sides, with each one taking up a place not occupied by another. If the Friends were kneeling side-by-side, five or six of us could place our foreheads on the threshold together. I love fingering the edge of the linen when kneeling. It feels thick and rich like the hem of His garment. The chamber is unfurnished except for the tall pedestals in the corners with alabaster vases on them. The center chamber, behind the lace curtain, is rich and filled with tall urns, golden candelabras with tall tapers, large and oriental electrical lamps, flowers and the golden symbol of the Greatest Name on the center of the carpet that covers the remains of the Bab.

The doors to the Shrines of the Bab and Abdu'l-Baha are tall, metal, coated in rich enamel paint and totally quiet when opening and closing. They are double doors and only one is used when just a few of the Friends are visiting.

The Shrine of Abdu'l-Baha has three chambers similar to the chambers devoted to the Bab. They are closer to the steps that lead down to the bay and are different in color and decor. As the walls and light in the Bab's Shrine are white and bright with rich wine colored carpets, the color of the Shrine of Abdu'l-Baha is apricot. The color is not from paint but from the glow of the large lamp that sits on the floor just inside the inner chamber. Its glass shades are colored like a peach or a soft warm summer fruit. The threshold in this chamber is a doorway with the door eternally open. It, too, is draped with a white linen cloth with a gold vase with flowers and blossoms that lay to each side. Two of the Friends can share this threshold, and, like the Shrine of the Bab, the resting place of the Master is covered with carpets and the Greatest Name. Flowers and beautiful vases are placed around the edge of the carpet. If I were a carpet maker, what greater gift could God give me but to have the work of my hands in such holy spots?

DAY SIX, SATURDAY, NOVEMBER 30th, 2002

Still warm and in my bed, I awoke to Suzanne's presenting me the most beautiful prayer beads. It was my birthday, and Suzanne had asked our friend, Jaleh Burns, to make them for me, and they were amazing. Ninety-five large beads of turquoise separated by much smaller beads of coin silver tucked into a round leather pouch. I took them to the Shrines and let the holy energy bathe each and every bead.

It was our sixth day, and we were on our way to Akka, the Prison city. There we visited the ancient city and the prison that held Baha'u'llah and His family. We were not allowed to enter the prison itself and spent many hours walking the streets of one of the oldest cities in the world. Its history has been recorded for thousands of years. The walls, windows openings, and arches are pitted and worn. Mortar has fallen away from many of the large stones and they appear loose and about to fall.

We visited many places and were told about the Bahai's that had lived there. It was dangerous for them. They suffered, and many died.

The city is on the far end of Haifa Bay and the smell and sight of the ocean surrounds it. We watched people work. Some were lifting a sunken fishing boat to the surface of the water. Women were hanging laundry out second story windows and sweeping the entrances of their homes. It wasn't a comfortable place for us to be, and we were watched without smiles.

Later we were bused to the House of Abbud, then Mazra'ih. We looked out windows, up stairs, and across courtyards where Baha'u'llah had lived. At Mazra'ih I was shown a worn, square toed pair of slippers that were His. Of all the precious sights I saw that day...the slippers touched me the deepest.

The bus delivered us to our hotel just in time for dinner. Suzanne walked me to a restaurant where we had dinner, and we celebrated my birthday. A Baha'i couple from North Carolina joined us. We talked about our day and about being Baha'i in our hometowns.

DAY SEVEN, SUNDAY, DECEMBER 1st, 2002

Our day started with a walk from the Pilgrim Reception Center across the street to the Monument Gardens. Here the remains of The Greatest Holy Leaf, Baha'u'llah's daughter, The Purest Branch, son of Baha'u'llah, Navvab, wife of Baha'u'llah, and Munirih Khanum, the wife of Abdul-Baha rest. In this beautiful garden, monuments were constructed which reflect the same ancient Greek style that is shared by the other Baha'i buildings on the side of Mt. Carmel. We read prayers at all the sites, and then returned to the Reception Center where we boarded buses and drove to the site of the future Mashriqu'l-Adhkar (House of Worship). The location is on the high end of Mt. Carmel before it drops into Haifa bay. The view is spectacular. Standing there now is a massive monolith surrounded by formal gardens filled with exceptional flowers with leaves I hadn't seen before.

We visited the International Baha'i Archives which was the first Edifice built on Mt. Carmel. It is filled with very personal items of the Holy Family and the early believers. Our guide on this visit was Mrs. Khan. Upon entering the building she unlocked the tall metal doors that opened into a small entrance room. She then opened the inner doors and we found ourselves standing in a long room with a ceiling several stories high. The floor was a green tile and the outer walls of both the main level and the balconies, on both sides, were filled with bookcases and other pieces of display furniture. Large Persian rugs covered the center of the floor and upon them were display cabinets, placed back to back, up and down the length of the room. A massive table with a huge oriental vase occupied the center of the room. The wall on the far end of the room was filled with a large two-story stained glass window of red, blue and gold glass. It had a powerful effect on the room. Several massive crystal chandeliers hung from the ceiling.

We spent several hours looking at Writings, clothing, photographs, drawings, calligraphy, swords, books, art work, and many, many personal items that have great meaning to the eye that looks at it, and little if it is described by words.

DAY EIGHT, MONDAY, DECEMBER 2nd, 2002

We were up early and had our usual breakfast of fish, eggs, fabulous breads, cheese, cheese, and cheese, lots of extra wonderful quiche, cabbage rolls and bowls of fresh vegetables. Now that we are in the days of Chanukah all of these foods are more wonderful than normal.

We then went down to the street and flagged down a taxi that quickly drove us down the mountain to the Reception Center. The tour buses were ready for our next adventure, so we loaded up and were on our way to the Bahji Mansion.

I loved being in the Shrine again and laid my new prayer beads on the threshold. We then toured the Mansion, which is filled with artifacts, and the rooms that were occupied by Baha'u'llah and the Holy Family. We spent several hours viewing it all, and felt that many more hours could have been used.

Next we had our lunch, which we had made during breakfast at the hotel, and visited with other Pilgrims. Visiting has become an exceptionally enjoyable experience. We have tied up with a Persian family that lives in Australia. They have two adult children who are in their early twenties and remind us of our kids.

We then drove to the House of Abdu'llah Pasha. I had not seen this house before and enjoyed sitting in the room that had been occupied by the Master and watching the bay. There was a strong wind kicking up the waves.

The Ridvan Gardens were our next point of visitation. There we prayed, got cold from the wind, and enjoyed oranges from the trees on the property, just as Baha'u'llah had done years before.

Around dinner time we jumped out of our bus at our hotel and ordered a sandwich. We had learned that food is always presented in large Israeli portions, so we shared one, and then returned to our room.

On the last day of Pilgrimage we will visit the Holy Shrine for the last time. I don't expect to return to Haifa, and am sad, and yet OK with that realization. I am deeply in love with my Faith, and this experience has given me a richer depth and understanding of why I love it. God has always blessed me and continues to bless me each day of my life.

DAY NINE, TUESDAY, DECEMBER 3rd, 2002

I have seen a Bahji' that very few Baha'is have seen. The day began with a brisk wind racing down Hanassi Avenue. It pushed us back as we hailed our cab and chased us down the road to the Reception Center. Shortly after we arrive we discovered we had another free day. Suzanne said there were no commitments for the day, but I doubted her. I tried the Center phone without success, and I was not satisfied until our guide said, "You have a free day." Her gentle smile forgave my lack of faith.

We decided to visit the Monument Gardens, Master's House, resting place of Amatu-l-Baha, Ruhiyyih Khanum, and drive out the Bahji, where we would again visit the Shrine of Baha'u'llah.

The wind mixed itself with a light rain and our umbrella popped inside out and was useless. Suzanne properly folded it away before we visited the graves of Bahiyyih Khanum, Mirza Mihdi, Navvab, and Munirih Khanum. The Monument Gardens are directly across the street from the Reception Center and easy to access with a loaned key. Several friends had asked for prayers to be said in these Gardens, so those requests were fulfilled.

We jumped on bus number twenty-three and rode down into the old city of Haifa, where we walked down narrow streets, stacked with homes and buildings that had the look of being old and enduring. Across the street from the Master's House, a large section of a city block is now the groomed garden and resting place of Ruhiyyih Khanum. She was the wife of Shoghi Effendi, Guardian of the Faith, and grandson of 'Abdu'l-Baha. She had come to Haifa as a young woman and lived all her days in the Master's House. She had written books, managed households, and traveled the world in service to the Faith. With our loaner key, we entered the garden, enjoyed its beauty, and said the prayers we had promised to pray. Suzanne described Ruhiyyih Khanum as "no shrinking violet."

With a locked gate behind us, and block after block of unbelievable cultural beauty before us, we set off to explore. We ate in a local restaurant filled with workingmen who watched us for a few moments as we dipped our pita into the tahini and filled it with fresh vegetables. They soon lost interest as we enjoyed our early lunch.

We wandered across a small section of the city, taking pictures and delighting in the open markets, and the freshness of the fruits and vegetables offered. We peeked into toy stores and fabric shops, and giggled with delight as our eyes feasted on streets and alleys that held views we had never seen before. Our trek ended at a Sherut station, where we climbed aboard a van for the hour drive to Bahji'. By the time we arrived, the wind had decided to behave in a way rarely seen by locals. It continued to mix itself with rain, and pushed itself up to a serious storm. The cypress and eucalyptus trees that separate the sections of the Bahji' gardens were swinging like Chinese yoyos. Branches snapped and limbs fell to the ground. The normally leaf-free lawns and walks were stacked with fallen oranges, mixed with branches and greens that had been bent further than their ability to flex.

I walked for a bit, taking pictures, then joined Suzanne in the Shrine. I pushed my bag and shoes under a tarp held by the man who guards the entrance and entered. The door closed behind me and the sound of the storm softened. For a while I watched the treetops dance by sections of the windows that surround the top of the room and then I succumbed to the tranquility that surpassed the storm. An hour passed, and then we left and returned to the storm. Many more branches had fallen, and the wind continued to search for others that were weak and unable to resist. We dashed for a long distance until we reached the protection of the Information Center.

Another group of Pilgrims was having tea, so we visited with them until they boarded their bus and headed for another location. We weren't happy about our having to walk all the way down to the highway to flag down a sherut, and were delighted when, after only a few minutes of walking, we saw one coming our way. We waved him over and jumped aboard. He returned to the parking lot and waited there for half an hour, attempting to fill the van before he returned to Haifa. A half empty sherut doesn't make much money. We didn't understand much of the Hebrew that was spoken by the other passengers, but we all handed the driver money until he was happy, and we headed back to Haifa.

Once in Haifa we tried to board the Carmelit, but it was closed due to the Shabat. We found a cab close by and, for a little extra, we were soon back at the hotel.

We rested for a while, and then walked, with more than a little help from the wind, down the street, until we found an open restaurant where we had soup and bread. Most everything closes during the first two hours of Shabat, so we were happy with the food we had found.

After our dinner we caught another cab that drove us down the hill to the Reception Center, where we had heard one of the Hands of the Cause would visit with us. We then ended our evening attending the Pilgrim Farewell and Prayers in the Shrines. Suzanne and I shared a delightful and significantly bonding moment when, together, we laid our heads upon the threshold in the Shrine of the Bab. It felt like we fused another part ourselves together. Our shared love of the Faith is the best part of our relationship.

We were tired after our long and adventuresome day, and were ready to sleep when we reached the room. We knew we were leaving Haifa the next day and wanted to store up energy for the travel. Our Pilgrimage was almost over, and we both knew that we would probably never return to this most holy spot.

Thursday December 5, 2002
Florence, Oregon

I made arrangements for a sherut to pick us up early in the morning. We had planned on seven of us making the trip and ended up with only five. It made our shared cost a little higher, but we didn't care. The drive to Tel Aviv took ninety minutes, hand we had lots of time to kill before our flight. We had been instructed to show up three hours before our flight for a strict security clearance. The hotel was happy to cancel our room for that evening and we saved one hundred and twenty five dollars.

My sitting-in-airport skills improved. Appreciating powerlessness must have something to do with it. The security felt like going through a program designed and operated by youth. They had lots of big impressive machines and seemed to be training each other as they went along. We got to keep most everything we packed except for the power cord to my computer. It looked dangerous so they kept it with a promise it would be in the mail by the time we took off. It was probably on our airplane.

We flew and sat and flew and sat and flew and sat. The time between our bed in Israel and the motel in Portland was over forty hours. I often found myself in a light sleep that helped pass the time. Upon our arrival, we hailed a cab to our motel room, and for the next twelve hours we slept. I had dreams about painting Holy Places and remodeling Baha'i Centers. We'll see what is in store for me.

We're in Eugene! We arrived mid-afternoon and spent the morning with Jamie and Skylar, showing them the posters we purchased at Haifa's Department of Tourism. Jamie picked one of them that I will have framed for her. We went out for a little lunch, watched a few minutes of our homemade videos, and before long we were completing the last leg of our long trip home to Florence.

OUR TRIP TO THE HOLY LAND

Our trip home took forty-two hours and left us exhausted. We spent a couple of days getting there and a couple coming home. For ten days we visited the Shrines, gardens, places of historical interest and wandered the streets of Haifa and Akka.

I watch too much CNN, so I felt more than a little discomfort flying into what I feared was about to become a war zone. I promised my kids that I wouldn't ride busses and broke that promise, finding comfort with the people, all forms of transportation, and the food.

While we were there we visited with many of the Jewish and Arabic citizens. The Jews had just begun their Hanukkah and the Arabs were ending their Ramadan. Several Jewish people said, "This is not a very happy Hanukkah because we know that war is at hand."

There were good roads, many of them were freeways filled with new cars. The traffic was heavy at times, and the cars were mostly from Europe and Japan. I only saw a handful of American cars. The busses I promised my kids I wouldn't ride were modern and very space-aged in design. It felt a lot like home. Not home in Florence where we don't know what traffic is, but home like Eugene or Portland.

I was also surprised to see shopping centers with Office Max, Home Depot, McDonalds, KFC and many other American businesses. Amongst the Hebrew and Arabic signs would be a bright and glowing "Drink Coke" with bottle caps on both ends.

It is a strange thing when you see a beautiful, new BMW driving down a cobblestone road under an ancient city arch built two thousand years before the birth of Christ, or the old cigarette smoking Arab leaning against a long-standing wall with a cell phone against his ear.

I saw lots of food for sale in many small street front stores. The produce, whether it was in a poor area or affluent one, was always fresh and presented beautifully. Their burlap bags and baskets of dry goods were clean and called to be eaten.

We were warm there. We found ourselves in short sleeved shirts with jackets left behind. Most days we enjoyed seventy degree weather and were surprised to find forty degrees in Florence.

I went to Haifa to treat my soul and found that all of me benefited. Walking the streets of this Holy Land was good for my body. I also learned to further appreciate the importance of the world religions coming together and the need for unity and peace. The Writings of my Faith say, "This is a new cycle of human power. All the horizons of the world are luminous, and the world will become indeed as a garden and a paradise...the gift of God to this enlightened age is the knowledge of the oneness of mankind and of the fundamental oneness of religion."

ELWAY 2002

Jamie was with us and the walk on the beach was windy. Elway was his normal self and charged the surf and all the endangered plovers that flew just out of his reach. He would scoop his mouth full of sea foam and just in time scoot out from under the crashing surf. Watching his graceful bounding always entertained Suzanne and me, and today with Jamie, it felt much like showing off our child.

I dropped the tailgate on my pick-up and lifted the camper hatch so Elway could jump in. He had unbelievable grace and lacked fine motor skills. As a result he always looked good even if he knocked his head getting in to the truck.

I parked on the street across from our home leaving the driveway open for Suzanne's car. Our neighbor, Pam, was backing her truck out of her driveway as I opened my camper hatch and let Elway jump to the street. He was running down the curb as I waved to Pam and gave her the OK to drive on by before we crossed the street. With a smile and a little goose of her truck's motor she accelerated past us.

Out of the corner of my eye, I saw my one hundred and twenty pound apricot Shepherd prance in front of my truck and across the street. Seeing the truck upon him he dropped to his haunches and extended all four legs in front of himself. Pam hit her brakes. Like a bundle of sticks his legs slid in front of the skidding truck tires. For several horrifying and immobilizing feet we stood and watched the tire grind the flesh and fur from Elway's legs until it climbed upon them and stopped. His howl pierced the neighborhood's tranquility and broke our frozenness as we dashed to his aid. Jamie caught the terrified eyes of Pam and screamed, "Back up, back off of him." Pam now shared our immobility and was slow to engage her transmission's reverse and back off of Elway who was biting at the tire like a trapped wolf. Finally her rear tires squealed and mixed with Elway's howl. The backing tire brought the sound of snapping bones and I said, "Oh God, he's broken his legs." With my flat hand against my chest I dropped to my knees beside him. In an explosion of motion he gathered his legs under himself and propelled himself to the curb where he dropped to his chest.

We three were upon him to assess his damage. Pam stood behind us with her hands cupped over her mouth. "I didn't see him. I am so sorry." Together we comfort her with words of, "It's not your fault, Pam. You couldn't see him."

I was anxious as Elway rose to his feet and stood. Blood was oozing from all his legs as he licked and attended to his wounds. We walked him to the house and laid him on the floor where he allowed us to doctor his injuries.

Several days have passed now and Elway is stiff and walking. His eyes glow and the flesh missing from his legs has formed a bizarre pattern of vertical and horizontal rips that are reminiscent of an abstract painting. Suzanne took him to the beach yesterday and he made one charge at the plovers, and then contented himself with walking beside her. The plovers won't get off as easily next time.

POEMS BETWEEN THE FATHER AND SON 2003

Hello dear father.
Now I snuggle into sleep
Snug and tight in my sheets.
A candle I will soon light,
To keep me warm in the night.
A book will be read,
And thoughts in my head...
Will bounce and play
The night away.
I'll have a dream or two,
For that's what sleepers do.
In the morning I will wake,
And perhaps pancakes I'll bake.
Tee-he, Tee-ha my rhyme is done,
I hope it made you smile; it was lots-o-fun!

Love yaw, Love yaw,
There's none above yaw!

The Son

Hello there son, how do you do?
It delighted me to hear from you.
A poem from you is such a treat,
Your words sure rhyme and have a beat.
I sit today in my big office chair
Wishing that I wasn't here, but there.
We would find a coffee shop and sit,
And tell life stories as our drinks we sip.
You could boast and spread your feathers,
While I lean back, it can't get better.
I wish that you were close at hand,
So together you and I could stand

And watch our lives and days go by
And share our growth, our laughs and sighs.
This Father loves his Son today
And appreciates all that he has to say.
I know that God gave me a gift
Of Jordan Gabriel a son to kiss.

The Father

A poet you are ties true
No one can rhyme as you do.
We laugh and play throughout the day,
As our words babble and brew.
Ahhh, yes, coffee would be grand.
It's always nice to have the hand
Of the father who I love so much
As we talk and share such and such.
To sit, to chat, to play, to bat.
To laugh and giggle and sometimes wiggle.
These are the joys that life can bring
For two people whose souls do sing.
Yes, songbirds of life that's what we be.
You and I, you and me!
Yet, like night and day, hot and cold
We are not together but apart a fold.
Perhaps a fold in a map. Yes that's right.
For soon the map will open when a plane takes flight.
Into the air I will zoom
Although I'd rather ride a broom.
Landing softly on the ground
Full of laughter without a frown.
The Dad, The Dad, I'll shout with glee
And you and I shall play, yes sireee!

Love ya!
The Son

To climb your mountain of excellent prose,
Leaves me hanging on an edge with only my toes,
So please reach out and take my hand,
I don't want to fall on that hard land.
I lift you up and sing your praise
And will humbly write you on other days.

The Father

SIUSLAW RIVER COFFEE ROASTERS 2003

"Thanks for joining us. Our next song has a long lead that is not normally heard except in recordings by Mel Torme." The gray bearded host stroked his guitar and a sweet clarinet slipped in as Swanee River filled the room. The building, once an outboard motor shop, was now a blend between a coastal gift shop and coffee bar that was heavy with ambiance and light on space. Thirty folks, all over the age of fifty and most closer to seventy, packed themselves into the spaces left between display tables and potted plants. As each song was performed, the six musicians, each draped with his personal style of old age, skillfully used their instruments and voices to broaden the smiles and tap the feet of their audience.

We had been told by Leah, a long time music buff, that these old men were past professionals, or at least damn good musicians, who had found a corner in the Siuslaw River Coffee Roasters on Bay Street, and made great big band and blues music from 8:30 to 10:00 am on Sunday mornings. We had known about the event for a month before this morning when we woke early enough to walk down to Old Town and check it out.

There's a large community of retired folks in Florence and many have had rich and active lives. Finding places to express their talents is often a difficult task, but when a spot is found, it becomes an immediate hot spot. The Coffee Roasters had become the Sunday morning hot spot.

The banjo player, a local dentist and probably the only member of the group who stills works, got the group together. I had to tell him, when it was all over, that he had the most beautiful banjo I had ever seen. It was gold on gold with Ivory accents. When he took his moment in the light, he could run that banjo up and down the scales and never miss a stroke. Such a happy sound I haven't heard in years.

One old retiree who danced with my wife several times said, "I believe the guy playing the guitar heads up the water department." He wasn't sure, but had heard that from Mabel Lynn the other woman he was dancing with.

There were two trumpet players. They both had their silver hair slicked back and one of them would lunge to the side and push out his hand with an extended finger. He didn't do it all the time. Only when the music was really swinging and he wanted to mark a musical point. The first time or two he made his slick move, I thought he was heading for a tumble on the floor. The other horn man wasn't as active and sat on a stool. He would pop a metal mute into the end of his horn, close his eyes and wash us all away with his soft, sweet sound.

The two fellows on the guitars may have been a little younger. The tall one with the beard, the possible head of the Florence water department, was the main vocalist. His voice was gentle and you had to lean your head a bit in his direction to catch all the words. Like the old horn blower, he had a sweet, sweet sound. The other guy was short and round. He wasn't looking for glory. He just wanted to play and fill in the holes left in the music by the old guys.

The instrument that seemed to capture the lost sound of big band best was the clarinet. With a fresh haircut and a solid perch on his stool he slipped Benny Goodman into the room and lit the dance room ball.

Like the round guitarist, the drummer just loved drumming. All he had was a single snare and he rapped and tapped it to all the rhythms the others wanted to make.

Six old men and a room filled with old happy people. Life in Florence is a wonder.

KAUAI 2003

We wanted to spend the Christmas week together and chose the island of Kauai. Suzanne and her son Jason, Jamie and her son Skylar, Jordan and his wife Erica and I were guests of the Makai Club. During our week on the island we spent lots of time in Hanalei where we shopped in the Saturday Farmers Market, played on the beach and admired the long pier that runs into the pounding surf.

We ate Opah (moon fish), Ahi and tiger prawns, between playing in the bay with surf and boogie boards, building sand castles, watching casual beach people and admiring the prehistoric mountains that surround the bay and keep their tops dipped in ocean crossing clouds. It was a Merry Christmas.

FLORENCE CAFÉ 2003

If you stood on the Florence Bridge, which has spanned the Siuslaw River for seventy years, and tossed a Frisbee down Highway 101 it would probably hit the Florence Café.

It's an old block building built like a twisted shoebox on an oddly shaped lot. For the past dozen or so years a gal named Val owned the café and kept it a favorite eatery for locals and visitors alike. Val was considering a change in her life, so when Bill Hall offered to purchase her business she said…yes. Within weeks Val's Florence Café became… Hall's Florence Café. You could hardly tell the difference except for the Iron Cross Harley Davidson mounted in the display wall where the candy racks had hung.

Bill often talked of his Italian lineage and the love everyone in his family had for food. Not just "flip it in a pan and heat it up" food, good authentic "you know how to prepare it correctly" food.

As Bill's Realtor, I had the opportunity to eat with him and his family in their lake side home above Lake Woahink. Bill was truly tickled if you liked his home cooking and when dining out together, he would take one bite of an entrée, lean his head back, close his eyes and emit a, "hummm this is really good." He would then start talking about every spice in the dish and how the chef had prepared it. Bill was born to own a restaurant.

The outside of the restaurant didn't change much with Bill's ownership. He added fresh paint to the exterior walls and had the old "Florence Café" neon sign repaired. It hadn't glowed in ten years. Black signage painted on the front windows boast a half a dozen specials and their reasonable prices.

Most of the old crew kept working and the new menu highlighted many of the old favorites and the new offerings that were pure Bill Hall. Big Bill's Omelet was so big that if you ate it in one sitting Bill would put your name in the local newspaper. He also has the rapidly growing and famous, "sing for your dinner" Thursday. The evening's best singer enjoyed their dinner on Bill's tab. I didn't deserve the win...but enjoyed a free dinner myself.

CHOWDER, BLUES AND BREWS 2003

Early in September Florence hosts the Chowder Blues & Brews. It's a weekend long event with live blues music, great clam chowder prepared by local restaurants and excellent Oregon-based microbrews.

Over half of the Event Center is filled with vendors selling sea food plates, classic pizza, finger steaks, pasta, and, of course, chowder from Oregon coastal clams and other sea delicacies.

On our way we drove through Old Town, parked our car, and watched the cyclists complete Cycle Oregon. These folks, many of them my age, had ridden their bikes from one end of Oregon to the other. As it turned out, we were the finish line for the adventure and it was a pleasure to watch faces as they rolled across the line. Suzanne and I asked each other if we were up to that kind of commitment, and we agreed with a joint, "Nah."

By 1:15 p.m. I was happily seated in the front row of the Events Center' flat floor stage, only a few feet from Doug Randall, an exceptional keyboard man, who I have admired for several years. He was raised in Florence, and I had been helping him and his brother purchase a beach home. Doug was taking his turn at the ivories playing in an impromptu jam. It seemed like everyone that was performing during the weekend gig kept joining other groups on stage and the music was exceptional.

We kept wandering back to the food vendors grabbing crab, shrimp and lots of clam chowder. Entries from throughout the coast vied for the title "The Best Chowder on the Oregon Coast." A grand prize award of $1000 was awarded along with a jumbo traveling trophy.

The emcee was the indefatigable Paul Biondi. He was also the music director and kept everything moving and the dance floor full. After the Jam, Bobby Lindstrom and his Blues Band took over until 8:15 p.m. Bobby sweats more that any singer I have ever watched and his blues are very blue.

The Boomer Band took to the stage and knocked us all over with old-fashioned rock and roll. The band features Lee Garrett who co-authored with Stevie Wonder "Signed, Sealed, Delivered I'm Yours."

By the time we walked out of the Center my blues hungry soul was full and I had eaten a little of every yummy seafood available and toped it all off with BJ's ice cream. When we dropped into our hot tub to enjoy the star filled night, we realized that most of our home chores were unfinished ... and that was OK!

AFRICAN GRAY 2003

She wants him! She wants him in her mouth and between her teeth. She wants to sink her long canines deeply into his turkey like flesh. He drops his voice and rattles off a full unintelligible sentence backed with, "Come here, Elway, come on boy," and then tops it off with a screeching whistle. Dropping to her hindquarters and squinting her eyes she rolls back her lips exposing her fangs. He loves the attention and does a one legged swing down to her level and freezes in his upside down position as she loses all control and attacks.

Jenny is our Sheltie and she hates our African Gray parrot. She hates him because he calls her Elway, the name of our big Golden Sheppard, and because he talks and shouldn't. Reno, the parrot, is very smart. He is completely comfortable in his cage and exercises his brain by developing new moves and sounds for Jenny's benefit.

Both animals are healthy except for the Sheltie's extra pounds and the Gray's bare chest. I understand Jenny's extra weight, and have been totally perplexed by Reno's removal of chest feathers. When people see him they seem to wonder why anyone would keep such an ugly creature, or maybe they think we are into bird abuse. It doesn't matter…our home is a pet farm.

We have seed shells and millet mixed with dog hair moving around our home in stumbling size dust balls. The weekly Rainbow vacuuming produces a wet mass of pet residue that looks more in need of burying than being tossed in the garbage.

We are a social couple, Suzanne and I, and our pets provide our company, and us, with ample entertainment. If the dogs are slow on the draw and a visitor can make it to knocking on the door, we can expect an animal racket of embarrassing proportions. In turn Reno will start yelling in my deep voice "Elway, Elway come here." The house sounds like a kennel with an echo. Once I have gathered up the dogs and herded them into the bedroom, Suzanne can consider opening the door. If our visitors are new they are often displaying sheepish expressions, mixed with discomfort, and maybe a little fear.

I have considered having fewer animals and find little support. Neither of the dogs or the parrot has offered to leave and Suzanne would block the door if they tried. I have discovered that with the passing of time one can adapt to most anything, although it still is upsetting to have Reno greet me with Suzanne's warm voiced "Hi, Honey!"

DOGS ON THE BEACH 2003

The dogs are always excited when I drop the tailgate of my old Ford truck. After moving to Florence it didn't take long for them to figure out that an open tailgate was an invitation to heaven. Heaven can be found in many places around Florence and our favorite is the piece of open beach north of Driftwood Shores.

We have two great dogs. Elway is a German Shepherd and Jenny a Sheltie. They both are seven years old and live for the beach. We clip them to their leashes until we get to the sand and can see if there are other dogs to be concerned about or not. If the beach is clear we let them run. There are few sights more beautiful than a rich orange sun setting on top of the rolling surf, with a broad ribbon of light dancing across the water, and the silhouette of your dog bouncing across the top of the surf's sea foam.

Elway is a great hunter wannabe and drops into a deep crouch as he slowly creeps up upon the beach birds. The bottom of his chest is reflected on the wet sand while he makes his charge and the birds casually lift into the air above his reach. Elway has never caught anything. He has several problems with his hunting efforts. The first is that the birds are much faster than he is; the second is the stick he grabs in his mouth when we first start our walk and he refuses to relinquish until we return to the truck.

The beach is always changing. No two walks are the same. One day will find bright sunshine and a calm that almost puts the surf to sleep. Another day will have rain spinning down the beach like a tornado dragging itself from one beach stump to another. My dogs don't care. The beach is the beach and that is what they live for.

ALL THINGS CONSIDERED 2003

The sound of the radio tuned to "All Things Considered" is filling the background of my office. It's late in the winter, February 13, 2003, and there is talk of war. The State failed to pass Measure 28, and unemployment is everywhere. The local Emporium store is closing. It's the only store in town where you can buy a pair of shoes.

I had a great 2002 and made good money in Real Estate. I am fearful that 2003 will be hard. I tend to slide into negative thinking and want my cup to be half full, not half empty.

Yesterday I had the dogs groomed. It costs fifty-five dollars. They smell great and are beautiful. It is fun to be a bit extravagant, and paying for dog grooming is an extravagance for me.

The weather has been exceptional for this time of year, with lots of sunshine and little rain. Today it's raining. I am printing up envelopes for my monthly newsletter. I enjoy writing and having folks read my stuff. I enjoy reading my words, and am always hopeful that others will feel the same.

We have two new Baha'is in our community. John and Marcia Lang have moved here from Bend and are a wonderful addition. Tuesday night Suzanne, John and I attended a local high school basketball game. Our team is in second place in the league and Marist is in first. The game was great, though we lost by a couple of points. It was four dollars well spent.

Jordan just called. He was at work and wanted to take a minute to say "Hi." Both he and Jamie often call me. I feel loved by my children and am proud of them. Jordan talked of being tired. He is recovering from a nasty cold. Jamie said she was a bit under the weather also. Hummm. I think I am feeling a bit crummy also. Maybe this blue attitude of mine is the bug. I'm tired and am going to call it a day. Maybe tomorrow will be wonderful.

ERICK'S COFFEE HOUSE 2003

I feel relaxed, enjoying the view of the Old Florence Bridge as I drive south on Hwy 101 to view a new listing. It is mid-morning and the rain is mild. The windshield wipers are on delay. Sunshine bursts through a cloud, my eyes quickly close and I fill my lungs to their depth with a fragrance that always brings a smile to my face. The Siuslaw River Coffee Roasters are roasting.

Erick's Coffee House sits on the river's edge in Old Town and is close to the footings of the bridge. I often join friends there, and we talk about some things that matter and others that don't. "Hi, James! Twelve ounce house in glass?" they ask as I walk through the door. "Yes and a sixteen ounce for John. He should be here in a few minutes," I reply, as I pull my coffee card and a few bucks from my pouch.

For years the Coffee House was an outboard motor repair shop and was skinned in corrugated steel with no insulation. It has had several owners and each has added to the transformation from a place of repairs to a nest for friends. Tucked in the open rafters is a model train track that probably works and almost disappears as it winds from one beam to another, and daily maintains the silence it has kept for years. The tables are separated by chin-high walls, which afford privacy as regulars yell across them with warm greetings and waves. Two pellet stoves pump out heat from opposite sides of the room and make tables close by most desirable.

The back of the Coffee House opens to the covered deck, where tables and chairs await the hearty customers that want to view the river and snuggle down, as they inhale the rich coffee and the coastal air. Just inside the deck door is a private corner, which is home for a coffee table, sofa and a chair or two. I rarely sit there. It's hard enough for me to leave after an hour of coffee and friends. I can't imagine how long I would stay if leaving the comfort of the sofa was part of the deal.

Erick has packed the walls and a few shelves with books and lots of creative gifts that are big hits with the tourists and the locals when birthdays and anniversaries sneak up on us.

The young folks, who work the espresso machine and take our money, banter and rub a bit of their youth on us. Most of us appreciate it, discovering a little of our cool in our responses.

Warmed by coffee and friendship I leave and can count on hearing, "Take care James! We will see you soon."

LOVES MY MOTHER 2003

Here we go again! We have been on the road for a little over an hour and are half way between Florence and Philomath. Suzanne is teaming up with Jeanine and they are presenting another component of the Teacher Development Program. They are expecting twenty or so to attend. I am support staff and transportation.

The Baha'i Cause and how happy we are that we share our Faith is the topic of our early morning conversation. Words disappeared for a while and I wander in my mind as my eyes delight in the beauty of early morning in the north end of the Willamette Valley.

Being beside and with Suzanne is like curling up in a mink lined nest. Our lives are filled with serving the Faith, our family, work, and all the daily efforts we apply to keep our lives enjoyable. During all these labors she maintains an attitude of joy, and is pleased with the choices she makes. She is an endless funnel of love, giving herself away in her service. She does not consider anything more important than people, and savors bringing happiness to others. What others consider precious material treasures, she views as givable and assesses their value in the happiness it brings others? Her son, Jason, once captured her essence by saying, "Everyone who knows my Mother loves my Mother."

Suzanne has talked about the women in her family and how they are often five foot tall and sometimes less. They tend to be full and curved women who live long lives and celebrate their days on this earth. I love the way she tucks under my arm, how we shift our shoulders and wind our arms to be close and fit in the tiny theater seats. I like the nighttime spooning and the easy body shifts that keep us close and comfortable.

We stop mid-way on our trip for a potty break. It is a public park, and I sit behind the wheel as she shuffles across the wet early morning grass to the bathroom. She's all dressed up today with her black outfit with the seashell necklace I bought her for Valentine's Day. When she returns, I watched her face. Her salt and pepper hair is long and frames her eyes and smile. She's all lit up. It is 7:30 a.m. on a Saturday morning, she had just used a cold porta-potty, her shoes were wet from the morning dew, and she had a, "I get to play on the beach smile." It's the most beautiful sight and I get to see it so often. Goldie Hawn is Suzanne's favorite actress and they share the same smile.

Sharing space can be difficult for some people. I am blessed and feel like a piece in a spinning puzzle that always finds its spot and the fit is perfect. I'm sure that the reason my nest is so soft and I fit so well is due to Suzanne. She celebrates me. She accepts me. She isn't looking to improve or change me. She likes the way I fit in the puzzle. She appreciates my growth.

We share family. She has hers and I have mine. She makes mine hers and celebrates their lives and victories like hers. She wears their accomplishments and accepts their shortcomings. She extends to them the unconditional acceptance she has for me.

I have often wondered why God gave me this gift of a woman. It seems as if I am being prepared to do important things, and this nesting time is teaching me about God's love and how it should be expressed.

HARLEY DAVIDSON 2003

It was Saturday afternoon and I couldn't believe it. My daughter and I were having a wonderful time walking through all the people dressed in black leather and the motorcycles and that had gathered on Bay Street.

The Rhododendron Festival is always great and this year was not an exception. The sky was coastal blue and the clouds that passed across it were fresh and white. Florence was the clouds' first view of land since their formation over the Pacific Ocean, and they were fat and full as they paraded above Old Town.

Jamie had escaped all the hustle and bustle of Eugene, and we were arm-hooked and blissful as we stood in front of the Beachcomber Tavern and watched a huge pack of freshly arrived bikers roll to a stop in the middle of the street.

On the four blocks between the bridge and Harbor Street, there were hundreds of Harley Davidsons. The bikes were all backed into their slots and were draped with their owners and those who rode with them.

The new arrivals slowly began their performance. None of them would smile as they sat on their bikes and looked over all the taken parking slots. One and then several hands could be seen cranking their leather tasseled throttles. Quickly their chromed and massive engines roared in response as the full pack joined the ritual. The pedestrians stopped and the bikers stood and turned towards them

I couldn't have kept a smile off my face if I had been paid. Everyone grinned as they raised their hands and mixed their cheers with the Harleys' roars. Front brakes were applied and, in a sitting position, rear tires began to spin as several bikes broke their rear tire loose and filled the street with smoke and the stench of burnt rubber. It lasted longer than I would have thought and then it stopped. Smiles were everywhere as the newcomers kicked their bikes back into gear and cruised away. I looked at my daughter, and all the other faces around us. We had just been welcomed to the Rhododendron Festival.

DEPRESSION! 2003

Hi, Sweet Niece! You seemed concerned about your depression and the direction it took your Dad. Let me tell you a little about your Dad's... my brother's...last months. I have never felt very good about that time. I was in the process of ending my second marriage and moved from Eugene, Oregon to Selah, Washington where I rented a little duplex. Steve and I spent lots of time together and we walked and talked - talked and walked. He was very unhappy in his marriage with Sue. He hated it that she had closed the avenues of communication with you and your sister. He hated it even more that he had allowed her to do that.

Steve watched me move away from my bad marriage, which was ending primarily because my wife, like Sue, hated my children. One day, close to the end of my marriage, Jamie said to me, "Dad, I will never bring a child of mine into a home you share with Shirley." It was the last straw for me, and I felt that Steve took courage from my action when he chose to separate from Sue.

Ending a bad marriage isn't easy. Even unhealthy patterns of living have a degree of comfort that you lose when you separate. Steve and I would talk a lot on our walks and he would remember the depression he slipped into when the marriage between your mother and him ended. He made an attempt on his life at that time and didn't want to fall into the same pattern now. It was his greatest concern, even before he separated. Once he did separate from Sue, he felt himself slip into the familiar spiral. He would, with such ease, talk about suicide as an option to solving his problems. It was like one of three doors before him, and taking his own life was perfectly OK. I would respond with, "That isn't an option, what about this and what about that." Giving consideration to my counsel wasn't a part of his processing. He didn't seem to think beyond himself to those that loved him. I never understood it, though we often talked about it.

He did seek medical assistance, and was loaded with meds that may well have been the reason for his inability to take a more complete assessment of the choice of suicide. I moved away from the duplex we had shared for a short time and returned to Eugene where I was entering a new relationship with Suzanne. He was disappointed in my leaving, and sad that we wouldn't be doing the projects we had talked about.

Like you, I haven't figured out his depression. It's easy for me to make myself a part of what went wrong and in some way think of myself as responsible for his decision to kill himself. I don't want to do that to myself, and hope that you won't do it to yourself.

DEAR WIFE 2003

I know that you are mortal and that life could turn and take you away from me. What a loss that would be. I am so connected, unified and blended with you. Even with the support of all those that love me, I would be alone without you. I could sit at the foot of the parrot's cage and listen to him greet the opening door with your voice. I could wrap myself around your clothes and bury my face to smell you. I could call your cell phone and listen to your greeting. I could sit in the seat of your car and hold the wheel. I could play your computer games. I could read your mail and watch old musicals. I could pray and sit on your painted lawn furniture and feel closer. If God chooses to bless me with one more day together, I will hear your car in the drive, open the door and feel you in my arms one more time. Your Husband

MONDAY NIGHTS 2003

Slats of pine, nailed and finished, are pressed into use as the table's top, which provides the surface for the expression of my appreciation. A handful of years ago I returned from the bramble bushes of spiritual isolation and was allowed to climb beneath the cloak of God's grace and protection. I begged to be there and promised, like all desperate souls do, to be grateful in my thoughts and actions.

I push the vacuum, dust the surfaces, polish the wood, scrub the floors and on the slats of pine I prepare food for my friends. They, like me, have explored the bramble bushes and discovered scratches, scars and the hollow void of being alone and exposed.

We fill the kitchen as we load our multi-colored dishes with soups, vegetables, fruits and bread. With our physical appetites satisfied we talk of our spiritual paths, our journeys towards God and we are, like all desperate souls, grateful in our thoughts and actions.

CHAIR 2003

It's a monarch of a chair. Last summer, maybe the summer before, we were in the desert near Phoenix. Frank Lloyd Wright had built a home there, and being fans of his architecture, we wanted to see it.

Hot was the weather on that sun drenched and windless day. The courtyard offered no escape and when the relief that bottled water could offer evaporated, I walked into the house and found the most exquisitely furnished room.

In the corner beside an eccentrically designed floor lamp was a chair like nothing I had seen before. They said Wright liked it, and that the creator was named Stickley. I found myself slowly approaching and appreciating its box and slat design as art and far from it's puffed and stuffed sofa sisters who fill most furniture stores.

It was heavy with a finish that was hard and clear. I could see deep into the grain of the crosscut oak and knew that grandchildren could pile on its broad and bench-like back and arms. I skimmed my hand around the two hundred and seventy degrees of flat wood stock and slid the finished corner into my palm as I backed myself over its cushion and unhurriedly lowered myself.

I allowed myself to be enveloped by the chair, and as my eyes closed and the breath of my lungs passed my lips, I scuffled with the practical and sensual parts of myself, acknowledging that I desired ownership of such a chair.

FIFTY-NINE YEARS 2003

I have been on my spiritual journey for fifty-nine years and am more in love with my Creator today than I have ever been. I began my love affair with God as a young boy. I remember worming and wiggling across the benches of my father's church as I watched him kneel and pray beside my big sister, who would interrupt her reverence to cast me her look of death in judgment of my childlike behavior.

Like a little sponge, my growing brain soaked up information about God, and I was in acceptance of everything I was taught. I knew that God had created all the people and I knew He loved us all like my father and mother loved me and my brother and sister.

I don't remember how old I was when I became uncomfortable knowing that only the people who attended my church would go to heaven. Lots of kids on my block didn't attend to my church, and some didn't even go to church at all. As a young boy I loved my friends. I didn't like thinking they weren't going to go to heaven with me. My Dad told me that God takes care of everybody, but the teachers at church would shake their heads and have little hope for those who didn't believe as we did.

My knowledge of our planet and all the different religions that were practiced added to my confusion as I moved in to my early teens. Why would God make all those people and not open a path to them as He had for me?

Because of this unanswered question and other youthful concerns, I found myself apart from my church and my understandings of truth became murky and unstable. Years passed and I married and had a wonderful daughter, who I wanted to teach about God, like my father had taught me. I began a search, which took me through several churches and landed me on the doorstep of a woman who introduced me to the Teachings of Baha'u'llah and the Baha'i Faith. My questions were answered and I learned that God had opened a path to Him for all of his creation. There was only one God and only one religion and all the people on the planet were one. Like a swimmer diving into a pool filled with spring fresh water, I immersed myself in the Teachings of my newly discovered Faith and was delighted.

As years passed and my appreciation of my Faith grew, I developed a desire to travel to the side of Mount Carmel in Haifa, Israel, where beautiful shrines have been built to hold the remains of Baha'u'llah and the One who came to prepare the His way, the Bab.

The pride of Haifa is the Baha'i Gardens, which cover the sun-bleached Mount Carmel like an ornate blanket of lush green grass, bejeweled with white marble buildings that bring to mind the beauty of Greece when its ancient buildings were new. The centerpiece of the Garden is the gold-domed Shrine of the Bab, which captures your eye as you absorb the terraces and fountains that climb from city streets to the mountain top, which blends into the Mediterranean blue sky.

I first viewed the Gardens as my tour bus rounded a corner and suddenly, as if a magician had quickly pulled away his cape, I saw the point of my adoration. I crossed my chest with my hands and gasped. "It's the Shrine! Oh, sweet God, how beautiful it is."

Bahai's fully appreciate that the Messengers of God; Zoroaster, Abraham, Moses, Buddha, Krishna, Jesus, Mohammad, the Bab and Baha'u'llah are the channels God has given us to know and love Him, and that they all suffered in delivering God's message. I love Them all for their gifts. To walk on the holy ground that held the remains of the most recent Manifestations was a bounty beyond belief or understanding.

An apron of cool marble surrounds the Shrine. I slipped of my shoes off and placed them against the wall. Before entering the inner chambers and drawing even closer to this most holy spot, I chose to slowly circumnavigate the building. Beneath the massive arches that extended across my path to the tall smooth columns I walked and savored the coolness it gave my feet and soul. I found myself separated from the problems of the world as I prayed and thanked God for the many gifts He has granted me. I filled myself with His love that has been continually draped over me, and remembered when I learned to love Him at my father's knees.

ANOTHER MORNING 2003

They are my family and the start of my days. Mornings are often the same and I like that. Alarms ring, additional minutes of bedtime are taken while public radio packs today's news into my awakening mind. The parrot is squalling "morning" and the cats play their catch and conquer games across my quilt covered feet. The dogs, with their bladders full, spin in the hall as I shuffle past them on my way to make coffee.

With the coffee pot on, cats fed, and the dogs in their kennel, I make a breakfast that, more often than not, is a shake of soymilk, protein powder and frozen fruits. Suzanne does her fussing and softly talks to me from her bathroom, while I struggle with the parrot's continual squawks and trying to understand her words.

With her coffee in hand and my robe tightly cinched, I walk Suzanne to her car, where I stand, often in the rain and wind, while she starts her car, secures her seat belt, and rolls down her window to receive the drink and her goodbye kiss.

It is then, with my newspaper in hand, that the cell phone rings and I greet my son. "Hi, Son, how are you this morning?" For the next twenty minutes, with my earpiece in place, I prattle on with him as he commutes across Portland to his teaching job. We talk about everything and miss being together.

I read the paper, drink my shake, say my prayers, shower, press my shirt and dress before my wife calls to let me know that she has arrived at the Newport Bridge and is close to her work. We talk about her drive, her teaching schedule for the day, and her plans for the evening. It's usually a short visit ended with "I love you."

My daughter calls on her way to work, with her son strapped safely in the back seat. I can hear him playing with his toys, and after we have shared our own well-being, we include him for a few minutes. She and I like problem-solving and laughing at our human condition, and marvel at the ability of others to affect our feelings of gladness.

With my soul refreshed, my body nourished, and my need to be loved and to love my family satisfied, I open the door and begin my day.

MAZATLAN 2004

We, towards the end of March, flew off to Mazatlan, Mexico with our friends John and Marcia Lang. Together we did some things I promised myself I wouldn't do, many things we had planned to do, and a few adventures that surprised us.

We stayed at the Marina El Cid, which impressed us with its marble floors, tropical plants, smiling employees dressed in uniforms, and ornate tables, where charming women smiled and invited us to attend timeshare presentations. We responded to their smiles and did the one thing I promised myself I wouldn't do.

Our room reminded me a bit of Italy and its coastal hotels. The rock hard sofa was crafted with white stucco and padded with colorful cushions. Relief trims tastefully decorated the walls and were painted bright colors that were handsome. Glass doors opened onto small balconies that overlooked the marina and pool. Sadly the bed had a plywood hard mattress designed for therapy, not comfort.

We quickly learned the best way to get around town...Pulmonias. They are open air taxis that share their little piece of road with cars, bicycles, motor bikes, buses, trucks and a mule-pulled cart or two. We were glad to ride, not drive, over the crowded cobblestone roads.

Several times we enjoyed the resorts exceptional buffet of pork, fish, beef, rice, vegetables, and dish after dish of Mexican delights I had never tasted before. Mariachi bands were always playing love songs, and the weather was warm.

Cooing pigeons and pelicans, with their massive wings and heads cocked, swooped across the fresh waters that were opened by the departing fishing boats. Some black birds with golden-ringed eyes landed on the gentle slope of the resort's wading pool and drank its warm water.

We visited the big cathedral in the center of old Mazatlan. The church was exceptional with its ample share of gold and stained glass. Our wandering took us to the Market, or Mercado, where we admired booth after booth of fruits, vegetables, meats, fish and endless rows of clothing. We loved it.

It was my plan to attend a bullfight. The other three weren't interested, but were willing to keep me happy by attending. I double checked the time of the fight and was disappointed to discover the next fight was scheduled for the first week of May. We were two months early.

We rode a pulmonia to the Golden Beach where there were reports of good shopping and excellent food. Most of the stores were closed and a restaurant Marcia had heard about was open. Poncho was its name and the view, the service, and the food were exceptional. The women shared a seafood platter that was massive and beautiful in its presentation. It was a dish Poseidon would have been proud of. John had a more typical Mexican dish and I had one of the best T-bones ever. We spent the dinner forking tastes of this and that into each other's mouths. The food was only part of the wonder of the evening. Poncho's is on the high side of the beach and we were looking down on miles of warm sand, blue ocean, and sun lovers. There was a white-eyed blind man that sang Mexican songs like Caruso. There were brown and young bodied college students, poor locals, working families enjoying family picnics, smiling people riding horses, first-time sailors hanging on the edges of fast sailing catamarans, Mariachi singers in sand-filled sandals; patio bound business men enjoying a Sunday social meeting, and lots of kids running up and down the beach.

Down the block from our resort we visited La Casa Country and watch their floor show. It started with Mexican folk dancers, then a singer who could hit unbelievably high notes, followed by the waiters doing cowboy line dances. We had a great time.

The boat traffic was heavy in the mornings. I enjoyed watching the bright white crafts following each other to the oceans outlet like pearls on a string.

John, who loves baseball, learned that the game was professionally played in the Mazatlan area. The teams had names like the Hot Chile Pepper Pickers, Stone Suckers, and the famous Tomato Pickers.

We visited the land of bad stings, Mialpiqus. There were lots of bees, tarantula and spiders looking to bite someone. Suzanne had an overwhelming fear that she would be bitten while using the primitive bathroom. We all understood.

I found a very interesting tortilla making machine in one of the little shops, and sat for a long time watching it work.

All the villages we visited that day reminded me of the Mexican set we saw at Universal Studios that was used for old western movies. The only thing that was missing in the real villages was the water rushing down the dry gulch on command. All our villages had dry gulches that remained dry.

We bought a handful to tortillas and munched on them as we drove to Concordia, which was called San Sebastian during the Spanish days, and was founded in 1565. This larger village had an exceptional church built in 1765. There was a little old lady that walked around its front doors with a note in English telling the tourists that she was poor and needed money to buy her medicine. There were also dramatically suffering statues which had lots of blood and grief.

Suzanne found a couple of dresses at a vender's stand in the plaza where students gathered to catch the bus. I bartered for the dresses and, as Suzanne walked off towards our waiting bus, she couldn't stand the bargaining process; I worked out a deal with the old lady that pleased me and satisfied her. Both dresses were beautiful. Suzanne wore one of them to dinner later that night when we took John and Marcia out to celebrate John's birthday.

My favorite village was called Copala. This tiny tile-covered place was in the Sierra Madres and was the same age as Concordia. The steep hillside it was built on added to its charm. Children on burrows wanted to sell you pictures of them and their animals, while others sold little pieces of bark that were carved to look like their town.

The church was at the town's high spot. Inside its large and wood-carved doors, a glass coffin with the crucified body of Christ laid to rest. It's not hard to believe that Christ suffered and died for our sins after visiting a few Catholic churches. We had a good lunch and enjoyed looking over the arched walls that were draped with many colors of bougainvillea.

Another day we saw a walkway that wound itself around a massive rock in the Mazatlan surf until it reached the top where an old stone rail capped the boulder's top. We saw several young men there and one, who was dressed in a black pair of shorts, stepped to the top of the rail, crossed himself as a plea for God's mercy and protection, and dove the thirty-five feet to the ocean surface. He quickly popped up, swam to the side, climbed to the walkway, ran to where we stood in admiration, and held out his hand for tips.

We spent an hour on the Sea of Cortez, sailing first to the Mazatlan lighthouse, then to a small rock capped with sea lions, and at last to Deer Island, where we spent the day. The Island was only a few blocks long and maybe four hundred feet tall. It was covered with scrub plants, rocks, sand, and lots of critters that bite. We were advised to stay on the sand and not venture off to other parts of the island. There were thatched palm huts and a stone structure where the banana boat, kayaks and snorkel equipment were kept. We spent our day playing, eating, and enjoying new friends. I delighted in watching Suzanne buck across the

Sea on the back of the banana boat, as she and her fellow riders were dragged across wave after wave, then ending in a flip that tossed them all into the water.

Our week in Mazatlan was great and we were all pleased with the souvenirs we carefully packed and dragged home. A few of them didn't arrive in one piece, but the tiles for our bathroom remodel did, and they look wonderful.

INTOXICATED 2004

My client had planned to show up at his new riverfront home around 1:00 p.m. He was a little late, and I was early. The day was exceptional, and I wasn't in a rush to get anywhere. Doug, a local contractor, was adding square footage to the riverside deck that he had originally built years ago. I knew that Bob and his wife Rachel would be delighted with his work.

I picked a step close to the top of their staircase, which gave easy access to the beach, and sat with my back against a rail support. The tide was high, and the flow of the river was at that magical place where it appears to stand still and is covered with a smooth surface like a glass tabletop. At the base of the steps, the water was clear and the river's sea life was displayed better than most aquariums. Several seals that were attracted by Doug's working noises were sitting twenty feet off shore watching, as if they were sitting in underwater stadium seats. An occasional otter would circle around them and playfully disappear under the surface. The sea gulls that are always over the river were exceptionally creative in their flight. There were several black cormorants perched on nearby pilings with their wings spread wide to dry in the warm fall breeze.

I was touring new listings with Mary, another client who was interested in the area. She was content to take a break with me and enjoy the wonder of the Siuslaw River, which is such a big part of why Florence is so extraordinary.

Five years ago when I, with my wife Suzanne, decided to make Florence our home, I was attracted to the pace of life. We aren't the classic sleepy town, but rather a community of vibrant and stimulating people who have developed the skill of enjoying the world we live in. Throughout the summer our community is filled with busy vacationing folks who are satisfied with just a week or two of our yearly lives. Some, after a taste of true coastal bliss, become intoxicated and make Florence their home. Others promise themselves Florence as a future reward for years of hard work, and ask me to provide them real estate information sheets until the time comes when they can join the happy community that lives on the banks of the Siuslaw River.

WINCHESTER BAY 2004

If I'm not careful during the summer months, I can spend too much time working and miss out on many of the reasons I chose to live in Florence. With several busy weekends piled on top of each other, I made a commitment to play... and I did.

Suzanne and I got off to a slow start, due to my needing to clear my desk of a few real estate items that had piled up during the week. As committed as I was to having the whole weekend free, I wasn't completely successful. With work behind me, I washed our little aqua colored convertible and lowered the top. We weren't looking to get anywhere fast and slowly drove south on Hwy 101 through Gardner and Reedsport until we arrived at Winchester Bay.

The weather was great with blue skies and sweet ocean breezes. It's nice, when your top is down, to slide down in your seat and watch all the beauty of the coast flicker by. We played a great Cat Steven's CD my son had given us a week or so before. The sound of those old tunes made the drive perfect.

Every year Winchester Bay has a car show. This was our first year to attend. Driving into the harbor area is a visual delight. Turning west off of Hwy 101 you drive downhill through a couple of blocks of old residential homes which open onto a broad span of measured mooring slips, lots of sea water, old sea weathered shops and restaurants all wrapped together by high, tree-covered hills. It feels like the land is cupping this little harbor away from the ocean with its fingers open just enough to allow the boats to slip in and out.

Between the homes and the mooring is a long street that runs parallel to the ocean. This is where over three hundred cars were lined up to be judged and admired by the crowd. Tucked behind each car were the owners, relaxing in their folding chairs and answering the endless questions we all asked as we admired their restoration and customization skills.

Most of the owners are old guys like me. Few young folks can afford this hobby and, in all honesty, these cars are reminders of the 60's and 70's when driving hotrods was what you did on a Saturday night and none of us could afford anything new.

With very little encouragement motors are started and the rumble of V8 engines echo around the harbor and out to sea. Heads turn and faces smile as the RPM's mount and pipes pop. The night before they had a loud pipe and tire smoking contest. I wish I had known.

We followed the crowd to a seafood Bar-B-Q and selected a dinner of crab, salmon and halibut topped off with coleslaw, "corn on the cob" and clam chowder. I was amazed how well it was all prepared. We shared our outside table with some folks from Eugene, who knew Suzanne from her years of working in Eugene, and a custom car owner from Salem who told lots of hot rod stories.

Back in our little convertible we drove past all the custom cars and waved to folks who could tell we were having a great time. On our way home we stopped at a garage sale and drove up to the Episcopal Church on the hillside above Gardner, where you can watch the three rivers blend before they enter the Pacific Ocean. One of the neighbors next to the church invited us to join them on their deck to enjoy the fabulous view. We were tempted, but extended a thank you and drove back down to Hwy 101 and north to our home in Florence.

I had accomplished my goal and discovered yet another reason I love living on the central coast of Oregon.

MOM 2004

Under the broad brimmed straw hat where the face of a farm girl, her arms filled with fresh flowers, should have been, I found my mother and the remains of her mind. The appearance of the hat and its placement on her head is a mystery, while the class to wear it and tilt it just so was not.

A fresh spring smile on any face would flatter the floppy edges of the hat's straw brim, while the face I saw, with its withered and twisted lips, rejected the season and captured the loss and discomfort of winter's gloom.

With cheer and high spirits, I seized her hands while she growled, protested and pushed me away. With her cheeks in my grasp and a kiss on her lips she paused her assault and withdrew her kick. "Hello, Sweet Mother…do you know who I am? I'm your son and I love you as much as I can."

With her eyes more angry than filled with fear, she tilted back her head and squinted her eyes as she examined me and searched her mind. She paused with a smile and grabbed both my hands. Her head tilted and her brow drew down as she said in a whisper, "Who are you old man?"

CHOWDER BLUES 2004

As I craft these words I am sitting in my second story office at Prudential Real Estate looking through French windows watching leaves fall from plum tree branches. A soft breeze is moving by, as the unflawed and endless blue sky rests on top of our little community nestled on the beaches of the Pacific Ocean. I am sporting my new Chowder Blues and Brews shirt and looking forward to another night of great music. Last night Suzanne and I sat in the front row and listened for hours. We danced to a few irresistible tunes like "Mustang Sally" until my feet and her knees would have no more of it.

I love it when Florence has its celebrations, and the Chowder Blues and Brews is probably my favorite. On both ends of the Events Center there are the food booths that specialize in chowder and seafood. The center of the room is filled with bandstand, dance floor and chairs for all of us who aren't comfortable standing for an evening of music.

James Heintz

GOOD DEAL 2004

Writing the check wasn't the problem. The problem was the decision I made four months ago when I got the "good deal." A flyer was circulated around the office that the owners of an upper-end listing, were selling most of their furnishings, including a bedroom set.

Suzanne and I have used an old bed that her grandmother used for years. It was a double and worked much like a funnel directing us both towards the center. We were fearful that a morning was in our future that would find us paralyzed or piled together on the wood floor under the bed.

Everyone knows that folks who have lots of money buy the best, and that was the premise I operated on when, with a cavalier flash of my checkbook, I purchased the queen bed from hell. It wasn't until a week or so later, when I had the time to pick up my extraordinarily good purchase, that I realized my mistake. Grabbing the mattress, and expecting the weight of quality, I was surprised at its lightness. "Ah, I must be built of some space-aged materials that provide unbelievable comfort," was my cautious hope against an immediate knowledge that a mistake had been made. The box spring, which is a misuse of the word in this case, was pine slats stapled together, topped with cardboard and covered in cheap cotton. It did none thing but elevate the mattress, which would prove to be far from futuristic.

I had a powerful taste of disappointment in my mouth as I slid the mattress on top of the box spring and closed the gate to my camper top. "Damn! Why don't I tell these people that their bed was junk and not worth twenty-five dollars let alone two hundred?" I took my hit, pulled up my pride, and took it home, where I put it on its frame, made it up, and forced my wife to sleep on it for months. As the old double bed was a hole to get lost in, this new torture device was as hard and flat as my desktop.

There have been many mornings that we could have "slept in" and couldn't. Pain drove us both from our bed, and that particular day we sat on opposite sides of our bed and looked over our shoulders at each other. "I wanna new bed, Baby, how about you?" "Yah, Baby, I want a new one too," was her reply. She would have suffered a few more months with me, and then the day would have come when her pain would have overridden her desire to protect my pride. I didn't want to wait.

The check for the new bed was many times the amount I paid for the other mattress and it was a great deal…or that's what the saleslady said. If there is a God, and I believe there is, she will be right.

OCICAT 2004

She was asleep and both cats were perched on her blanket-covered hip. They had stacked themselves on top of each other and were simultaneously turning their heads from side to side, like those plastic wall clocks with the wagging tails. It was early and I was rushing from the guest room, where I keep my clothes, to the bathroom off the master bedroom and had captured their attention.

Months ago Suzanne and I had decided to purchase an Ocicat. I had been checking out the local cat pound for several months in hopes of spotting some kind of cat I could make a connection with. I had been unsuccessful. When Suzanne's son sent us pictures of his new Ocicat, I knew what I wanted.

We searched the web and discovered that they were not common, and that if we wanted a kitten soon, we would have to travel to Los Angeles to get it. We had planned a trip to visit Jordan and Erica for Erica's graduation from Grad school at UCLA and decided to come home with a new cat.

In one of the communities packed around Los Angeles we found the Veterinarian who was the Ocicat breeder we had decided to buy from. Her office was expensive, and we were directed to a visiting room where several kittens were delivered and left with us to decide upon one.

The Ocicat is a spotted cat originating from interbreeding of Abyssinian, Siamese and American Shorthair, and it is the only spotted domestic breed bred to look like wild cats. The kittens that were playing around our feet were little gray white fuzz balls, with hints of dark spots. They were shy and looking for places to hide. There was one exception, and he was an exception in every way. If you had poured and lightly whipped chocolate into vanilla bean ice cream and pressed that pattern on a fat small kitten you would have seen this exception. He yowled, which this breed of cat doesn't do, and wasn't shy like his brothers and sisters. I picked him up, as Suzanne did one of the others, and we both spent time looking at these gorgeous little creatures.

"Oh, Honey, I just love this one. What do you think?" were Suzanne's words as I glanced from my ball of whipped chocolate towards the kitten she was holding. The Vet, who had timed her entrance perfectly, entered the room and explained the difference in markings and the great value and near, if not show quality, of the kitten Suzanne was holding. Mine, on the other hand, was a mistake, and would be sold for half price. All eyes were on Suzanne's selection and I, well, I couldn't let go of mine. "Baby, I love this little messed up one, and he's half price," were my words as she, with confusion, looked in my direction. We talked and talked and at the end of our decision making process. Neither of us was willing to part from our choice.

The next day we boarded our plane without our kittens. They were too young to be apart from their mothers and, although we were empty handed, we flew home pleased with our purchases. Several weeks later Suzanne flew back to LA and returned with our kittens.

My guy we named Carrumba and the little show cat was Scheherazade. I called her Zod. Life with our Ocicats has been delightful. The dogs were slow to share their space, but after a few weeks of cautious introductions, everyone settled down to an agreed upon union.

Our life has been delighted and entertained by our cats and I am fairly confident that Suzanne, although she would never admit it, and like me, likes Carrumba best.

CARRUMBA 2004

His weight can be felt as he stalks across the blanket that is spread between us. Behind him the covers sag while his paw reaches out over the drum tight spread between our shoulders.

Vibrating our eardrums his purr swells as he continues on his trek towards the head of our bed. Stepping up on my wife's shoulder he lowers his weight and reaches out for the bound edge of the blanket and pulls it back and away from us.

At another time we might have rejected his request and pushed him away. This early morning we find him delightful and help him in his lifting as he slips down between us and joins us under the covers.

VARAOOOOMM! VARAOOOOMM! 2005

Early this summer, towards the end of May, we had our Rhododendron Festival. There is so much to love about our first celebration of the year. We pack our streets with visitors from all over the northwest who bring with them their toys. The most common toy is the Harley Davidson motorcycle.

Our Old Town's Bay Street is only five maybe six blocks long and on this weekend there isn't room for a single car. Backed in against the curb are hundreds of motorcycles. The folks that ride them are draped on their bikes, each other, and against every building and lamppost. Black leather and skin are their uniforms, with lots of tattoos added for a color.

The bikers have been coming to town for years and are a fun and happy part of the Festival. I have often wondered, as I have weaved myself through the packs of bikers, if their parents had stood in the same spot with their leather and bikes twenty-five years ago.

If you pause to admire a particular bike, the owner will often join you in minutes to listen to your praise and boast about the beauty of their bike. Sometimes they will tell stories about the old days when bikers were scary and their behavior was a bit more on the rowdy side. Others discuss their legal or medical practices back home.

My grandson likes it when they pull their bikes into the street's center and "light them up." I don't know where he learned the term "light them up" but the bikers seem pleased to respond as he yells at them from his perch on my shoulder.

Saturday night is always exceptional. While our Old Town fills itself to the top with Harlies the shopping center at 18th and Highway 101 does the same thing with Hot Rods. When the sun sets on Saturday, the two come together on Bay Street. The bikers pack a little tighter, while tourists and locals join them on the sidewalks. When everyone is as cozy as sardines the Hot Rods begin their cruise. For the next several hours the Rods, with their loud pipes, custom bodies, and gregarious paint jobs, slide past the bikes and all us folks who make up the best of cheering gauntlets.

SQUALL 2005

Wind whips around the drops of water clinging on naked tree branches

Blue sky blocked by rain-gorged clouds so thick their movement seems undetectable

Final leaves red and rolled vibrate and flutter on long lasting stems

Blankets of fallen leaves and unpicked fruit cover the last of summer's grass

Sheets of rain stand tall and rush across the street like day ghosts in chase

Sounds like rattling sheet metal fills the room as rain pounds and probes the window frames

Huffs and puffs push and pull the sky while birds take shelter and abandon being at wing

Moments of calm seem ominous as the lungs of the storm fill for another blow

I think of warm fires and blankets while the morning sun slips beams of light under the belly of the nighttime squall.

BIG BOY DISPLAY 2005

Our plans were to have a late birthday party, then walk down to the beach lot by the Coffee Roasters and watch the fireworks. My grandson, Skylar, was having his third birthday and much of the family was coming to Florence for the celebration. Skylar's mother had let us all know that he wanted a Spiderman birthday, and we were making that happen. We filled the ceilings of our home with black yarn looped and tied to look like a massive web. We then sprinkled the house with plastic spiders and stuffed a blow-up Spiderman doll in the middle of it all.

When my grandson walked in and saw all the family, decorations and the cake surrounded with balloons, he was delighted.

Florence also delights in its celebrations, and the 4th of July is not an exception. Our Old Town has a riverside street which runs between several blocks of old buildings that have been restored or rebuilt to remind us all of days gone by. The buildings are filled with restaurants and shops that celebrate life for the young and old alike.

On the 4th they pull a barge to the center of the Siuslaw River just a short distance up river from the beautiful old bridge that has spanned the river for over seventy-five years. From this location the fireworks are launched to the oooooooo's and aaaaaaaa's of all who watch.

Hours before the formal fireworks are ignited; Old Town is packed with folks toting their legal and safe fireworks while they search for the perfect viewing perch to set their camping chairs. The docks of the marina, which quarter our fleet of fishing boats, are the first to fill, as the fisherman sell off the last of their tuna catch. As the sun sets, the sand banks of the river, the boardwalks, and all the open land and parking lots for blocks around fill up.

This time, when the sun is setting and not yet down, is when we all set off our private stock of fireworks. By the time the "big boys" start their display, we have filled the air with smoke, the squeals of fireworks and all of us hooting over the displays.

When the first massive boom rattled through the mountains bordering the Siuslaw River, my grandson climbed into my lap and laid his head against my shoulder. Together watched the wonder of fireworks against a star-speckled sky reflected over the water of a river on the beautiful Oregon Coast, and made memories for both of us.

SIXTY YEARS OLD 2005

My son, my baby son, called me from a chair lift on Mt. Bachelor, and we talked about it being his thirtieth birthday. Three days before my mother had celebrated eighty-five years of life, and next month, on the thirteenth, my daughter will be thirty-seven. I stand before myself today and see a sixty-year-old man who is happy. If pressed I could talk of my body chemistry which has the ability to sabotage my well being and which is also a common topic of conversation between my daughter and myself. It seems that she, like me, can have "wonder" all about and still stand on the side of the curb and watch happiness speed away down the road. We have both learned many tricks that are effective tools for controlling our runaway moods and agree…that if we use them we are happy.

Six years ago I dove into one of life's grinders and have rewrapped and packaged myself. Going into the process I had lost my rights as a Baha'i, had ended a second marriage, closed a business adventure with bankruptcy and embarrassment and I was living in the garage of a friend.

The grind was painful and could have been terminal, yet, with God's grace and those that love me, I continued. My first blessing was regaining my rights. My love for Baha'u'llah was never in question, just my poor judgment. With my divorce, sincere regret, and the passage of time, I was again a Baha'i in good standing.

I was given the gift of a life's partner who is perfect for me. Suzanne walks, talks, prays and plays beside me. She loves and accepts me and those I love. She directs my vision towards God and love. She keeps fresh air in my lungs and sweetness on my lips.

The pieces of myself that are not filled with my relationship with God or Suzanne are packed and seasoned by my children. Both of them are an interesting mix of their mother and me. Jamie is very familiar with my tests because many of them are hers. She and I understand the difficult path and the effort it takes to continue. She understands that if we stop, we sink. She and I tend to lead with our hearts, without the caution our wisdom could offer. We tend to jump out of planes and think about the parachutes later.

Jordan comes at me from my other side. He is careful and plans. His mistakes are most often bad luck rather than poor judgment. He manages his heart, loving fully and deeply after he feels trust and safety. Like Jamie, he keeps his body strong and well, and pushes away the blues and sadness with exercise and good food. He looks for laughter and makes his will happen. Jamie worries about today while Jordan worries about tomorrow.

Mama takes me back to another time and the wealth of my childhood. She is always where I leave her and reminds me that my days will also have their end.

Our home is filled with dogs, cats and Jason's parrot. The walls are covered with art and prints of places we have visited. The windows are large and the floors are patterned wood with furniture and furnishings from the age of Deco. My homemade tables and lamps give me boasting privileges, while their imperfections are ignored.

Important people pass through my days, leaving their influence on my mood and heart. Skylar, my grandson, has filled more picture frames in our home than all the others. His hugs and smiles rush me back to parenting my children and all the delights I experienced in those irreplaceable years. Gregg, my son-in-law, and Erica, my daughter-in-law, love my children, and I love them. Jason is my wife's greatest source of joy, and is patient with my side of the family. The Baha'is come and go, leaving their love for Baha'u'llah, each other, and us, in every fiber of our home. I discovered my sister, Judy, in middle years of my life, and I love her and appreciate her knowledge of our shared lives, and her husband, Mag. I have many nieces and nephews who reach into my life with e-mails and pictures that remind me, for them, I am the man my uncles were to me.

You can see through to the clear cellophane of my wrap that I am well packaged and richly packed. The spice of life runs through every fiber of my being, and the label on my surface says "zesty with ample shelf life."

GOLDEN YEARS SUCK 2006

So much of what was important to my parents is gone. My sister and I sold or gave away most of it, and the few items we kept are special and valued, with one exception I don't understand. Hanging in my father's garage for years was an eight-inch square of knitted yellow yarn with mustard colored letters that said, "The Golden Years Suck."

When I was younger and my body's painless performance was a given, I recorded Dad's sign in the "old fart" part of my brain. That sign now hangs on the wall in my garage and my appreciation of its words grows with each passing year.

Dad was probably my age when he first hung it. I hope he didn't have the aches and pains I do. If I live as long as my father, I have twenty-three years to go. I remember him climbing under his house to repair plumbing a couple of weeks before he died. The thought of such a task drives my hand into my pocket to inspect the dollar section of my wallet, and lament the high costs of plumbers.

My son has asked me to help him with several remodel projects, resulting in my growling like a bear as exhaustion drained my happy disposition. A handful of years ago I could swing hammer and pack lumber all day, while thinking nothing of splinters and cuts, then tack a few more hours into some remodel project of my own.

Today…today I sit on my butt and spend hours at my keyboard knocking out real estate forms and reports. My medicine cabinet is full of herbs and pharmaceuticals, which I take several times a day, attempting to calm the protests of my body. Diabetes, high blood pressure and cholesterol, anti-inflammatory for aching joints and scars down my chest from by-pass surgery fill my medical chart. My once chicken-hawk eyes are gone. Without bi-focal glasses, I couldn't read one pill bottle from another. If my dogs aren't eating my hearing aids, I wear them, and still misunderstand much of the conversations around me. My feet scream in pain two blocks into a walk around my neighborhood, and things are growing on my skin that belongs on lizards. If I don't bend correctly, my back rolls out and I spend time on my chiropractor's table. I can't imagine what twenty-three additional years will do to me.

I think the "suck" sign gave Dad a good laugh. I think it has polluted my mind and is destroying my body. Maybe it's some kind of voodoo and if I toss it, eat less, and exercise more, I might feel better. Do you know anyone who deserves a little bad karma?

PRAYER POLE 2006

With November only a handful of days away, we came and sat on the flannel mats that protected us from the morning mist coating the benches beneath the canvas gazebo. We are accustomed to summer, with its sunshine and warmth, and are surprised by the blanket of fog that wrapped itself around the garden.

The misaligned brass latch on the cedar box attached to the prayer pole was opened and several hand written prayer requests, one in Spanish, were removed and inspected in, hopes that the dampness had not blurred the letters. Green moss climbed the base of the white picket fence that borders the garden and many of the flowers collapsed and withered as the fall season passed and the sun's warmth withdrew.

Some of the friends arrived on bicycles; others drove cars. Bundled in winter clothes we, alone and in pairs, passed through the arbor and greeted each other as we gathered beneath the gazebo where we nuzzled together. There seems to be a degree of wonder between us as we look at each other faces and appreciate the effort each of us had expended to be together in the garden. Steaming cups of coffee and tea were set aside as we opened our prayer books and wiped the haze from our glasses.

Joining us, the birds on the power lines that are draped over the garden, pulled their wings tight against their bodies and side-stepped until they, like us, were close and cozy.

The morning prayers that misted from our mouths, skipped across the blades of damp grass, wound themselves up the trees and past the birds, seemed different than those whispered between walls and under ceilings.

We enjoyed our time with our heads lowered and our thoughts directed towards our Creator. Each of us took our moments, and when we were done, we folded our blankets and returned them to the basket with the prayer books and the requests from the prayer pole. We hugged each other and talked about the day and week ahead as we committed to gather together next Sunday under the gazebo in the middle of the garden.

HAVING FUN WITH MOTHER NATURE 2006

Life in Florence is filled with excitement. If our great restaurants, local theater, excellent coffee houses, festivals, terrific hunting and fishing prospects aren't enough to enthuse your life…the weather will.

This winter was filled with pounding rain and high winds from the mountains to the coast. Storms buffeted the coast with sustained winds of thirty to forty mph and gusts up to sixty-five.

The Siuslaw River spilled its banks near Mapleton, where the homes are perched on high foundations and stilts. They are prepared for the heavy winter rains and consider it a small price to pay for the privilege of living on the edge of one of the nation's fish-rich and beautiful water playgrounds.

I love sitting in my second story office and watching the trees swing their branches back and forth like a congregation praising God in a hand-raising church. Showing property was always fun when my clients, who were moving from Southern California or Arizona, hadn't yet learned the pleasure of a face wash by Mother Nature.

The best of it all for me, during the winter rains, was sitting by my fireplace. I have mission style chairs and divans that have wide wooden planks across the back and arms. It's on these flat surfaces that my cats like to lay as they watch the fire and me, while I rub the backs of my dogs with my slipper-covered feet, and listen to the wind and rain whip about my cozy home.

I love winter in Florence.

TUXEDO 2006

My friend just rented his tux for our cruise in September. He shelled out two hundred dollars. They have several big deal dinners on our ship that require formal attire, and we want to participate. One of my office buddies said, "Ya know, James, you can go to the Men's Wearhouse and buy a new tuxedo for two hundred dollars." I had just finished talking with one of the Mr. Formal rental shops and had a quote of one hundred and seventy-five dollars for coat, slacks, shirt, vest and tie for a tired, God only knows how many times it had been puked on, used outfit. With the information shared by my buddy, I decided that is was worth the additional $25.00 investment to get a new one. What fool wouldn't agree?

When we arrived at the Men's Wearhouse, Adon greeted me. He was an older gentleman who was very polished, and came with an entourage of several nicely dressed women, who followed him and were there to support him in his assisting me. They quietly stood to the side and held the shirts or ties he grabbed from display tables and racks. They reminded me of Vanna White, and properly displayed their products when asked to do so, presenting me with an array of combinations. Adon would slip a coat on me, let me view myself, and then turn my back to the mirrors so I could watch all three Vannas clap in approval, like British women at high tea. He would then hold a new tie up to my neck and another clap and sweet nodding of the heads would occur.

I completed this delightful experience owning several silk bow and long ties, two dress shirts, tux coat and slacks, with vest, and an inflated ego that only cost me five hundred dollars.

PANAMA CANAL 2006

September 24, 2006

John and Karen Robertson talked us into taking a cruise. Our ship was the Sun Princess and we sailed from Seattle, Washington to Fort Lauderdale, Florida, through the Panama Canal. On the way we visited San Diego, California, Cabo San Lucas, Acapulco and Huatulco, Mexico, Puerto Caldera, Costa Rica, Cristobal Pier, Panama and Aruba.

While aboard the ship, we enjoyed excellent food, great accommodations. Our stateroom included our private balcony, where we drank morning coffees and ate fruit while watching flying fish and other wonders of the ocean. The cruise also provided great entertainment. The stage performances were in a huge theater in the bow of the ship. The shows were composed of young dancers, singers, actors, comedians and often a classic lounge lizard. We learned to love and hate the lizard.

While at sea I discovered that if you hang onto the balcony rail and lean your head out over the side, you can see the ship cut through the waves and get a better feel of the speed we were traveling. It's a long way down to the water. There were days when all we could see was water. The view disarmed me, and as we walked the decks and watched folks bask on lounge chairs and eat yummy fat-making goodies, I tried to relax.

One night we dressed up, Suzanne had her hair done, I brushed the cat hair off my tux and we wowed everyone. We went to the center of the ship and visited with the Captain and crew. It was very fancy...just like all the pictures.

We had delightful High Teas, with fancy pastries and fancier waiters. We walked the teak decks around and around the ship. I loved those walks and always felt better when we worked a little exercise into our day. There were informational lectures and expensive Art Auctions. Lots of money was spent. Sitting on my hands seemed like a good idea. One day we even attended a ballroom dance class. I want to be a good dancer...I also want to be rich.

During our Cabo San Lucas visit, we hired a taxi to drive the town's old streets, then south to San Jose. It was there that we shopped and found some fun stuff to bring home. The temperature was in the high nineties and walking the streets got a little rough towards the end.

On our way back to the ship we were aboard an open tender and I talked the captain into letting me take the wheel and sail us out to our ship. Wheee!

Often we would sleep while the ship sailed to a new location and would wake up in a new harbor. I remember getting up in the blue waters of Acapulco with its rugged headlands and beautiful city. Suzanne and I stayed to ourselves that day, keeping the visit delightful and simple. We browsed the Museum of Masks, giving us a rich taste of culture. We wandered through a handful of old streets and purchased a dollars worth of tortillas that were hot off the press, and made by a proud older woman just for us.

We couldn't keep the sweat out of our eyes, so we took a taxi back to the ship and were poolside in a matter of moments. The cool water washed away the heat and relaxed us as we lounged away the rest of the afternoon reading books and talking with folks from other countries.

One morning the village of Huatulco was our morning view. It was the best. The beach was filled with lounges and umbrellas, with brightly colored buildings with palm leaf roofs. We walked down the new pier we shared with a Mexican war ship and soon our feet touched sand and we were on the perfect tropical beach. It was very warm and the water was perfect. We spent most of the morning floating like two bobs on a line, while colorful fish glided between our feet. Sadly we didn't remember our masks, so we didn't snorkel. That's something to go back for.

Huatulco has many little bays, and our fellow travelers who went to see some of the other beaches said that they were all wonderful. The water was crystalline with rich coral reefs. The rugged mountain range behind the town was in the early stages of development, with several large and unfinished buildings.

We left the ship around nine in the morning and had to be back on board by a little after noon. It was a short visit to the perfect spot. Everyone said that they would have given up our visit to Acapulco for a couple of days in this tropical Eden.

The ship jerked about that afternoon and interrupted my nap. With some degree of anxiety, I observed that winds had kicked up and the sea was covered with white caps. Suzanne was all smiles and didn't act like we were on a sinking ship, so I tried to calm myself. They told us that there was three miles of water under us. God…it could take a week to sink.

We had dinner with John and Karen, and then attended a stage performance of "Tribute." It was a dance and song presentation of music from the fifties through the seventies. We enjoyed it a lot, and then joined in a Sing-A-Long at the piano bar, where the piano player had been doing this for over 20 years, but still managed to keep it fresh and fun for us. Now that's an art. By the time we went to bed, the seas were fairly whipped up and I was a little uncomfortable.

We began our next day on our balcony where we had breakfast and coffee. The seas were calm again, so I had a feeling that God was watching out for me. It was a day at sea, so the pace was slow and easy. We attended another dress-up that evening and ate at the Steakhouse. I wore my white Panama suit and was kina cute with my sandals and one of my big flower linen shirts.

Next morning the captain anchored the ship off shore and we used the tenders to take us to Puerto Caldera, Costa Rica. Once on land we were greeted by drivers inviting us to use their taxis. We hooked us with a tour guide and a driver who had a nice van and were willing to show us around for fifty dollars a person. We had a great time seeing tropical rain forests with crocodiles and lots of wonderful birds. I had a Toucan sit on my hand. I could tell he admired my peckable eyes. There were iguana and many other critters we didn't know. We also visited a furniture store and saw the most beautiful furniture you could imagine. Some of the mountains we drove up and over were over thirteen hundred feet above sea level. Looking down across the rugged terrain to the sea is a thrill.

One of the churches we visited was made of steel, like a ship. When you banged on the wall it rumbled. It was filled with all the things I've learned to expect…crucified Jesus Christ in a glass coffin gilded with gold and lots and lots of candles.

We bought a hand-painted ox wagon. We had them ship it to our Oregon home. I don't know what is wrong with us.

We stopped for lunch on the top of a mountain in the middle of the rain forest. It was like being in a tropical tree house. The view and calm were beyond your best dream.

We did lots of walking and putting through poor little villages where most folks were on bicycles or had Japanese cars with hot rod or no mufflers. In one village, where we stopped for a snack, a dignified white-haired man was training an elegant dappled stallion on a bougainvillea-lined gravel lane. It felt like we had stepped back a hundred years and it was beautiful.

Sailing under the Bridge of the Americas is a big deal so we got up very early in the morning to experience the dawn crossing. We sat in our plastic lawn chairs for three hours while we waited our turn to enter the water channel beneath the bridge. The view of the moon passing over the city of Panama made the getting up early worthwhile.

You may be surprise to know that it's hot in Panama. Our ship had only inches of space on either side as we slipped through the locks. The locks raised our ship eighty-five feet above sea level to Lake Gutan, which we sailed on as we crossed Panama, then locks again, lowering us to sea level. The Pacific and the Caribbean are both the same sea level. Each lock is one thousand feet long and one hundred and ten feet wide. The distance from sea to sea is fifty-one miles and it took us all day to make the passage.

The Canal was not what I expected. Much of it is very narrow and the lake between the locks is full of ships of every sort waiting for their chance to slip through the locks. There are also little islands covered with tropical trees. I swear if my arms were a little longer, I could have harvested coconuts as we sailed past.

Once through the locks we visited Cristobal Pier for a few hours. There I bought my Panama hat, to match my too-hot-to-touch Panama suit, before we sailed on to Aruba.

I don't have much good to say about the island of Aruba, except we had a great day of snorkeling aboard a pirate ship. Suzanne, in choppy seas, snorkeled over a sunken ship in about sixty feet of water. She saw the ship, sharks, and barracuda. I was so glad I didn't get in the water with her. I am certain there is a shark out there waiting to eat me. This is a conviction Suzanne doesn't share.

I took a tarzanesque swing on a rope attached to the mast and dropped into the most beautiful aqua blue sea you could imagine. Nothing bit me. It was a great day.

We had expected to catch a cab once our pirate ship landed and were disappointed when we had to hike nearly a mile to a hotel, where we found a taxi and road back to our ship. It was too hot to be enjoying a mid-day hike.

We spent the next two days at sea and were ready to return home when the Sun Princess sailed into Miami, Florida.

The trip was truly grand.

GETTING UP 2006

Alarm sound as dogs jerk heads from tightly spooled bodies.

Cats without dog foolishness remain bed curled and motionless.

Eyes welded shut against rolled and grinding fists find partial and blurred vision.

Floored feet and conscious pain testifies to shallow and fitful sleep.

Bed partner rolls and blanket wrapping confirm the solitude of this morning rise.

Hands brace back and neck bones crack while drooping chin rises from gray haired chest.

Dogs abandon bedside guarding and avoid shuffling feet while bathroom lights glare and push me into sunlit hours.

LAST QUESTION 2006

A year has passed and layers lay between me and the moment I held her lifeless body. It was practical to lift her…not pre-planned at all. Her body was on a gurney, a hard chrome thing with cold and comfortless leather pads. The sheet she had suffered on was drawn around her like a rice package tossed at a wedding.

I entered the room enclosed by accordion fold-backs. They were tired after years of being pushed open and closed, and were closed this day to provide the privacy needed when one touches and examines the body of their dead.

As a boy I found a naked and dead baby bird at the base of our maple tree. The sight moved me. I picked it up and placed it in a white handkerchief my mother had stuck in my pocket. I remembered laying the bundle on a rock when I picked up my dad's shovel to dig a small hole and bury it. The spring wind was blowing and lifted the corner of the kerchief and exposed the little bird, which looked so much like my mother today, naked, lifeless, phenomenally vulnerable, and yet not.

In recent years I have been lifting mom in and out of beds and cars. She was weak, thin, and would have been easy to pick up if I had been one of her grandsons, but I managed. Today I needed to raise her body up off the gurney to clean and prepare her for burial and to wrap her in a warm, fresh cloth.

I slid one hand under her neck and across her back and with the other I cupped her bent knees. I drew her body to my chest and moved her up and off of the red leather pads.

Oh my God, how different she felt. It felt like her bones were going to escape their connections to one another and slip between my arms and pile themselves at my feet. I held her tightly as my wife stretched the new fabric across the table's surface. Mom's face rolled into my shoulder and her eyes opened.

There I stood with my dead mother in my arms. Her eyes were open and only a few inches from mine. I was overwhelmed. The moment was too great and all I could think was, "Hi Mom! Am I doing this right?" It was the same question I had asked my mother for my entire life.

OAHU HAWAII 2007

Sunday February 11, 2007

We wanted to vacation with my sister Judy and her husband Mag and decided that Makaha Bay on the island of Oahu would be perfect. We found each other in the airport, picked up our luggage, and were on our way in a rented Chrysler convertible. We stacked our excess luggage on the trunk lid and drove up Highway One from the airport at Waikiki. We felt the population fall away as the lanes of highway diminished, then opened onto two lanes running beside the beach parks that are permanently occupied by folks whose homes were elaborate weavings of blue tarps with clear plastic windows. I thought, at first, that I was seeing a life style choice, but later discovered that housing has become a major problem in Hawaii, and many of the low income people have been forced to the west side of the island where public parks have become their homes. The minimum wage is around six dollars an hour and apartments start at twelve hundred dollars per month. It's a dollar formula that doesn't work for many of the Hawaiians, who are proud and unwilling to work entry-level jobs.

Iz filled our convertible with wonderful Hawaiian music while we wound ourselves up the highway through Pearl City, Waipahu, Nanakuli, Maili, Waianae and Makaha. Most of the buildings we drove past were modest, and we wondered what our accommodations would be like. Just a bit past Makaha, on the far end of the bay, stood the very nice sixteen story Hawaiian Princess at Makaha Beach. This condo was unlike all of the other area buildings, except a smaller sister building just to the north.

We pulled off the highway and drove up the road to our hotel where we were greeted by a security officer. Our accommodations were great with rolled rattan and leather furniture, suede sofas, tropical ceiling fans, marble counter tops and colorful wall hangs. We ooed and aahed as we slid open the sliding glass doors and stepped into the eighty degree breeze. The turquoise surf piled thick rolls of white trimmed waves on the coarse beach sand, where colorful umbrellas were planted over sun bathing guests. Children ran strings of looping footprints down the freshly washed beach, while snorkeling swimmers and boogie board boys enjoyed themselves in the surf. We were beyond enchantment as we settled into our lounge chairs on our lanai and relaxed after a long day of travel. We felt a little uncomfortable knowing that many of our neighbors were living in tents.

Our lanai was fifteen stories plus a foot or two above the heavily crashing surf. There we watched several memorable sunsets and quietly sat together, commenting on the hues of orange and gold the sky had displayed.

Every morning of our stay we watched green turtles swim at the edge of the surf, while early morning walkers left their marks on the freshly washed beach. In the afternoons we watched humpback whales play with their babies and flap their massive flippers against the surface of the ocean.

Our beach was just around the corner from the renowned North Shore, where big surf is famous. Several days our surf was bigger than me, and I was content to watch it from the shore. Other days I happily waded into the ocean until it swept me off my feet and left me bobbing like an abandoned ship.

One day when the surf was big, we watched one group of boys playing a bit beyond the surf and one of them got into some kind of trouble. His mama charged into the surf to help him, got knocked down by the wave, and was washed back to the beach three times, desperation and determination mounting with every trial. Seeing the predicament, a young surfer paddled over to the boy, pulled him onto his board, and delivered him to the mother. It was hard to watch her powerlessness. Imagine her joy as she held him close.

We took several road trips, visiting the Dole Pineapple Plantation, the Polynesian Cultural Center, and way up the east side of the island beyond Kaipapau Point and North Shore where long boards were stacked everywhere, gift shops lined both sides of the street, and kids rode buy on their bikes with short boards tucked under their arms. We also spent time in the parking lot of the Aloha Stadium near Pearl Harbor where three times a week vendors fill the lot with canopies and wares. There are blocks and blocks of cheap tourist stuff.

After our shopping adventure at the Aloha Stadium we drove into the University area where we visited with Aunt Theresa. She is my father's big sister and will be ninety-six in a month. We had a long visit and all of us walked several blocks to a nearby restaurant for lunch. She's a delightful old woman who is a real lover and accepts most everyone... bumps and all.

We had a last beach walk together. Judy and I strolled out to the southern point of our little bay and found a gourd mounted on a rock. It was dried and the top of it was cut off and covered with a fabric, which was tied with a hemp cord. It had a Hawaiian name and then below that it said White Boy 1945 – 2006. We wondered if it was someone's ashes.

SAN DIEGO 2007

Conventions are always the same, with flashing lights, booming music, and the hollow, yet enthusiastic, master-of-ceremonies, who pours macaronied words of success and encouragement over the participants. Under this puffed canopy endless awards are presented to participants celebrating their successes. They, with waving arms, winking eyes, and pointing fingers, bounce across the stage, while the unrewarded from their offices jump to their feet, discharge air horns, and scream like children at a birthday party.

Even the bait of an evening with the Beach Boys was capitalistically delayed hours while the company president was pushed, on her elevated stage, from one end of the frustrated convention floor to the other. Like an Indian princess atop her undulating elephant she threw her head back and laughed as she tossed New Orleans Mardi Gras necklaces to the masses at her feet.

Even though they were badly delayed, the Beach Boys' show was the highlight of the convention. There were only a couple of the original guys performing, but the others knew the music. The lights and sound system were good, and the moment they began filling the room with "little deuce coupe" their old fans rushed the stage. The old guys needed and received help when the music went beyond their energy and tired vocal cords

It's kind of hard to see age claim the stars of our youth. I appreciated being there to hear their music. Some didn't.

The brokers from our office decided to get together for dinner at a famous Italian restaurant in the Gaslight district. Suzanne and I rode the Trolley into the area and walked half a dozen blocks to the restaurant, which was very cool and reminded me of a place Tony Soprano would eat and entertain his gangster friends. The service and food were exceptional, as was the price.

Behind the Convention Center there's a long boardwalk that edges much of the San Diego waterfront. After the morning session, the owners of our company invited us all to join them at the Long Board Café, which was on the boardwalk. The atmosphere, as one might guess from its name, was an old surfer's delight. We admired carved coconut heads and boards that have been away from the surf for many years. The food was good and we teased each other as we watched other tourists come and go.

With two days of corporate America behind us, we settled into our delightful world of putting around and went to the Zoo. Thirty years ago I visited the San Diego Zoo with two children in tow on a hot summer day.

This trip we were minus the children, the weather was cool and all we were concerned about was our feet. We began with the bus tour, which helped us to appreciate our inability to cover much of the Zoo's offerings. Wanting to photograph the Black Mamba for our grandson we began with the Snake House where we settled for a snap of a green mamba which wasn't black. He will notice.

We then walked through monkeys, apes, gorillas, ox, lions, tigers and bears until we questioned our ability to hike to the red trolley that would transport us back down the hill to the neighborhood of our accommodations.

The two young women of color not much more than seventeen or eighteen years old boarded our Trolley and sat in the back. They were small girls weighing half that of the average men packed on the benches around them. Both had book bags and were probably students from the nearby college on their way home, or maybe to work. They didn't talk with each other and kept their eyes diverted as one listened to her Ipod and the other read a book on her lap.

A man, a bit on the ragged side, sat on the edge of a bench occupied by one of the girls and took more than his fair share of space. She asked him to give her a little more room, "Thank you, sir." He replied with a deep chuckle, "Don't you worry about it little girl, I have daughters your age at home." Good God, I can't even begin to tell you what happened next. Both of those young women took off verbally whipping that man and every other man around them. At first I thought it was a game between friends, but am pretty sure it wasn't. All male hands were in the air as they leaned back on their benches with big cautious smiles, topped with large and surprised eyes.

It went on for several minutes with an occasional, "Whoa, whoa, girls…now calm yourselves down." This call for calm only served to amp the already high volume of female indignation that continued through several stops. When the women stood, adjusted themselves and stepped off the trolley all the young males had their heads against the window shaking them with amazement as the girls, high in pride, walked down the street without a backwards glance.

It had taken us several days to develop Trolley and bus riding skills and now we felt comfortable enough to make the connections to Sea World. One hundred dollars traveled from our pockets to theirs as we passed through the gates. We were surprised at the excellent lunch we had at the Calypso B-B-Q, and were pleased when we arrived early for the Shamu Show.

I had mild expectations of entertainment at the killer whale show, and was taken aback when I was emotionally touched by the flavor of the show and the impressive performance. The trainers, athletic looking young folks in wet suits, were able to frolic with, stand upon and play with these massive mammals with a surprising level of affection. Many times I found myself with my hand over my heart and my breath taken. It was also extra delightful to watch the children and their parents laugh and enjoy the experience together. It brought up great memories of early years when Jamie and Jordan were young and being enchanted with the wonders of the world.

We spent hours wandering from Beluga to shark to dolphins and then bears. At each display we found ourselves hanging over the rail and delighting in the animals and their relationship with us humans. Mammals are truly exceptional.

We ended our day with our feet, despite our new coil shoes, tired. Looking for a shortcut to the bus station we sneaked out the student gate, which was a one way passage, and found ourselves outside the park, and as far from our desired location as we could possibly be. Having found Suzanne's short cuts and diversions entertaining on other adventures, I kept my spirits high and smiled as we trudged around the parks tall fence to our bus. We felt blessed when we arrived and found a bus on the edge of departure. The driver was standing outside his bus finishing the last drag on his cigarette and was willing to wait as we waved to him and increased our pace with our last specks of energy.

The San Diego convention was less than wonderful and our playtime together was, as always, great.

STATE CHAMPIONS 2007

I was the last car in the parade and proud to be there. Our town is small, so when our high school team is fighting for the state championship of our league, it's a big deal.

That morning I drove across the coastal mountain range to Eugene, Oregon and attended Florence's championship game in the University of Oregon's Autzen Stadium with my friend Steve Earnshaw.

The stadium, which holds fifty-five thousand fans, was sparsely populated. With a bundle of a thousand or so Florence enthusiasts clumped around the fifty-yard line, we looked like the bow on a colossal Christmas wreath. A little extra fluff was added to that bow by the folk from Sisters who sat beside us and supported their Outlaws.

Under a sky that spat rain and dried itself out with sunshine, we watched two well matched teams battle for the championship. Together we cheered for our youthful teams and made an impressive amount of noise. The game ended in a tie and was followed by overtime and the crowning of our team as victors, twenty-one to fourteen.

Steve and I enjoyed a top-down drive back to Florence in our convertible, and complimented ourselves for taking the time to attend the game.

Later that afternoon the soft sound of rolling surf that blankets our town was disrupted by the wail of an emergency siren. Quickly the sound doubled and then grew even larger as horn honking and other alarming sounds chimed in and demanded the attention of the entire community. Was it a tsunami?

I quickly determined that our victorious team was returning to town after watching four other squads fight for the championship of their leagues. I wanted to watch the celebration, so I jumped in my car and drove the few blocks between me and the center of town, where I discovered every piece of emergency equipment our city owned lit up with sirens screaming. I sat at the intersection and watched fire trucks, ambulances, patrol cars and volunteer equipment escort our team into town and back to Siuslaw High School. When the last car went by I slipped into the procession, turned on my flashers, hooted and hollered, as I proudly brought up the end.

I love living in Florence.

HEART ATTACK 2007

"Jeeze! This is one hell of a panic attack," I whined as I rolled to the side of the bed and sat up. Twice Suzanne had gotten up, dumped her PJs on the floor and put on her bra only to have me change my mind and return to bed. An elephant was sitting on my chest, pushing pain up my neck and across my shoulders. I hated the thought of going to the emergency room and leaving with a huge bill and a diagnosis of stress. "OK…OK let's go," was my resigning whine as the pain continued to mount, despite two doses of Lorazepam.

She has always stood beside or behind me when the choices I needed to make were about me. Tonight it was a struggle for her to hold that position as my pain mounted and I hesitated to do what needed to be done.

It had all started around ten p.m. and should have passed in a few minutes, or at least reduced in intensity with time and Lorazepam. Tonight it was different. As hard as I tried to explain and minimize my circumstances, I was afraid.

We walked through the emergency room doors shortly before midnight, and with my history of heart disease, I found myself on a bed, poked with needles, and wired like a cheap robot in a matter of minutes. "We aren't sure what is happening, Mr. Heintz, but blood tests are showing enzymes that indicate a problem with your heart. We will be keeping you overnight just to keep an eye on you while we gather more information." They tucked me into another bed down the hall and away from the Emergency Room. Suzanne curled herself up in a chair, and we spent the short night sleeping poorly and worrying about me.

Dr. Powley came by early in the morning and talked about his surprise to find me on his hospital roster. He surprised me by ordering an ambulance to transport me to Sacred Heart Cardiac Unit in Eugene, where I would be under the care of a specialist he held in high regard. Dr. Padgett is a fresh-faced fellow in his early fifties who is the head of the Oregon Heart and Vascular Institute. He was pleasing to talk with and secured my confidence quickly. It was his plan to conduct an Angiogram Saturday morning to answer all his questions, and then possibly make a fix or two, if necessary.

The bulk of Friday evening was spent with Jamie and Suzanne, who filled the room with love and laughter. We were all anxious to find out my diagnosis.

I awoke Saturday morning after a night of visits from many staff members all determined to stick me with needles and draw my blood. My first visitor was a woman who shaved all the hair off the left side of my groin. She handled me with a flip and casual flair that caused me several hard swallows and serious mental adjustments. She took a long time and made statements like, "you wouldn't believe all the strange things I have seen since I started this job." I presumed and hoped that I fell into a category she considered normal, and was grateful when she completed her task.

The rest of my morning was filled with needles, the switching of my IV from one arm to the other, no food, and a wonderful visit from Jordan, Erica, and the return of Jamie. Suzanne was at my side always and tried hard to keep her spirits high and hide her fears.

Shortly before I was rolled away for the Angio, I was talking to my CNA about being shaved first thing in the morning and she seemed puzzled as to who had visited me and why they had shaved the wrong side of my groin. She consulted with her RN and returned with a little hand shaver, trimmed me up in a couple of minutes with great discretion, and asked if, by any chance, I had seen a name tag on the woman who shaved the other side. Humm! Was I the victim of a phantom shaver?

Dr Padgett had thought that I would be on his table by mid-morning, and I wasn't. Mid-afternoon, and after his lunch, my turn came around. It seemed that folks who had problems more serious than mine kept taking my scheduled turn. The process was quick and uneventful, leaving me with an unexplained time loss. They rolled me into the room, slid me from my bed to the procedure table and three minutes later the hour long process was completed.

Dr Padgett informed me that I have a heart murmur. It's not a big problem now and will be watched with hopes that a proper diet and exercise will keep me off the surgical table having a valve replaced.

The experience was difficult and expensive. It scared me and has motivated me to take better care of myself. My wife and children watched over me and filled me with gratitude. God continues to bless me with being loved, and with more time to love.

THE DEATH OF A GUY I KNEW 2007

As I drove down the long driveway towards one of the most elegant homes in Florence, I saw Big Bill's black lab trotting towards me. She had a clear plastic cone wrapped around her neck that was designed to protect her ear that was plastered with fresh stitches. She looked anxious and when I spotted the blood dried around the edge of her cone I wondered what she had been through in the last twenty-four hours. I knew the blood wasn't hers and didn't want to think about how she got so much of it on her.

"James? This is Billy. My dad is dead," were the words of his son. The conversation was shocking and learning about the suicide death of someone I had known pushed my mind into disbelief and promoted action. Between my deep sigh and soft groans I asked Billy to tell me what happened. A story was told of addiction and depression leading to hopelessness and his father's death. His mama, my friend Barbara, took the phone from him and added more anguish that she ended in a favor asked. "James, he shot himself in the head with a shotgun and made a mess. I can't bear the thought of seeing it and wonder if you know anyone who could clean it up before we arrive this afternoon." Barbara went on with talk of loss and responsibility. I tried to comfort her with my words and knew she was beyond anything I had to say other than…"don't worry. I will have it taken care of before you arrive."

I called a contractor friend with a pressure washer and met him at a corner close to Bill's house. I fed the code into the locked subdivision gate and drove down the road edged with fine homes and grand yards. Once parked behind Bill's truck, James dropped the tailgate of his truck and began to remove his washer. When we began our walk down the slate path to the lakeside patio, we noticed the lab had jumped into the back of the truck. She wanted to escape and had hoped that the truck would be her way out.

The view of the lake was beautiful and to the right of the steps leading down to the water's edge a large pool of blood could be seen. It had caked itself against the stone wall and ran down the edge between wall and walkway. Some had slipped away and fallen on the dirt beside the wooden steps. It was still red and had thickened in the day between it being spilt and our arrival.

We rolled out the washer and hooked up the hoses and James began his washing. Gallons of water flowed across the blood that stained the water red for far longer than we expected. He washed and washed the mess over the steps and down the hillside until it was clear and thought the task was completed only to have the blood rise out of the stones and pool again.

James talked of his depression that morning before my call and his hesitation to accept my request for his help. "I'm glad I came here today," he said. "This man had money. He had a great house and his truck out front I dream of owning and yet…here I am washing his blood away. Today I appreciate being alive. I'm a pretty lucky guy." I agreed with him. We pulled the lab from the back of the truck, loaded up James's equipment, patted the poor old dog on the head, and drove away.

FLORENCE FIREWORKS 2007

When the sky slips below the underskirt of night and the smell of cheap corner stand fireworks has filled Bay Street's atmosphere... the 4th of

July fireworks begin. Like a sleeping behemoth, a barge floats in the middle of the river, anchored to the muddy bed below. From the deck of the barge the first boom sounds and all the spectators stand in front of their collapsible chairs and begin the "Ohhhs and Ahhhs."

ELWAY 2007

He's lying on the braded rug and I'm slumped in my prairie chair. Biting on my knuckle, a new habit I'm developing, I glance over the top of my eyeglasses and watch the dog…my friend for the past eight years. He's beginning the process of getting up on all four to walk down the hall where a soft cedar mat awaits him. It's a slow process and his hind legs respond poorly. Rounding the loveseat he glances over his shoulder and seems to say, "I'm going to bed. Is there anything you want?" "Goodnight Elway," is my response. He turns and sways down the hall vanishing into the bedroom.

He was two when I adopted him at the local animal shelter. I was delighted to find such a beautiful red & black German shepherd. He was over a hundred pounds then and added another twenty as the years passed. I could only guess his history and was sure someone was devastated having lost him.

Together we have spent wonderful hours sharing the space around the fireplace and walking the ocean beaches. The sunset memories of his silhouette bouncing over the surf are eternally recorded.

Today we are sharing ageing. He can still trot the water's edge, but the sea gulls hardly lift their wings as he passes. I grab the arms of my chair and slowly pull myself out of my stiffness. His golden eyes still sparkle as the word "walk" reaches his perked ears. I drop to my knee to connect his leash rather than the "bend and clip" of past years. His teeth are yellow and ground to flattened stubs. I have taken up his practice of afternoon naps. He barks at back yard intruders from the sitting position. I find movies more appealing than remodel projects and yard work.

I wonder if he wastes his time wondering which of us will die first. The books say he could live several more years. I'm in hopes that I can do that also. He's been a great dog.

CARRUMBA 2007

After five days I had began to implement little tricks to make his absence acceptable. Carrumba, my beautiful Ocicat male, slipped out the door with his sister Saturday night when my visiting daughter took her new puppy out for a midnight pee. Suzanne discovered his escape when she let the dogs out in the morning and found Scheherazade on the back porch curled up under a patio table.

We searched every free moment, walking the neighborhood streets, handing out flyers and asking all to keep an eye out for him. Several days passed as we suffered with our broken hearts.

Several concerned folks called and reported seeing him, "I saw him jump over the fence. I could tell it was him by his big fluffy tail." We appreciated the call, though our cat's tail is shorthaired. Another kind neighbor talked of a mid-night yowling fest between his cat and Carrumba. He promised to call us at any hour the next time he heard him.

After a meeting on Saturday night, and during our drive home, we received another call. We met the neighbor who pointed to a yard two blocks from our house. "He dashed across the street in front of me, and I feel sure it was him," were her words. The neighborhood twelve-year-olds were on the street playing when we arrived. In no time at all, flashlights were gathered up and the search was on, Suzanne, myself, and a passel of excited boys.

Within moments Suzanne's flashlight beam fell on Carrumba's hindquarters as he dashed away from the search party. "It's him, Honey. It's him," were Suzanne's words. There was too much commotion for Carrumba to feel safe, so he dashed into a back yard and disappeared.

We both deeply appreciated the kids' help and with our own flashlights in hand we scooted them into their homes and continued a quite search. I lost track of Suzanne as I wandered up the block to peek over fences and into back yards. In a beam of light the eyes of cats glow. It's a great give away.

"Honey...Honey! I've got him. Come and help me," was Suzanne's anxious call. She had spotted him in someone's back yard and had turned off her flashlight and talked to him. "Come here, Baby. It's OK. Come here Carrumba," was her soft call. He came and allowed her to slip her hand around his empty belly, lift him to her chest, and hold tightly. Carrumba was OK with the tight hold, even when Suzanne stumbled in the dark and fell to her knees. That was when she called out to me and heard my big feet clumping to her aid.

Once in the car it took only a few moments before we were safe inside our home. We watched in pleasure as his sister cautiously checked him out. With her approval he went directly to his food bowl and was curled up on a pile of unfolded laundry within the hour. When we tucked ourselves into bed with dogs on both sides of the bed and the cats curled up at our feet, we felt gratitude. When you've lost hope and are given another opportunity to love a little more, one's heart is intoxicated with gratitude.

PAINTED HER UP 2007

A handful of days stand between this moment and Thanksgiving. History promised gray skies and rain or at least morning mist and wet grass. The French doors of my office stand open and the bright sun is reflecting off parked cars and passing traffic. Above the tired lupines and curbside shrubs, the glass-clear sky forms a light blue mantel over the neighborhood. Highway traffic flickers as a variety of trucks and cars rush north and south like the river's salmon making their final journey up the Siuslaw River.

I had hopes of customers; yet find contentment in the quiet of the day. If I hadn't demanded floor time I might have been on the river in our little red boat. This year we purchased a fishing license, tuned up the motor, painted her up, and named her Skyboy. Three or four times we have had her out and watched others pull in their catch while we consoled ourselves with beautiful weather and easy recreation.

A sudden change has blanketed the sky. On the hills east of town a slash burn has taken command. The sky that was blue has become soiled and unattractive like the hem of a wedding dress dragged across a dusty field.

The fish probably weren't biting anyway.

THANKSGIVING DAY 2007

I massaged my feelings in a dozen different ways and still ended up feeling shortchanged. There wasn't much merit in it all and yet…my hurt feelings were in place and were quite unwilling to change. We would be alone this Thanksgiving.

The mother of my children wanted them to be with her, and I wanted them with me. She got my daughter, grandson, and son-in-law to commit. When we lived closer to each other it was easy for the kids to squeeze a little time in with both of us. Now three hours stand between their mother and me, and this year I am too far away. My son out-foxed everyone by having Thanksgiving with friends who live close to him in Portland. He and his wife have invited all the relations to gather at their home for a big pre-Christmas dinner and visit. That frees them up to do what they want on both Thanksgiving and Christmas with nobody upset or that's their hope. Suzanne's son will be watching football with friends' three states away and too short on time to come home.

Suzanne and I talked about the day. We considered going to a restaurant, cooking for ourselves or asking a few folks over to share the afternoon. We elected to share our food and time and asked three kindred souls to join us. Julie, John and Colin were in the same boat as Suzanne and I and were pleased to accept our invite.

We spent our morning cooking and cleaning and were on schedule when our doorbell rang a little before two in the afternoon. Julie, who always arrives early, walked in with smiles and good wishes. Minutes later John and Colin appeared with bouquets of flowers. John dug into his coat pocket and added a couple of cans of cranberries for our dining delight.

The turkey lived up to his name and was a little slow getting cooked. We spent the extra hour visiting and getting to know each other. Suzanne offered us shrimp hor'deurves and her special dipping sauce. They were scrumptious, and held off our hunger while we cranked up the temperature on the bird.

About the time our stories were getting personal, the turkey was done, so we gathered around the table. We all said a little prayer with good thoughts for the families we weren't with and a deep appreciation of each other on this Thanksgiving Day.

Several hours of eating, laughing, teasing, and contentment passed before we cleared the table and brought out the pies and ice cream. With coffee and tea, we finished our holiday, and thanked each other, and smiled in our victory over lonesomeness and self-pity.

WINTER STORM 2007

The warm winter storm pushed massive winds across the beach, forcing treetops back and closer to the ground than ever before. We were chin deep in our hot tub watching the trees around our yard stand on the toes of their roots, and then settle back into the dirt. The battle between the winds and trees lasted days, with victories claimed on both sides.

Most nights, before we tuck ourselves into our bed, we spend half an hour relaxing in our hot tub that sits on our back yard deck and is fully exposed to the elements. Normally we delight in cloud formations sliding across the moon, or clear skies dotted with glowing planets and stars. This night we felt like Alice at the Mad Hatter's tea party spinning in our hot tub, moments away from being lifted and tossed into the next block.

After ten minutes of staring at each other's disturbed eyes floating inches from the water's surface, we popped out and slipped into the security of our home.

The excitement of winter storms is one of the exhilarating parts of life in Florence. The next morning we found ourselves sitting in our car in a little turnaround at the north end of Kla-ha-nee. We were separated from the ocean beach by ten feet of whipping beach grass and sand dunes. Our car rocked with the blasts of wind that pushed and relaxed like the breath of some storm god. With wipers wiping, we watched the surf stand taller than most buildings in Florence. On the horizon, where we would most often see a slightly arching flat line, waves chopped and slammed against each other. From these monsters we watched smaller, yet mighty, waves shove their way across each other and onto the beach.

Today all is calm. Droplets of water hang on the pencil thin branches of the maple tree outside our office window. Broken branches have been cut and picked up while the last of the fall leaves have been dispersed across the city and anticipate raking.

It's wonderful living in Florence and knowing that tomorrow's weather will probably be different than today. An old saying you often hear around town is, "If you don't like the weather…wait ten minutes and it will change."

LIGHTHOUSE 2007

The storm had wrapped itself around the Head Keeper's House, and the night-cloaked path, which climbed through the wind-pressed trees, offered little protection. The one hundred and twelve year old Heceta Head Lighthouse was at the end of the steep path that ran south and high above the house. It was there, on that high and rocky head, that its beacon cast beams, like the spokes on a wooden wheel, across the sheer hillside over Devil's Elbow, and out to sea. Looking behind ourselves and through the besieged trees we could see the Christmas lights wrapped around the Keeper's House. The glow of the lights twinkled as the swinging branches and lashing rain battled to block our vision. The ocean, white with churned waves, offered no sight of the normal deep-water blackness before vanishing under a curtain of rain.

We had spent several delightful hours in the Keeper's house singing Christmas carols, drinking hot-spiced cider and eating snicker doodles. The Community Chorus had carried out their holiday tradition by performing one major concert in the Events Center, half a dozen visits to nursing homes around town, and a couple of smaller performances in unique locations like the Heceta Lighthouse. Despite the bad weather, twenty folks showed up in their red Santa hats, white shirts, and Christmas scarves to sing a dozen classics as part of a fundraiser sponsored by the Lighthouse Association. As an additional enticement, the Association opened the Lighthouse for night tours. These tours rarely occurred and were intended to be a treat for the participants.

The extent of darkness on the path and the ease of misguided steps weren't appreciated until we climbed beyond the glow of the Keeper's House and lost all sense of direction. It was these short moments of disorientation that heightened our appreciation of the other visitors who had the wisdom to bring flashlights. Like small pinholes of light they appeared and granted new confidence to our steps and lightened our hearts.

There was little dialog on the path. It was as if we all were on some seafarers' pilgrimage to a point of light that had guided and protected sailors for over a hundred years. The storm itself amplified the importance of the lighthouse and we, sure footed on the cliffs of Oregon, could only imagine being aboard some squall-battered ship working itself up or down the coast of Oregon, and having the illuminated security of the lighthouse cutting through the storm to guide and protect.

The lighthouse had two smaller buildings that sat at its foot, like building blocks dropped by a child. They had, in past years, served as storage rooms for the kerosene cans that the poor lighthouse keeper, or one of his assistants, would pack up the steps to the lamp. With the changes of time and the addition of electricity, the stoutly built buildings were used now for storage, and, in recent years, protection for the tour guides. For hundreds of feet around the sides and face of the head, all trees had been removed, and had left the three buildings exposed to all the weather the ocean could create.

When we left the mouth of the sheltered path, we were shocked by the intensity of the unbridled wind. Our umbrellas, long before blown inside out, were now being wrenched from our hands. Only with the greatest effort were we able to protect their exposed ribs and fabric from the ripping wind. The small door to the kerosene building was open and a much smaller light than the beacon above us offered an inviting protection. Inside we found our guide, who was delighted to share her knowledge, and prepared us for our visit up the lighthouse. With new information and ample expectations, we dashed from our block-shaped room, to the round base, to the lighthouse. Another light-bathed door stood ajar, and we dashed inside to an exceptionally delightful sight. The interior walls were mortared red brick, recently stripped of their plaster finish. A steel spiral staircase wrapped itself against the wall as it climbed level after level, to the beacon that spun on its brass rollers at the top. Step after step we climbed, looking up and down as the beauty of our ascension changed, and our expectation of seeing the beacon heightened.

The lenses, which look much like the headlights on a turn-of-the-century car, were mounted on steel bands, and turned on big brass rollers. A pair of sun-like lamps glowed, casting beams of light in eight different directions. As with many pilgrimages, we were allowed only a few moments in the hallowed space that housed the beacon, and after one full rotation, we were directed back down the spiraling steps. When we reached the bottom and walked outside, it seemed as if the storm had calmed. Our hike back down the path was blessed with many flashlights enroute to their pilgrimages to the Heceta Head Lighthouse, and even though the storm had calmed, we were pleased to reach our parked car.

BEND 2007

It's cold and the roar of the ocean is not to be heard in Bend, Oregon. Unlike our ocean side community, where we view the sky through tall lush evergreens, the central Oregon sky is big. It's like standing in the middle of a vast open field on the top of a mountain. Must be why they call it a high desert plateau.

My nose and eyes remind me that it's much dryer here, and there is no wind. Rarely do trees in Florence stand motionless.

The colors I am accustomed to don't exist on this side of the mountains. Coastal green is rich and vibrant, while the countryside around Bend is a muted sagebrush brown. White mountains spring up on the plateau's edge like coffee filters placed here and there on a child's picnic blanket.

We rented a condo at Eagle Crest. Its large basalt fireplace, with light birch cabinetry and comfortable wine-colored rich leather furniture, is surrounded by large light-drenched windows. The dark mahogany dining table is long, and the tall backed leather chairs are elegant enough for Cardinals to use while electing their Pope.

Eagle Crest was all dolled up for the holidays. Electric Christmas-light figures, most having nothing to do with Christmas, line the golf course. There were cowboys, golfers, exploding cannons, cow skulls, a chuck wagon, a fishing boat, a spouting whale, an eagle, and all the regular stuff. Jamie and Gregg drove up for one day with their new car.

They drove us to Redmond to watch their Christmas parade. We were amazed at the turnout in the twenty-degree weather and the hospitality of the town. One Mexican restaurant was ladling out delicious hot chocolate. The woman filling the cups said, "It's an old recipe my Mama has made for years."

It was dark and the floats were hard to see. The little twinkle lights weren't bright enough to light up the faces of the kids riding on the farm and heavy equipment trailers. The floats passed in pods, leaving long periods of time when the street was empty and lined with searching spectators.

The next morning we drove south of Bend to the High Desert Museum. It had been years since any of us had visited it, and we were amazed at the expansion and the lack of visitors. The place was ours. We discovered a great little cabin on the hillside behind the main building. It attracted us by its curl of smoke rising from the chimney. Inside we found a woman was dressed like a pioneer woman and talked to us as if she were from the turn of the century. She was the highlight of our visit, capturing our attention and imagination for a long time, as she answered our questions and talked of her life in cattle and horse country.

After the kids left, Suzanne and I filled the balance of our holiday reading, enjoying the fireplace, and winter walking the resort.

WONDERFUL WINTER DAYS 2008

During the months between December and June, Florence is determined to attract seventy-five or more inches of rain. The rain makes us beautiful, keeps our air fresh, and cleans everything. Knowing that days of rain can be depressing, the Florence weather queen interrupts the moist days with half, and sometimes full, days of glorious sunshine. This past week she spoiled us and stacked five-fifty to sixty degree sun-filled days together.

It was perfect timing for us when our daughter Jamie and her family came to visit. We spent hours on the beach looking for treasure and introduced Poochie, Skylar's dog, to the surf. He is just a fluff of a dog, who claims his father was a Shiba Inu and the mother was Shih Tzu.

He looks like a very little Chow Chow with an extra coat of long fine hair. Skylar loves the little guy, and we all laughed when the surf, laced with foam, rolled up the beach and captured him.

Skylar found an excellent walking stick, customized and finished to perfection by the surf. It was fun watching him prowl around the beached logs with his new staff as he looked for ocean offerings hidden by the surf god. Skylar's step-dad, Gregg, spent several early morning hours on the beach with Poochie, long before the rest of us rolled out of bed and drank our first cup of coffee.

We drove north on Hwy 101 and visited Devil's Churn. Skylar wanted to see the ocean's power up close, and this particular piece of beach is dramatic. The ocean jams tons of sea water up and into a long and deep crack in the ancient lava flow. When the ocean runs out of space it tosses the water high into the air before it collects itself and draws back, preparing for the next surge. When the tide is very low, the Churn is emptied, and only sand fills the chasm between the rocks.

The hike down the hill offered a great view of the ocean below. On our visit it was a rich cloudless day and the blue sky was breath-taking.

Poochie had ample energy for the trip up and down the steps, while Skylar, who had less oomph, complained about the climbing part of the adventure.

We made a short drive south and found ourselves on Cape Perpetua's Neptune Beach. Gwynn Creek was high, so watching her dump her fresh and crystal clear water into the ocean was great. Skylar wanted to wade across the creek and visit some of the tide pools on the other side of the Creek, but Poochie resisted, so they didn't.

Our next stop was the Heceta Head Lighthouse. The area is named for Captain Don Bruno de Heceta of the Spanish Royal Navy, an explorer whose expedition passed along the Oregon coast around 1775. Heceta Head's light first shone in March of 1894. It stands two hundred and five feet above sea level. Its light is visible for over twenty-one miles. When they were carving out the building site for the lighthouse, over one thousand barrels of blasting powder were required to create a flat table on the rocky cliffs. Skylar and his parents climbed to the top of the lighthouse and inspected the massive lenses. Suzanne and I contented ourselves with the view from the bench in front of Keeper's House.

We ended our adventure with lunch at Travelers' Cove on their sun-baked patio that stretches out towards the river. We had our waitress pop up the first table umbrella of the season, and we tossed French fries into the air for the seagulls to catch.

RED FIGHTING KITE 2008

All that is left of the weekend is some sheets that need washing, sand in the cracks of the wooden floor, and half burned pieces of wood in the fire dish. Jamie, Gregg and Skyboy filled our days with hours on the beach, hotdog roasting, kite flying, dog walking, sandrail riding, and visiting.

Skyboy and his parents began their visit riding the dunes in a four-person sandrail. It was electric blue, and the driver wore a full-face mask with the American flag embossed into its plastic. He was an old salt who claimed to be retired and had been driving the dunes all his life. As we watched them leave the parking lot and rumble down the sand trail towards the ocean, I knew they would have an exceptional time.

Suzanne and I entertained ourselves watching other sandrails load up and take off for the dunes. Their passengers were also excited, but none of the other drivers had the cool and patriotic face screen.

When their rail returned and rolled into the parking lot, smiles beamed below their goggles and all hands were waving high in the air. Skyboy jumped from the front seat, after releasing his safety belts, and proclaimed his courage and willingness to do it again.

The red fighting kite with the long blue tail was a bit to handle in the brisk beach wind. Skyboy had been flying his small kite on a string that he wound up into a unit that looks like a plastic fishing rod. On his next birthday he will be seven and his asking to fly the two-stringed fighting kite seemed, to me, a bit beyond his abilities. I handed him the spools and questioned the capability of his little hands to hold them. "I can do it Grandpa. Just let me try," was his moan, as I stood behind him and gave instructions. "Grandpa!!! You don't have to hold my arms…I can do it," he said as he respectfully rolled his body out of my arms. I stepped back and watched. The kite climbed high into the blue sky, then stalled and dove towards the beach. Just before it buried itself deeply into the wet sand, it snapped to the side and skipped along the smooth surface with the tip of its wing inches from contact. It then leapt towards the sun, spinning like a rocket out of control. When it reached its high point in the sky, it calmed and waited until it again dove looping like a downed fighter plane towards the ground. Again, seconds from destruction, the kite flipped to the side and, in phoenix like style, joined the passing sea gulls circling above us.

For an hour I stood just beyond the length of his lines and watched him, with one of his eyes squinted, squat and twist as he completed maneuvers I would not have attempted. Occasionally I was asked to re-launch his kite when the rules of physics were pushed beyond reason.

With sand in all the places sand likes to be, we left the beach and returned home to the hot tub and an hour-long soak shared by grandfather and grandson. "Grandpa? Do you believe in ghosts?" That was the start of a long conversation about body and spirit. In one example he said, "Grandpa…do you see that B-B-Q? It's nothing without the fire inside it. It's just like us." We talked for a while, and I found his spiritual insights more impressive than his kite flying.

Our back yard is very enclosed and feels much like a private park with benches, swings and a wonderful fire dish. Many magnificent and wind protected days have been spent in that yard and lots of marshmallows, chocolate and Graham Cracker s'mores have been eaten after polish dogs with mustard and relish.

With another visit recorded, Suzanne and I stood at the bottom of our driveway and waved good-bye to our daughter, son-in-law, and Skyboy as they drove down the street. God willing we will have many more weekends like this, and be blessed with good minds that can savor the memories.

MY DAY AT CATLIN GABLE 2008

Catlin Gable is on one of the hills that pepper the perimeter of Portland. The morning drive with my son was filled with good coffee and his pointing out the bike path he travels when he is not driving his father to visit his school. Jordan has been teaching there for several years and is proud of his employment. We park his car and wander across the campus towards his classroom. On the way we pass groves of evergreens and acres of grass, with buildings sprinkled here and there. In open spaces and special corners, play equipment and art from other decades adds interest to the already stimulating environment.

It was Disco Friday, so my son was wearing a shirt from the late seventies that I could have owned. He walked into the kid-packed library, slid a DVD into a player, cranked up the volume, and filled the room with music from my young adulthood. Mirrored balls spun, reflecting prisms of light, while projectors splashed patterns of color and the images of students dancing across the large screen that covered one end of the room. Jordan was in the center of the floor, encouraging everyone to raise their hands and form the letters YMCA. Even the parents on the sidelines, who couldn't resist the musical call, bounced their bodies about in ways their kids had rarely seen as they held their waving arms above their heads and formed the letters along with the kids. Song after song was played as Jordan taught the kids moves that were popular in the eighties. Donna Summer would have been proud… so was I.

His classroom is open and light filled. Rectangular tables with blue Formica tops horseshoe an open area that is filling with his students. On the floor and in a circle, all the students gathered and discuss the day and accomplishments to be shared. I was introduced and sat in a traditional chair on the side. Stiff bones and no flexibility denied me a place offered to me within the circle. At the students' request, I shared my greatest embarrassment and received consoling words and smiles of appreciation. Suddenly the circled students, with Jordan's lead, leaned forward and pounded their hands on the floor. Silence followed, and then another class in the building responded with a similar rhythm. Silence…another class entered the pounding procession. Patterns changed and other classes' sounded in with new rhythms until the communication between rooms ended and the focus returned to the fifth grade room.

Spirit birds in vibrant colors hovered high in the open cedar ceiling, and greeted me as I joined the students in Peggy's room. It was filled with instruments and would remind you of a studio used by a Marimba band. Long and tall drums of natural wood, and some painted with rich reds, sported skins of leather pulled across their tops. Students moved them from corners to open spots where they played them with delightful skill. Native flat drums with their massive rings and leather surfaces were held by ropes crisscrossing their open backs, while padded mallets awaited the opportunity to strike the skins and fill the room with their ancient and deep-rooted sound. Handsome wooden xylophones, some small, others massive, remained in their places when the student/musicians slid up and under them. Bowls and boxes filled with hammers and sticks with colorful pads were removed and caressed before being put to work. Flutes, recorders, gourds with bead wraps were removed from their boxes and placed close at hand. The piano was tucked in the corner behind charts of lyrics and poetry. The young piano player was hidden by the vertical soundboard as his fingers began to tickle the keys. Peggy moved through the room. As each child entered, she attached invisible cords of control on each and every one. Slowly she infused a unifying song of music into the ears of each and every one. They gave voice to the song and circled around her as their voices tightened and blended together. With a twitch of her eye and a flick of her finger they complete one musical task and move to another. Together they wander from the music Shakespeare would have heard in English courtyards before the performance of Hamlet, to "Hit the Road, Jack" where boy, then girl solos rose above "Don't cha come back no more, no more, no more."

When boys being boys began the smallest wandering towards natural disruption, Peggy pulled the string ever so slightly and focus returned. As I watched these children and their teacher, I could not keep smiles from my face, even if it had been my desire.

The class ended and I was invited to join some of the students in their language classes. "James, join us in our Japanese class...no, no, James, come to Spanish with me."

Later in the day the fifth graders joined the little students in the second grade room to share the stories they had created and bound into handsomely decorated books. The energy in the room was delightful. With pride and confidence, the older students gathered up their charges and found open space at one of the many round tables that filled the room.

With soft but excited voices, the reading began, and the small children listened and glanced first at the book, then at the reader. Their expressions were often that of respect and awe. The authors excitedly read, pausing from time to time to appreciate the smiles that were directed towards them. When the readers completed their books, they closed the colorful covers and slid them across the table for the listener's study and approval. With hands held their chins and leaning on the tables, the authors watched as the listeners examined their booklets.

Having tapped my foot to Disco, participated in class room communication, shared my most embarrassing moment, rocked my body to Marimba music, watched children teach children, shared lunch, hiked the campus to attend to new and growing trees, I waved goodbye to late-leaving students and climbed back into my son's car, thankful to have been a part of a most exceptional learning environment.

2008 RHODODENDRON FESTIVAL

The kite flew out to sea as I sat behind my computer and wondered what I could have done differently. This past weekend was the 2008 Rhododendron Festival and my camera was packed with award winning photographs. There were close-ups of my grandson's smiling face reflected in the amazing paint jobs of vintage hot rods, and snaps of my daughter as she snacked on hotdogs with catsup squishing out of both ends. There were Old Town bikers, with their leathers open, lounging on their steeds under the eighty-degree sunshine, and the biker gal licking her ice cream as she leaned back on the pink, custom fender wrapped around her Super Wide 230 Series tire. This particular photo was seared into my memory as I felt the shutter click and spotted a massive blonde guy with a permanent sneer scarred on his face looking down on me as he said, "What in the hell are you doing?" I could only presume that he was with the woman who was looking the other way, oblivious of my taking her picture. My words rolled past my smile as I said, "Sunshine, hot day, beautiful blonde on a bike eating ice cream. What more could you ask for?" The pause was three heartbeats too long when he responded with, "Damn rights."

I slumped further in my chair as I remembered the endless panoramas down Bay Street capturing tons of chrome wrapped around hundreds of Harley Davidson's painted every color in the rainbow, and bent into shapes I had never seen before. Their owners walked the sidewalks and napped on their bikes as tourists, dressed in Tommy Bahamas shirts and straw hats, slipped between their tattooed arms and the women they were wrapped over.

The Davis Carnival filled the Port Authority parking lot and functioned as a colorful and gaudy spot on the black leathered Old Town. I was thrilled by the Ferris wheel ride I shared with my grandson and daughter. The view up and down the river was spectacular and the sky was bluer than the feet on a blue-footed booby.

My shutter captured the amusement rides, carnival tents, and hundreds of wandering children dragging their parents, with their hands full of red tickets, from one ride to another. My grandson conquered his fear of heights, and my lenses saw his joy as he tossed his hands into the air when our basket was whipped up and over the top.

I was pleased with the photos of the blue and white Rotary tent where my wife was working with Tawfik Ahdab to sell bottles of water to raise funds for the Rotary water filter project in Guatemala. The shot with several Harleys roaring past was the best, and captured the flavor of the day.

The Saturday night cruise gave me the opportunity to photograph every car on the move. As they pulled off of Bay Street onto Nopal, their angle was perfect, and the early evening light was ideal to capture their rich colors and gleaming chrome.

We have lived in Florence for ten years and the Sunday parade was the best I have seen. The bands, floats, flag bearing solders, cars, horses, trucks, trailers, and all the folks of import riding in convertibles and sitting on their trunk lids were fabulous.

At the end of it all, and in this chair behind my computer, I dropped my head into my cupped hands and moaned as I realized that I had deleted all my images before they were downloaded. Now they only exist in my memory.

MORNING PRAYERS 2008

On Sunday mornings around 10:00 a.m. the bench behind the Old Town gazebo holds several of my Baha'i friends and me. We gather there for prayers, and rarely miss a Sunday. The view over the Siuslaw

River is always spectacular as the tides come and go. Waves lap against the aged and deteriorated pilings that are the only remains of the ferry landing which was, in the early 1900's, the only means of crossing the river and traveling south.

During those days there were less than three hundred citizens in Florence. They supported the lumber mill, two general stores, two canneries, a saloon and the weekly newspaper. It wasn't until 1936 when the Siuslaw River Bridge was completed that our little community, which was dependent upon the logging and fishing trades, was connected with the southern part of Oregon.

The bridge is an excellent visual addition to the river, and the timber-covered hills that edge it. On most Sunday mornings the sky is clear and it is easy to see the bridge as it does its job and holds the traffic above and safe from the waters below. On some days, when it's hot inland, it seems to hide itself behind the fog that creeps up the river and, like cataracts, blurs our view of the tall towers and deco design. Winter rains, which most often respect our hour of prayer, rarely drive us off the bench and under the gazebo's roof.

We gather to pray for our community and to ask God to refresh and gladden our spirits, to purify our hearts and to illumine our powers. We pray for our departed, and ask Him to assist us in our daily lives.

It's easy to relax and meditate upon the Holy Words as seagulls and cormorants fish and entertain us with their skill. Most of the year, the boat traffic is nonexistent. In the warm summer months, though, fishermen and crabbers slowly negotiate their boats into the center of the river as they slip between the concrete pilings and under the bridge. They disappear as they motor west and down river towards the Pacific Ocean.

Sometimes morning walkers amble through the gazebo's garden and discover us as they wander down the path towards the platform that extends out and over the water's edge. They seem to know that we are praying, and offer respectful smiles as they share with us the bliss and joy of the view and the spiritual energy that is naturally a part of this little part of Florence, Oregon.

LIFE CHANGE 2008

Is change around the corner? The drive that was to begin the gentle wind-down process, after months and months of stress, was flipped on its hood as we spent two of the three hour commute trying, in vain, to save the only deal we had. Real Estate has been difficult and we haven't had a sale in five months.

Suzanne's son has his birthday this weekend, so she is flying to Arizona to spend some time with him. She needs the visit with Jason, not the last minute hassles of a failing transaction. By the time I dropped her off at the airport her bladder was engorged and her spirits dampened.

Last week Jordan talked about a job at Catlin Gabel that might be a good fit for us. He has been working for the prestigious school for several years. When the Caretaker position opened six months ago, we were slow to move, and another picked it up. When it came back around, because of personal issues with the new Caretaker's family, we were quick to fill out applications and express our interest.

It is my intention, while Suzanne is in Arizona, to check out the school campus and see if this Caretaker position might be a good fit for us.

It's hard to know what to do during these changing times. We need to make money. We love our Florence home. It is all fixed up and ready to protect and shelter us for the balance of our lives. Moving will require a level of energy we are unsure exists. We feel old in Florence, and wonder if being on a school campus might elevate our spirits and pluck us up and out of the atmosphere of aged that cradles our beloved Florence by the sea.

I will spend the weekend with Erica and Jordan while Suzanne is away. It's my intention to kick back, relax and maybe build something, take a bike ride, or just be lazy and visit. By the time Suzanne returns from her warm days with Jason, and I playing with my son and his wife, we should be ready to visit with Evie, the personal director of Catlin Gabel, and explore the option of being the Caretakers of Catlin Gabel.

SAVE THE DAD EXERCISE PROGRAM 2008

I asked him how far and he said, "Just a couple of blocks, Dad." I spent the last few days participating in my son's, "Save the Dad Exercise while Home Remodeling Program." I wanted to help him with a few small remodeling projects, and he wanted to help me establish a new exercise program. His primary tool in encouraging my participation was to mislead me with the words, "Just a couple of blocks, Dad."

We started by walking his dog three or four miles and then we tore a hole in his bedroom wall. We were looking for more space in the bedroom and were building a set of drawers into the unused attic space. It's always hot and sweaty work ripping walls apart and framing space for something different. My proposed two hour project became four, and ended only because Jordan had planned a bike ride to the Farmers' Market. He and Erica rode their new tandem and I, an old bike he had recently tuned-up. It took me awhile to master the shifter, and then I was able to keep up with them and their friends, Matt and Anna, who had joined us for the ride.

Our timing wasn't great. We arrived as the Master Farmer wandered through the rows, shaking her cowbell, announcing the close of selling. We grabbed a few plastic bags and filled them with nectarines and apples. I proudly tied my bag, containing four large apples and three barely ripe nectarines, to the metal bars under my seat, leaving barely an inch clearance above the rear tire.

We mounted up and began the pedal home. Within blocks the delightful ride down to the market was transformed into some kind of a Pike's Peak climb. My pedal partners quickly down-shifted and climbed up the road, while I fell further and further behind. After crossing several intersections at a speed so slow that maintaining balance was difficult, I spotted them waiting like roadside spectators. They all cheered, and I felt like a participant in the Special Olympics who could do no wrong. We repeated this pattern several times with the cheering getting louder at every intersection. When I finally reached level ground, I was pleased that I had been able to keep my feet on the pedals.

Several blocks from home the plastic bag that had been swinging over my slow spinning tire, like a pendulum in an old clock, dropped, and a hole was ground through the thin skinned bag, allowing some of my fruit to escape and fall to the street. I stopped, picked up my bruised fruit, retied the bag, and finished the trip home, where I gulped down several glasses of water and dropped into a chair with a beat up apple in my hand.

Jordan, less than five minutes after we had parked the bikes, asked if I would be interested in walking to the grocery. He seems to think of me as the high energy young man that raised him, not the beat up senior citizen I have become. "How far, Son?" I groaned. "It's just a few blocks, Dad," was his reply. A dozen or so blocks later, we reached the New Seasons Market and purchased the makings for our dinner. We returned to his home. As I walked up his steps, I surprised myself, and again felt pride.

The dinner was exceptional and when the choice of DVD's for evening watching was being discussed, I slipped out of the room and into my bed for a well-deserved sleep.

Following an exceptional breakfast I heard my son's words and knew that I was entering day two of my training. "Hey Dad! Do you want to walk the dogs with me?" My reply was, "Of course…how far?" He said, "Just a couple of blocks." We didn't head in the normal direction and shortly we were in a residential neighborhood that must have been built on an abandoned ski slope filled with moguls and peaks. I knew from my experience the day before that if you go downhill, you would, sometime in the walk, have to climb back up, and I was right.

Finishing up the drawer remodel took several hours longer that we expected. In my professional remodeling days, I was pretty good at estimating the time needed to complete a project. In recent years, I usually miss.

When we finished, and after we put away our tools, I heard my son's voice calling from the shower, "Hey Dad! Do you want to ride the bikes or walk down to the Coffee House with me? It's only a couple of blocks away."

GOOD REASON TO MOVE

"Dad…I'm just unwilling to have a kid that some babysitter would raise. Now if you and Suzanne would move to Portland that would be a whole different thing. I could drop the baby off on my way to work, pick it up on the way home, and would know that it had been well loved all day long," My son's words were often like this. If it wasn't about the baby, it was about the great times he and I would have if we were closer to each other.

We are in our second week of boxing up our home. A couple of weeks ago Jordan called and informed me that the position of Caretaker at Catlin Gabel School was open again, and that I shouldn't make the mistake I did six months ago when the job was posted for the first time in eighteen years. I took a week to think about it, and missed the opportunity. The young couple that took the job had to give it up, due to unforeseen family problems. The moment Jordan got the news, he called Suzanne and I and encouraged us to submit our application. We did.

We will begin our new job on the seventh day of July, and will move into our Portland home on the second of the month. Jordan is having his way and we are stepping forward in blind faith.

MOVE TO PORTLAND

Two and a half months ago Suzanne and I moved from Florence, our forever home by the ocean, one hundred and seventy-five miles north, and inland, to Portland, Oregon. The roof on our home was good for another twenty-five years, the vinyl siding required no maintenance, decks were built, the hot tub was full and in good working order, the yard was packed with the trees, plants and flowers we loved, and all the interior remodeling we deemed necessary was done or good enough for the next twenty years, or the balance of our lives with memory.

As if moved by an unknown force, we entertained an invitation by our son Jordan to interview for the Caretakers position at his school. We met with members of the Catlin Gabel board and were offered the job. We packed up our personal property, rented the house, quit our real estate jobs, said good-bye to friends, and moved from "God's little waiting room."

Every box we could buy or find in the trash behind local retail stores was filled with all the things we valued. The boxes we took from Webber's Fish Market were extra heavy and didn't pose a problem until they were packed and stacked in the hot garage. When we were completely packed and began loading the truck we discovered a problem. Even with our fabulous box packing and the skillful truck loading by the Camp Florence Felons, we had too many boxes and had to rent an additional trailer. Even worse…we had to leave behind several boxes containing God only knows what because every nook and cranny was jammed and we were out of room. In the dictionary where they describe those that are excessively materialistic, you will find a snappy photograph of Suzanne and me. Of course she is in the front of the picture and I am standing some distance behind her.

When we left Florence, Suzanne drove the Chevy station wagon with the cats, Jenny the dog and a trailer attached to the rear bumper. Jamie drove the Mercedes with so much stuff packed in its trunk she couldn't lower the top and enjoy the convertible ride she had anticipated. Jason drove the Jaguar, with Reno the parrot, and I drove the biggest truck U-Haul rents, with Elway sleeping between the boxes on the floor and my feet. The trip, although it was somewhat hillbilly, was easy, and we all arrived in good shape with very few broken items. With the help of Gregg, who was waiting at our new home when we arrived, we unpacked enough to set up camp for the night.

The next morning, our movers, who were much smaller that the three hundred pound plus guys in the photo ad, began the hard work of unloading. Suzanne sat a folding chair at the trucks ramp and directed every box to the room she deemed appropriate. Within two hours both truck and trailer were empty, and ready to be returned to U-Haul.

Setting up house was much easier than expected. Within days the walls were covered with pictures, and flowers were in a vase on the dining room table.

We were anxious about the move. Major decisions can prove disastrous, and we both found big cities good for visiting yet unacceptable as home. We were little town people who loved the intimacy of our coastal home with only eight thousand residences and no rush to do anything.

The "no rush to do anything" was one of the biggest motivations behind our move. Florence boasts an average age of sixty-three, so talk about failing body parts, proper foods to eat to maintain smooth functioning, and medications that work well for this or that malady made us feel old. The thought of living on a school campus with eight hundred kids held hopes of more youthful attitudes.

The Caretakers' house was good enough, and once filled with our furniture and art, it felt like home. The temperature in Florence keeps itself between fifty and seventy-two most all the year and colder or warmer days rarely blow in from the Ocean. Portland, on the other hand, gets hot. During our short stay we have had several weeks in the high nineties, and lots of days in the eighties. Even though I was raised in the Yakima Valley, a desert onto itself, my blood has become thin in Florence and was slow to thicken up and appreciate the heat.

The Caretaker's House has developed landscaping that needs lots of attention. In recent years she had been allowed to return to nature and many charming improvements are hidden beneath vines and branches. A fire place, cook stove and smoker crafted from decorative rock was lost below wisteria vines, and the shack behind the house, which needed many windows replaced, was a delightful green house. We were quick to plant inside the greenhouse and in the cinder block garden beside it, and have harvested cucumbers and tomatoes these past weeks.

Leaves have started to turn colors, and mornings are crisp when I do my early morning rounds. We are settled in and are having Monday night "Soup's On" for our Baha'i community and Friends. Suzanne has joined the Harmon Swim Center and is taking yoga classes on campus. She is my evening chauffer as we drive a golf cart around the campus to secure buildings and set alarms.

We purchased a GPS's just before we moved. It has made getting around Portland possible. I don't know what I would have done without it. We love it here. I didn't think we would recover from leaving Florence, yet we have. The young students are respectful and the school staff has proved to be wonderful folks who love doing what they do. It's great being a small part of it.

Jordan often comes by in the mornings. He rides his bike across town, so he keeps work clothes in our master bathroom. He parks his bike in our house, stretches, showers, and dresses for work in a quick fifteen minute visit we enjoy.

Suzanne has subbed in the lower school and looks forward to future days in the classroom. Kids have always been the joy of her life. We have both struggled with the free time adjustment and occasionally feel less productive than we want.

Several weeks ago we returned to Florence to pick up the boxes we left behind. The renter doesn't own a lawn mower, and our garage is now a storage room for his endless boxes of trash. Isn't life an adventure?

DEATH OF MY DOG 2008

Again he said "no" and I turned away from him and walked towards my car. All the rivets that had held me together popped half-way across the lot and fell with my tears to hot asphalt. I was shocked and unprepared for the muffled wails that escaped. Wails that were greater than the sounds I uttered after my Mother's last breath escaped her body. "Please…I won't cause a scene. Can I please sit with him while you give him the shot? I don't want him to be alone." The "no" was spoken with compassion, and I understood the young man cared. He was in his mid-twenties with thin lips, heavily pierced ears and eyebrows. I knew he was powerless and accepted the second "No" to my request to hold my dog while he died.

For over a month Elway had been weak in the rear end and the last couple of weeks I had to help him in and out of the car. Today I layer a blanked in the back of our station wagon offering him the only comfort I could think of. He was miserable and last night had been terrible. We woke to his deep and mournful wails as he puked puddles of thick white foam on the carpet beside our bed where he had been sleeping for the past nine years and wouldn't sleep another night. It was 3:00 am and we were both up attending to him as best we could, and cleaning up the mess. I took him outside and hooked him up to his chain while Suzanne began the cleaning. We quickly changed roles, as she took to his side and I cleaned.

I felt powerless to do anything and lost all hope when Suzanne went on the web, entered his symptoms and discovered that Elway's liver had probably failed. Before I rolled out of my bed with my dog's wrenching, I had begun protecting myself, knowing that the task at hand wouldn't be an easy one. Suzanne sat on the porch with him for hours and rubbed his head as Elway tried to muffle his groans and be a good dog. I left him in her hands and returned to bed.

When I got up in the morning Elway was still outside and in bad shape. His belly was swollen and he was on his side with his tongue lifeless on the grass. I could see that his puking had continued, and knew that he would probably be dead by mid-day.

I could tell by Suzanne's expression that she had already reached the same conclusion I had and was broken-hearted that we would have to put him down. I called the Animal Shelter and made arrangements. Elway was able to walk to the back of the station wagon where I loaded him up and, following kisses and tears from Suzanne drove him to the Shelter. I parked in the middle of the lot and went inside. They were busy adopting out a new puppy, so I had to wait. When my turn came, I stated my intent and was given a bill, instructed to pay it at the office, and bring Elway in. With the paperwork completed, I went to the car and opened the back. He couldn't do anything. When I slid him out of the car, he landed on the asphalt like a cheep castaway coat. I tried to help him to his paws and failed. His one hundred and twenty pounds were more than I could lift. I hated to leave him lying there, but did as I trotted back to the office to get help. I asked for a cart and a painfully long twenty minutes later the young man with the cart emerged from the building. I had been standing on the parking strip between Elway and the Shelter, fearful that if I got out of their sight they might forget about me. Together the young man and I loaded him onto the gurney, and when we reached the door I made my second plea.

Nine years my best friend and I couldn't support him at the end. Maybe tomorrow my not being with him won't hurt as much.

VIRGINIA 2008

"Hi Virginia, it's Jim! I understand you are dying," were the first words to pass between the two of us in months. "Oh, hi Jim! How are you?" "I'm OK, Sweetheart. Tell me about you." Her voice was little and with heavy breaths, she apologized. Even in her own death her concerns were greater for others than herself.

We didn't talk long. I thanked her for being my Spiritual Mother, and for introducing me to Baha'u'llah. We remembered the day, thirty-seven years ago, when I knocked on the door of her home and tried to sell her life insurance. She thought I was Baha'i and was right.

I cried as we talked, then she couldn't continue as her cough consumed her words. "I'm sorry, Jim," Virginia's daughter whispered, "Mom is having a seizure." "Tell her I love her," I gulped. I heard the daughter share my words and Virginia's weak reply, "I love you, Jim."

TOUGH WEEKEND 2008

In some ways the weekend was blessed, but only because it didn't reach a state of dreadfulness. Jordan banged on our patio door as he dragged himself and his bike into our utility room. He was upset and his ankle, knee, and elbow were red with blood and road rash. Although his bike route to Catlin School avoids most auto traffic, there are several areas where he mixes it up with cars, and it was there that he found himself in the spot all bikers fear. He was enjoying the smooth speed and control of his freshly tuned Scott CR1. The new shoes he was trying out for the first time felt pretty good, and he was exhilarated with his thirty mile per hour speed as he zipped down the bike lane. Sporting his colorful Cliff Bar outfit and his hi-tek helmet, he was easy for everyone to see, with the exception of the guy driving the Volvo. Apparently the Volvo driver planned to turn right across the bike lane at the next intersection, and was setting himself up for an easy turn by pulling into the bike lane. Seeing his circumstances, Jordan slammed on his brakes and slid as the Volvo shut off his lane and thumped him off his bike and down to the street where the concrete claimed its pound of flesh.

Fear, anger, pain, with a handful of other emotions, surged through his body as Jordan stood, assessed his condition, and walked to inspect his bike. The driver, a young man like Jordan, was extremely apologetic and accepted responsibility. With names exchanged, Jordan mounted his bike, which had lost some of its shine to the same road that had claimed a piece of him, and peddled down the street towards my house. He knew that there wasn't enough damage to him or his bike to trouble the Volvo guy, and he knew that he was going to be sore tomorrow.

Saturday night, following a cheap movie, I dropped Erica and Jordan off at their house. As I drove off, Erica felt another stabbing pain in her belly as she tried to unlock their front door. She had been complaining for the past twenty-four hours about cramps in her gut and wanted to go to bed. Jordan was concerned enough to insist that they go to the neighborhood clinic, and she reluctantly agreed. Once there, the medical staff seemed unconcerned and slow to address her discomfort. When she finally received the attention she needed, they discovered that she was pregnant and the baby had attached itself to the wall of her fallopian tubes. Now that the fetus had grown, there wasn't enough room, so the wall of the tube ruptured. Appreciating the seriousness of Erica's condition, she, with Jordan at her side, was loaded into an ambulance and transported to a hospital capable of addressing her ailment.

Our phone rang Sunday morning at 2:30 am. Jordan's voice was flooded with anxiousness as he shared their circumstances. Erica was in surgery and he wanted to believe that everything was going to be OK, but was fearful it wouldn't be. We dressed and were on the road in minutes. We were upset by their plight and wanted to be helpful in any way we could. The drive was too long, and then winding through the maze of hospital halls seemed endless. Suzanne's knee was acting up. In hopes of improving its condition before our Mexican holiday next week with Jordan and Erica, she had spent most of the day off of it. This endless trek down hospital halls wasn't good.

Jordan was soft and beat up by the time we found him. His man-of-steel position was weak, and his fear for his wife's life and health pierced through his thin plates of armor. Together we prayed, talked, and wondered before Erica's surgeon arrived and shared photographs and information that eased our concerns. She would be OK. Everything would heal. Another baby could come. This baby would not.

Suzanne and I ended our vigil at 6:00 am with prayers of gratitude. We thanked God for Erica and Jordan's health, and prayed for the little soul that spent such a short period of time with us. What a weekend.

A DAY IN OCTOBER 2008

The third day of October is half passed. I am sitting on the patio writing notes and drinking green tea from my red plastic Enjoy Coca-Cola glass. The sun hides behind gray-white clouds that push at the small section of blue sky curled up on the northern horizon. The neighbor's chickens are clucking their egg laying sounds as crows, high in the trees, squawk their endless warning calls. Douglas squirrels pack nuts into our small backyard and bury them between the blades of grass. Their tails dance a different pattern than their bodies, as other hiding places are checked before they scamper off to find other nuts. The roses and lilacs edge the yard and show early signs of fall as the first of their leaves begin to fall. The painting of the umbrella-carrying Frenchman watches over the garden and rolls one eye upwards as small planes fly across the sky. Jenny sleeps beside the patio as her unused chain winds across the asphalt walk. Yellow has climbed up the corn stalk and claimed the green of the cucumber vine. One tomato hides behind the late yellow flowers that promise more fruit in the fall days to come. Orange balls dangle from the Dogwood tree and look like nothing I have seen before. Dried and browned leaves have gathered below the greenhouse overhang and remain there, protected from the rains that are predicted.

This morning we stood and tapped our feet as we participated in Disco Friday. Once a month, Jordan, takes over the lower school library and fills it with spinning colored lights, screens pulsing abstract patterns behind images of guitar playing and song singing students. Packed in the large section of open floor between the shelves of books, librarian desks, and under several disco balls are excited kids, dancing to the pounding music. For thirty minutes, song after song flip through the system, changing everything from hip-hop to reggae. Occasionally a cowboy or bluegrass song will find its way into the mix and add a "Yahoo" flavor to the dance. Conga lines wind themselves through the crowd and grow as adults and children trail each other around the room and across the stage. As quickly as the beat of the music and the flash of the lights disrupted the respected silence of the library… it all ends. Kids hugged each other and parents kissed them goodbye, as they left for their day's work. Jordan, brow covered with sweat and disco shirt wet, greeted us and wished us a great day as he wandered off to his class with half a dozen kids in tow.

Across the Fir Grove and down the path, the Bee Hive is warming up for their Friday Sing. The kids that aren't old enough for the Lower School are busy singing their own songs. "Itsy Bitsy Spider" "Old Dan Tucker" and "Bayberry Tree" were a few of the songs shared by the kids and adults that surrounded the carpeted pit in the pre-school building. Like salve to the soul, these kid songs capture us all and, without inhibitions, feet stomp, hands wave above heads, and silly faces are made. Children watch the adults and find even greater moments of joy as they, with their parents, sing the songs their teachers taught them.

END OF THE SEASON 2008

We weren't able to plant our garden until the middle of July, but did spice up a few salads with fresh cucumbers and tomatoes. The herbs we planted are small, but did well and are the ones who get to spend the winter in the greenhouse.

This morning it was clear and cold. The news reported high thirties. Our backyard mole, who has daily constructed at least one mound of dirt in our little yard, seems to have taken the week off. Maybe he's done for the year.

The cinder blocks, which compose the growing areas for our garden, are mostly empty now, except for the three stalks of corn that are working hard to produce as many ears. Three plants still have a small basket of green tomatoes hanging on their pale green and withering vines, and the carrots have pushed a full crop of greens above their block, with only the tiniest of carrots in the dirt. The cabbage I harvested the heart from for last week's soup is wilting, as its slug-ravaged leaves soften and drape down the sides of the blocks. The hardy strawberry plants will ride out the winter where they are, and hopefully produce more fruit than the one red berry we found a month ago under one of its lush green leaves.

The weatherman is talking about rain tomorrow. I blew many of the leaves that have turned gold and brown and fallen onto our driveway into the neighbor's garden. I wanted to push them away while they were dry and easy to propel. I hope they appreciate the insulating and soil enhancements my leaves will give their shrubs and tucked-away bulbs. Several V's of Canadian Honkers passed over loudly, deciding whose turn it was to fly up front, while brown and gray squirrels quietly dashed about the grass checking on their hidden nuts. It has warmed into the sixties, and it's a wonderful day to be alive.

WHERE'S THE DOG? 2008

When Dad died, we became the caretakers of their dog, Jenny. Following the death of their beloved Ringo, a male Sheltie that had filled their lives with joy, my sister and I purchased them another dog. Although Jenny wasn't Ringo, she was a Sheltie, and Mom didn't like her. We found her, as a four year old, at a Sheltie rescue in Scapoose, Oregon close to Portland. She had been adopted a couple of times, but hadn't worked out for families with kids. Seems her herding instincts were strong, and nipping at the feet of small children seemed natural. Parents and kids alike disapproved of her inability to discern children from sheep, and her return to the rescue was threatening to end her life.

I was pretty sure Mom and Dad wouldn't be troubled by Jenny's need to nip, and my sister agreed. Suzanne and I made the drive to Scapoose to check the dog out, feeling fairly confident that she would be a good replacement. She was a bit shy and let us pet her. Her coat was beautiful, maybe even more beautiful than poor old Ringo.

I had thought that a rescue dog with Jenny's history would be cheap, but she wasn't, and before I loaded her into the car, I wrote the check for two hundred dollars.

It was then, as we drove away from the kennel, that I was introduced to one of her irritating behavior. She began to bark. At first I thought it was her excitement. Twenty miles down the road I realized that there was nothing I could do to stop her yapping, and tried to find that place in my mind where one blocks out the external world and seeks inner peace. I couldn't find it.

My Dad worked hard training Jenny and sadly died one month into the training program. We thought Mom would appreciate the dog's company now that she was alone, but she continued to dislike the dog. To ease Mom's life and to keep a promise I made Dad...Jenny came home with us. The trip was twice the delivery distance, and, to my dismay, Jenny was able to bark nonstop for five hours.

After our first couple of hours on the road, I turned to Suzanne and begged her to let me stop at a hardware store and buy some duct tape to secure the dog's mouth. Being a far better person than I am, she wouldn't allow it. By the time we reached Florence my attitude towards the dog was eternally scarred.

Years passed and many other offensive behaviors surfaced. At the sound of a jingling set of keys she would begin charging from one room to another, yipping at the top of her voice. She wouldn't retreat until we drove away. I have to presume she quit barking after our departure, and am still unsure. It had to be rough on our other dog and the cats.

If by chance she escaped her run or slipped a chain, she would wander off in any direction but home. Several times we had to rescue her from the local pound, adding more money to a bad investment.

One of her flaws was physical, and I am being harsh in holding it against her, although I do. She, because of her extremely long hair, would capture her stool in shitty little nuggets that she would deposit in the high traffic areas of the house. I always considered myself lucky to spot them on my bare footed treks to the refrigerator.

Jenny really doesn't like people and will snarl at some as she rolls her lips back exposing her possum like teeth. Others she just avoids and slinks off to distant corners, acting as if she has been violated by their presence. She was always on the creep and would snatch food from other pets, or us, if she could. There's a look she has that is best described as a princess that has been forced to live with trolls. It's a look she wears most all the time. Our other pets adored us and looked for opportunities to be close and affectionate. She didn't.

We had to modify our cat litter box. Jenny considered cat poop her personal box of Kitty-Roca and couldn't keep from eating it, despite our continual shooing her away.

As she aged she got fat and wasn't able to keep herself clean, so would often become infected around her external girl parts. I, the one who didn't like her, was stuck with the job of applying the medication. She knew I didn't like treating her and would lie very still. She didn't behave for Suzanne and would do her crazy possum retinue and nip.

Last week she wandered off. She had been keeping to the back porch, so as the months passed, we took to not chaining her up. It was one of the few times she had done something I liked. One of our neighbors spotted her on the run and we spent hours looking for her without success. It was as if she had vanished. After several days I began to appreciate her absence and found myself adding a little prayer of thanksgiving to my morning devotions. Suzanne was ashamed of me, but my feelings were true.

Suzanne called the pound several times without success and yesterday, on the outside chance they didn't know they had our dog; she drove the twelve miles to their facility. Jenny was there and today is lying on the end of her chain in a spot of sunshine outside my window. We spent another one hundred and twenty dollars on a dog I dislike. I am sure God is playing some role in this mix, and if I wasn't so locked into my dislike, I would probably get it.

$1,043.00 2008

The screw is tightening and the options to avoid the squeeze seem few. We, Suzanne and I, are semi-retired and are trying to live on a fixed income that is small. We do have savings, and draw from it every month to make ends meet. If we maintain our health and continue with our Caretaker job, we should be solvent for another ten years. If we live beyond that point, our social security and savings won't do the job.

The reason for the whine is the notification we received in the mail informing us that the cost of our health insurance will jump by two hundred dollars a month. Every month we will pay $1,043.00. What makes it worse is our having to pay a fifteen hundred dollar deductible and large co-pay every year. We are thinking that maybe no insurance is a sound decision.

BIGGER TABLE 2008

We need more space at our table, so I rebuilt the family dining room set to make it happen. The table is special. Mom and Dad, in the early

1950s, dug it out of a chicken coupe that was behind a barn on Uncle Don's farm. It was oak and covered with many coats and colors of oil paints that were slow to be removed, and skillfully replaced with half a dozen coats of varnish. When Dad completed the project, our family used the table for twenty years. When I got married, Mom and Dad replaced it with an elegant French set and gave the old one to me. The table had been with me all the years of my life until, in my mid-twenties, when my wife, who was thinning out our personal property prior to one of our separations, sold it at a garage sale.

When I returned home from my weekend drill with the United States Marine Corps Reserve, I discovered that she had sold all of my long play records and the dining room set. I was devastated. Years later, and in another State, a friend showed up at my shop with an old oak chair he wanted to rebuild and needed advice. I immediately recognized the initial carved in the back of the chair and begged my friend to sell me the set. He had been delighted with his purchase, yet valuing our friendship, and seeing my delight with his purchase, tossed his hands into the air and sold it to me. Its years apart from me would be described as hard use...maybe even abusive. I, despite my normal inclination to quickly finish projects, took lots of time and lovingly attended to all of its wounds until it was restored and proudly sitting in my dining room, where it belongs, once again.

Today we are living in Portland and have a weekly "Soups On" in our home. The evening, which has often attracted more than a handful of area Baha'is and their friends, is great fun, and helps me keep a promise I made to God. The table can sit eight of us, and ten, if we are willing to squeeze in a little closer.

I began the project with a trip to Home Depot, where I purchased several planks of oak, stain, polyurethane, and sandpaper. The supports under the table that allowed it to expand and contract were in poor condition, so I fixed the table size by replacing them with a pair of eight-foot long 4x4s. I attached the legs and the expanded tabletop to the 4x4s with oak dowels. I sanded it all down, stained and finished it with a look of rich red oak.

Suzanne and I look forward to lots of soup being eaten and friendships developed beside this table that has watched me live my life for almost sixty-four years. I would love it if most of the folks that have pulled up to it in the past could do it one more time. What a meal that would be!

DRUMMER

It's my understanding that the Catlin Gabel School rummage sale has been an annual occurrence for many years. They say it takes the efforts of one thousand people to make it happen. The last sale earned over a quarter of a million dollars for student scholarships.

On the first day of the sale Jordan asked me if I wanted to jump a bus with a bunch of his students and see the layout out before they opened the doors to the public. I took him up on the offer and was astonished when we arrived at the Convention Center. The school had rented two huge sections of the Center, and filled it with the donated items they had collected over the past twelve months. It was well organized, with signs hung over different areas, helping buyers find items of interest. Kitchen, shop, clothing electronics, treasures, art, toys, appliances, shoes, bedding, furniture, boat, and a car or two tossed in to make the sale interesting. I was amazed and wandered the different sections until I stopped in front of a midnight blue 5-drum set with cymbals. It had the floor tom, bass drum, power toms, snare hi-hat stand and cymbal, padded drum throne and sticks.

My daughter had been shopping for set, so I called her and we agreed that it would be perfect for my grandson, Skylar. I have never had rhythm or a desire to play any musical instrument, but my grandson might.

Suzanne and I have purchased him a keyboard and an electric guitar on past occasions, and thought that if we got the drum set, with his parents, he could be a band by himself.

He loved it and signed up to take classes at Eugene's School of Rock and Roll.

MISGUIDED DAYS 2008

I thought that she was someone else. My clarity was lost in a twenty-three year fog of forgiveness, misguided understanding and self-delusion.

I considered her a treasure beyond value, and she wasn't. Like a miser of love, I sacrificed all that I was and valued in my effort to retain her. All eyes watching told me the truth of my choice, and I denied their beliefs and championed her worth. Her heart belonged to herself and her commitment was tentative and often pulled away. "It's all about her, James. Can't you see?" I wouldn't, and the price of my loving seared my soul, mind, and body. "Such a foolish man."

Twenty years have passed and my life has moved beyond my misguided days. Recovering from obsessive love and moving into the clarity of honest living has taken all of this time. I am aware that the girl I fell in love with was wonderful, and she wasn't the woman I married. The girl of my dreams lives in my mind, and I see her from time to time walking with other boys. Her head leans on their shoulders…her kisses on their necks.

SNOW ON CAMPUS DEC 14, 2008

The metal frame of the window screen shakes as snowflakes, charging across the roof of the greenhouse and against the glass, fail in their attempt to penetrate the tiny fiberglass grid. Popular trees, weeks without leaves, swing their sky-seeking branches from side to side, like an artist spinning his empty brush before dipping it into the paint on his pallet. Smaller lilac branches shake with far less grace as snow-packed winds blast up the concrete steps and around the black wrought-iron yard lamp. Faded and yellowed rhododendron leaves tuck themselves tightly together under the massive lilac branches and watch the storm build. Confused flakes of snow, like schools of frightened fish, dash one direction, then another, without pattern or predictability. Blades of grass abandon their efforts against being covered and lay to the side as the snow deepens and presses them closer and closer to the frozen earth. The planks on the covered wooden deck capture their share of swirling snow for easy measurement when the storm has passed and are surprised how close to the house the wind can push the snow. Capturing and holding more snow than the other trees, the holly leaves become white and proudly display the dramatic contrast of their bright red berries. The unpruned branches of the climbing rose swing in the wind, like a long fluffy scarf wrapped around the neck of a winter jogger. Sudden blasts of wind push snow off the garage roof, obscuring vision and filling the sky with swirling white. As if denying the power of the winter storm snowflakes, falling over the harvested garden, gently spin and fill the raised beds with a soft protective blanket. A sparrow, captured by the closed green house door, pecks at the panes of glass in its foolish effort to escape. I, unlike my feathered captive, am about to suit up in my winter gear and wander about the school campus to assure myself that all is well in this newly arrived winter wonderland. I doubt I will see kids on the playground tomorrow.

SNOW 2008

The wire tomato frames that kept our crop up and off of the ground have disappeared except for the top rings, which are well over two feet tall. The rolled garden hose, hanging on the bracket beside the steps leading to the campus, shares the circumstances of the tomato frames, as does everything within my view. Below the three inches of fresh falling snow an ice crust holds a foot to three feet more.

It all began eight days ago and may continue for several more. Often Christmas in Portland, Oregon is green, but this year we are assured it will be white.

My escape from cabin fever is my Caretaker responsibilities. Several times each day I bundle myself up in my electric blue rain gear over a down liner, lace up my twenty year old Sorrel's, and tromp about the campus. The first snow day I was able to plow about on one of the electric Gators, but the snow depth immobilized them and I abandoned them to be rescued when the snow retreats.

AFRICAN GRAY 2008

It wasn't a good start and, considering my prejudices, allowing the bird in my house, was an act of love. It, because we don't know if it is male or female, came into my life years after Suzanne and her son Jason purchased him to offset the death of beloved grandparents and great grandparents. Jason wanted someone he loved to be around as long as he and the parrot, with a life expediency of seventy plus years, fit the bill.

When his parents ended their marriage and he went off to college, the bird remained in the care of his father, who called one day and said, "I don't want the bird in my house anymore and am going to give it away if you don't take it." Suzanne couldn't let her son's assurance of a life-long companion fall into the hands of some stranger so she said, "We want Reno." I have never asked why it was named Reno, but might guess it had something to do with the odds of losing a finger tip during an invited head scratch.

Parrots come with big black metal shit-stained cages, with tons of colorful and reflective toys hanging from the top bars. Glad that we brought the truck, I waited outside as Suzanne rolled the cage out of her ex-husband's empty home. We slipped it under the canopy, closed the door, and drove home to Florence. The cage was rolled into our office, where it had a great view of the back yard, and where the scattering of parrot carnage would have minimal impact on the rest of the home.

I couldn't get around my unhappiness at allowing such a noisy mess-maker into my house, and did my best to avoid contact for several weeks. When I made my first attempt to communicate with the bird, it squatted down on it's wooden cross bar, pooped, and then said, "Up yours, Fat Ass" which was a favorite nickname given me by the wife's X. I could only wonder what it took to make this moment happen and how he would have loved being a fly on my wall when Reno performed as trained.

Because of this and that, the bird has remained with us for the last seven or eight years, and has become my friend. It allows me to fondle its beak and rub its tongue on fingers when I twist its head from side to side. It also greets me when I come home with a "Hi, Honey," in my wife's sweet voice.

There continue to be problems that I overlook, and others that I tolerate. I tolerate the mess and the cost of feeding it. I overlook its shouting out "Yahoo" when we have friends over for prayers and singing. I tolerate it ripping the laminate off the wall next to the bars of its cage, and overlook it's growling in the voice of our dog, Jenny. The dog feels challenged and upset as Reno swings itself from side to side while hanging on the bars at the base of its cage. I tolerate it's yowling like our male Ocicat, that was guaranteed to be a quiet breed, and isn't. I overlook its pulling all the feathers from its chest…a practice it began at the X's home and has continued to this day. Visitors often look and say something like, "Oh my, where did its feathers go?" I tolerate it jumping into its water bowl, moments after we fill it, and splashing water all over the floor. I overlook the seed husks that pierce my feet and are cast several feet in all directions. I tolerate its efforts to destroy everything we hang it its cage for its entertainment. I overlook its endless daytime chatter and squawks of all the sounds I dislike most. I enjoy its learning new words and its intelligence. I like its staring me down when I am sharing the room with it, and its asking me, "Wanna peanut?" I enjoy its always thanking me for snack peanuts with a tongue click and a happy bounce to its shucking branch. I like its remembering the name of my dear dog, Elway, who died several months ago with its call, "Here, Elway, come on boy." It bothers me that Reno is only fourteen years old and should live to 2073, and I…with luck, will have 2028 carved into the stone atop my grave. What the parrot will do wit the extra forty-five years, I don't know. Maybe he will end up with Jason, who wanted him in the first place, or possibly riding on the shoulder of some space pirate with one eye and an "Aaargh!"

SUPER BOWL XLIII 2009

It's Super Bowl Sunday and the windows are fogged, frost is on the ground, and we have a new president. Interrupting my only morning to sleep in, my cell phone rang with a coach moaning about his inability to unlock the tennis courts and his students freezing to death. Once outside the door, with my lungs filled with clear and crisp air, my resentments around the early call pass, and my day was on its way.

Despite the day's blue sky, several blankets of dissimilar feelings have wrapped themselves around the world, and me, for several months. The excitement of Barack Obama is truly beyond words. So much greater than our nation electing an intelligent and knowledgeable man to its Presidency is our electing a man of color. We drove a stake deep into the heart of racism and closed it in a coffin that we buried deep in our soil and will hopefully never allow to surface again.

Obama looks at our Nation and the World with the same eyes of unity I do. I can't help but attach my dreams to the tail of his kite and do my part to reshape the way we all share this planet.

Money has disappeared. Money…the god of our nation....is half it's size and it has miniaturized self is hiding in the vaults of banks, while a world of worshipers wonder in fear. The loss of homes and jobs fill the news. The world is confused and is about join those that have placed their trust in the other God.

This afternoon in the media room of my son's home I will join him and his friends. We will eat bad food and watch a football game. For several hours we will all enjoy a timeout and each other's company.

FEBUARY MORNING 2009

The light covering of mid-night snow has melted and the freshly planted flower garden below the Holly tree pushes it's newly spread rich and black soil towards the beams of warm sunlight peeking over the roof of our home. The green and yellow striped hose is stretched out across the asphalt walk between the house and our freshly painted greenhouse. Swollen with pressure from yesterdays planting of Freesias, Ranunculus, Gladioli and Lilies it looks tired and threatens to rupture. The patch of grass beside the patio is rich and thick, less the two foot square where Jenny, our aged and overweight Sheltie, takes her morning pee. Leaves have not yet appeared on the branches and twigs, but color and tiny buds are forming, promising spring days without the cold and snow of winter. The ancient and moss covered branches of the massive lilacs, like the smashed and twisted paint brushes of tempera painting children, push high above the ever yellow and green Coleus that grows between them. Behind the greenhouse, that sports many new and freshly glazed windows, a pair of cherry trees snaggle their branches into the blue sky boasting a decade without pruning. The thermometer on the wall has 60 on the tip of its big red hand. Yellow and pink ceramic garden horses, suspended on their long green sticks, have their heads turned in its direction appreciating the day's warmth as drops of moisture drip from their outstretched bellies and legs. A large and nicely shaped clay pot sits empty beside the lilacs. Time and another day of gardening will fill it with something we will enjoy when summer comes and we share B-B-Q's on our large, covered deck. A winter fat squirrel dashed across the edge of the clay pot on his way to somewhere, reminding me that the time has come for me to join my co-workers in the school barn, where lunch is being served and dishes need to be washed.

ROMEO AND JULIET 2009

Many Catlin students wanted to participate in the play, so they cast it twice. Friday night one group performed, to the delight of staff, parents and stage lovers, and on Saturday night another group performed for Suzanne and I and another group of stage lovers. Everyone loved these high school kids who knew their lines, projected well, and acted better than many seasoned adults we have enjoyed in little theater productions.

We sat there for two hours in the beautiful Cabell Center watching these kids act, change sets, manage lights, sell tickets, and offer cookies and coffee during intermission. We have enjoyed other high school productions over the years and appreciated the skill and lack of skill displayed by those young actors. We never expected stellar performances, and always hope that they were having fun on stage and making lifetime memories. The Catlin kids were several steps beyond anything we had previously seen, and we were much more than impressed. Their performances, each and every one, were so exceptional that I worried about the fun we had wished for other high school actors. Maybe the brightest of the bright can have fun and achieve exceptional levels of performance. It's what I presume and hope.

SAMURAI 2009

She hates him. When he wants to play, she sulks. If he is being fed, she watches from across the room with the opportunistic look of an old and done-wrong fox. When we look the other way to admire the pup's playful pranks, she sneaks up to his bowl and rapidly wolfs down the puppy food that she later pukes on the rug. Her old stomach can't handle the rich food, but that doesn't matter during the gobble down time.

Ten years ago, when my father died, Jenny became my responsibility. My sister, Judy, and I gave Dad the dog following the death of his beloved Ringo, who was also a Sheltie and a great companion for my parents. Suzanne and I had found Jenny in a Sheltie rescue kennel. She had been adopted several times before, and we were her last hope for a successful placement. When we gave Dad the dog I respected his hesitancy to get another at his age of eighty-four, and promised to care for Jenny if he died or couldn't keep the dog. Several weeks later Dad did die, and I have been stuck with a most unlikable dog for ten years. I would have found her another home years ago, but Suzanne held me to the promise I made my father.

A week ago we drove down to Eugene to celebrate The Baha'i Days of Ha' with my daughter and her family. We had made arrangements to have two puppies delivered by the breeders who lived in Bandon, Oregon. They pride themselves on mixing small breeds. Ours had a father who was Shiba Inu and a mother who was one half Shih Tzu and the other half Shiba Inu like the father. They weighed five pounds, were ten weeks old, and looked a lot like little German Shepherds.

When the breeders showed up at the Sears parking lot, we spotted the pups in the back of their Subaru station wagon. They were in a wood frame puppy box, filled with wood chips. When they lifted the hatch, we saw our guys for the first time and couldn't believe how adorable they were. They were sharing their space with a Shih-Tzu pup on its way to someone else's home and were anxious to be out of the car.

We got all the puppy information and a bag of toys before we all loaded up in our separate cars and drove away. At Jamie's home we spent the weekend playing with the pups and watching them wrestle and sleep with each other. Jamie named hers Coco and we, from the recommendation of a fifth grade student in Jordan's class, named ours Samurai.

Once home in Portland we began to fully appreciate the wonder of our new dog. Most of his day is spent sleeping, and during the few awake hours great fun is had. The Persian rugs are peeled back from all corners and the carpet around the sectional serves as the lapping track where Samurai rips around and around until he drops and sleeps again. The last couple of days our Ocicat, Carrumba, has taken to chasing and being chased around the track by Samurai, while his sister, Scheherazade, watches and hisses when their behavior seems out of control. She, unlike her brother, takes life seriously and is not comfortable with another dog in the house.

Potty training is the part of puppy ownership that keeps many wanna be dog owners without dogs. It's understandable, yet always a bit of a surprise when the fantasy of having a pup and the responsibilities and time commitments involved collide.

Sammy's night cry reminds me of being a young dad and the pleasure I felt being with and caring for my newborn babies. For me, the pleasure of holding and caring far outweighed the hassle of getting up several times during the night. The night cuddles for babies and puppies are very similar, and the new life smell they both have warms my heart and brings sweet whispers to my lips.

We are one week into life with Samurai and, despite the little tests he provides, we are filled with puppy love. Jenny remains the only one in the house whose heart has not been warmed by Sam's sweet kisses.

BABY 2009

The phone rang and the first words out of Jordan's mouth were, "Hey Dad…Guess what Erica gave me for my birthday?" I could tell by the tone of his voice he was excited and appreciating Erica's ability to creatively buy for her husband I responded with, "What did she get ya, Son?" He quickly popped back with, "It's a baby, Dad." My hearing isn't great and Jordan speaks very rapidly like the fifth grade students he teaches so I replied, "A what? Gleefully he said, "A baby, Dad…Erica's pregnant." "Oh jeez…" I said as tears rushed to my eyes and my throat began to close.

They are thinking that it might be a girl and are only six weeks into the baby making process. It will be some months before they know if their guess is correct. They passed the PG test and Jordan said that a positive test is always correct while a negative one might not be right.

Being born on the thirtieth day of November myself, I may well share my birthday with my second grandchild. The world can always use another Sagittarius.

DISHWASHING 2009

The economy has collapsed, investments diminished, options for change vanished, and keeping the ship afloat is everyone's goal...including Suzanne and I.

In my sixty-fifth year of life, I find myself spending a couple of hours every weekday washing lunch dishes in the Barn. The Barn is a green cedar building that Catlin Gable School converted into a kitchen and lunchroom years ago. At noon I walk down the hill from our Caretaker's house, across the campus, and through the building's old double doors.

On the back wall there are cabinets and counter tops which are lined with coffee, tea, milk and juice machines. Squeezed against the old wooden wall and beside the storage cabinets sits a long line of freezers and refrigerators of diverse sizes and colors. They store many meals yet to be made. High above them is a bank of French windows that in earlier days would have cast their beams of sunlight on bales of hay and buckets of oats. Today it shines on the aged fir floor and the table and chairs that pack the room and offers the students places to visit and eat the delicious food cooked by Hen.

The ceiling is vaulted even higher than the white acoustical boards that have been carved to fit around the massive posts and beams. They support the insulation that keeps the room warm on cold winter days, but seems powerless to cool the building when the weather turns hot. The wall across from the refrigerators is uncluttered, except for the dirty dishes station, and offers the only view out of the room. Double doors are on both ends of the wall and between them bigger and brighter windows, like the ones above the milk machine, offer lots of additional light.

The ends of the room are walled off with the office for human services on one side and the kitchen on the other. I work in the kitchen beside a big three compartment stainless sink that is connected to a large sanitizing machine. Just off to my left, a small vinyl window offers me a quick peek at the outside weather, and supplies fresh air to cool me down.

My job isn't complex. I wash dishes, glasses, pots and pans. I wear a blue rubber apron and cumbersome black gloves. I melted my apron on my first day in the kitchen by leaning against a hot grill. I repaired it with a few strips of duct tape. When my dishes are caught up, Chris might ask me to help with the prep work and peel potatoes or slice tomatoes. On the day I melted my apron I was flipping grilled chicken while the cook served lunch to the students.

The kitchen reminds me a lot of the one I set up in the Ivy Street Coffee House in Junction City. It's small and many concessions had to be made to make it function. Hen, the department manager and head cook, is an exceptional fellow. His life story could easily be a book worth the read. He was born in Cambodia and raised in Viet Nam. He's in his mid thirties and would have been a child in Viet Nam during the seventies. Some of his stories he keeps to himself, and the ones he shares are amazing.

There are four women that work with me in the kitchen, and Robin, who works out front and takes care of the register, snacks and special events Hen caters. Chris, who, like Robin, has been working for the school for two decades, manages the team. She loves to bowl and talks of scores above two hundred. Sara is only twenty-three and is the second cook. She is full of young, bringing me many laughs. The two other women are Japanese. Yuriyo does most of the food prep and Yoko, who I help, is the main dishwasher. Both Yuriyo and Yoko are delightful and speak very little English. Yoko brings me glasses of water during my shift. She doesn't want me to become dehydrated and hurt myself. I love the way she offers me water with the glass elevated above her eyes and one hand flat on its base.

The dishwasher job brings my hours up to half time and makes us eligible for benefits. We save lots of money on our insurance, plus the coverage is much better. When I give financial consideration to the benefits, I appreciate how well I'm paid to wash dishes.

MEXICO 2009

I had looked forward to a tropical trip with Jordan and Erica for years. I worried that the Swine Flu pandemic was going to mess up our long-planned holiday. We made flight and accommodations arrangements months ago, but had to rearrange it all when our resort called informing us, only one week before our holiday, they were closing for the summer due to the dramatic reduction in tourists and the flu.

Jordan was concerned about taking his pregnant wife to a third world country, particularly the one where the flu was reported to have began, and was shocked when his fifth grade class ended its school year early due to several cases of the flu on the Catlin Gabel campus in Portland, Oregon.

We delayed our trip one week and were delighted when we arrived in De San Jose Del Cabo and found Casa Natalia. Erica said that last year it had the honor of being the best small hotel in Mexico. We had a wonderful time walking the nearby streets and swimming in our beautiful multi-level pool.

I awoke early the next morning and couldn't wait for my first cup, so I wandered up to the lobby. I found a hot pot of coffee beside a basket of red delicious apples. With coffee in one hand and an apple in the other, I returned to our private eighty-degree patio where, an hour later, we were served a tasty and beautiful breakfast by Cesar.

We walked about the town for an hour or so, then watched some dancers practice belly and scarf dancing on an outside stage. It was eighty degrees when we first saw them and ten degrees hotter when we returned a couple of hours later. To our dismay their hips and trinkets were still jiggling as they practiced the Persian dance.

On our walkabout we visited a church, lots of stores packed with merchandise with no tourists, and storeowners who were surprisingly tranquil despite the Swine Flu and the fear Americans had of traveling.

We paid a cab driver ten dollars to drive us out to Playa del Sol. It was the hotel we had accommodations with until a couple of weeks ago when they closed it for the summer. We wanted to have a peek at what we had missed. They promised to be helpful in finding us other accommodations and weren't. When we arrived at the resort, the staff would not let us view the property. Despite my best arguments, we were left standing in the parking lot, and out ten bucks.

We returned to the Nadia and enjoyed the pool until it was time to catch another cab to our next resort, the Me Cabo in Los Cabos.

My God! Me Cabo is beautiful and it is party central. Every fiber of the resort is shaking with the pounding beat of amplified techno house music. The sound never changes. It beats like a heart too excited to live for a long period of time. Most all the people are those beautiful ones, with young, scantily-clad lithe bodies. They have drunk too much and are behaving like they are all madly in love with themselves and want everyone around the pool to share their admiration. We felt out of our element and made minor efforts to move to another hotel. The Me Cabo has promised us a calmer day tomorrow, and the rest of the week. They said the big party days are Thursday, Friday and Saturday.

Jordan and I walked the beach and found all the others resorts to be calm and family oriented. We also found many Mexican peddlers dressed in white cotton and buried under pounds of jewelry, clothes, and blankets. Their parents must have been the people I talked to, and bought from, thirty years ago, when I drove my family, in an old school bus, all the way down the Baha to Cabo.

Our first adventure away from the resort was a search for a super market. We didn't find one that day, but did find several stores that had coke, crackers, dishwashing soap, and pornography. We walked Suzanne's legs off, so she was delighted when we found Johnny Rockets in a shopping mall and had American style hamburgers and fries for dinner. Jordan and Erica walked, while Suzanne and I delighted in a bicycle powered rickshaw ride home. Our driver, a very short and powerful man, only charged us seven dollars, and peddled his butt off getting us back to the hotel.

We gathered together on our fifth story deck and watched the soft wind move slowly through the palms and ruffle the miles of shear white fabric draped across private cabañas, arched doorways, and bamboo framed restaurants. We feel peaceful and were content to climb into our beds, which were side-by-side, much like padded slippers on a timid Mexican giant. I promised to not snore and made an internal commitment to sleep only on my sides. In the morning both Erica and Jordan complimented me on my quiet sleeping. I was proud.

Sunday morning is usually the day Suzanne and I go to Catholic Mass when we are in Mexico. This morning we spent three hours listening to time-share presentations so we could get discounts on some of the activities we wanted to do. God probably didn't support our decision. Before we joined the salesmen, Jordan, sensing my dislike of the circumstances, coached me to calm down and behave kindly. I appreciated his advice and was pleased to discover that his concern was unnecessary, because once they understood my retirement circumstances, they left Suzanne and me alone, and concentrated on Jordan and Erica who they found very attractive. I enjoyed watched them fend off all four salesmen who worked like a tag team, one following the other with an even better idea, until they gave us what they had promised, and we returned to our hotel.

Sunday was Fathers' Day and I felt loved by my children. One was with me and the other was in my heart. To celebrate the day we had dinner at La Fonda. The service was excellent and the food fabulous. We had Chili Relleno stuffed with plantains and cheese, Tacos with stuffed chilies stuffed with shrimp, refried beans and ranchero cheese, Chicken in Mole sauce, and Chalupa Originale. The four of us dined for less than a hundred dollars and felt extremely spoiled.

This morning Jordan and Erica walked to town. It was only a mile by beach, though probably twice that distance by Mexican sidewalks, which are a test in walking skill. Suzanne and I went to the beach and spent lots of time bobbing in the ocean. We were on the beach for hours, wandering back and forth from our umbrella covered lounging platform to the ocean. The breeze was warm and brisk and palm trees waved about like pom poms at a Ducks' football game after a touchdown. There were more peddlers on the beach than guests. The resort reports being full, yet almost nobody is around the pool or on the beach.

We were so pleased with the food at La Fonda that we returned this evening. I was brave and ordered a meal that wounded up being a chicken thigh and leg rolled in something close to straight cayenne pepper and baked. There was also a mound of rice and another of beans. The chicken skin was HOT and my tongue was pleased with the rice and beans. When we were done Jordan offered me a nibble of some thinly sliced vegetables he had in a separate bowl. "Sure," I said, and the moment he slipped his fork past my lips, I noticed his eyes and the slight turn to the corner of his mouth. I had thought my chicken skin was hot. It was nothing compared to this. I was alarmed as flame like pain ran from the back of my throat to the outer edges of my lips, which hadn't even touched the small bite I had been given. "Hot, Dad?" was his question as my body pushed water out of every orifice my head in its vain attempt to save me from the pepper's sting. Later we enjoyed some Flan that cooled my mouth and was the finishing touch of our evening meal.

The sea was choppy, which added to our adventure as we climbed into one of the glass bottom boats that run out to Cabo's famous Pelican Rock. We quickly zipped away from the sandy beach and soon saw an aquarium of tropical fish swimming below us. The boat's driver shared lots of information about what we were seeing, and then drove us from the Sea of Cortez out into the Pacific Ocean, where we took pictures of the rock formations. It was a Kodak moment as we all snapped shots in front of this famous landmark, struggling to maintain our equilibrium on the rocking boat.

In the early evening we walked down our beach in search of a restaurant that wasn't too expensive. We checked out several, and ended up eating at the Sand Bar, and were delighted. The women had a Mexican platter, and Jordan and I had sea bass. When Jordan asked if the fish were caught here, our waiter, a three hundred pound Mexican with a massive smile, said, "No," and then pointed to the surf behind us and said, "There." Very funny man!

The waiters built a fire in a fifty-five gallon half-cut drum on legs. The breeze off the ocean was cool, so Mexican blankets were brought to our table and wrapped around our shoulders. Jordan was slow to say yes, but after several waves of goose bumps on his arms, he relented.

In Mexico your check isn't brought to your table until you ask for it. No rush at all.

I bought a silver bracelet from a beach peddler, and felt pretty good about it until Jordan and Erica said, "Did you give him forty US dollars or pesos?" When I said dollars both of their eyebrows went up. "Do you think I paid too much?" I asked. Erica tactfully responded with, "If you like it, James...you didn't pay too much."

The beach vendors begin their early morning walk from one end of the hotel row to the other end. The folks that rent out the wave runners, glass bottom boats, sailboats, and kayaks set up for the day long before any of the guests venture out of their rooms. The beach restaurants place new cloths on their tables, and do all the other things restaurants do before their customers arrive.

Early mornings are quiet as fishing boats leave the little downtown marina, which is filled with humble fishing and taxi boats, small tour boats, a pirate ship or two, and many luxury fishing boats and private yachts.

I was proud of myself when I followed Jordan and Erica, who are known power walkers, up and down the sidewalks, which are dangerous with years of deterioration. The sidewalks are foot skill courses with stubbed toes and scuffed knees for the losers.

"Almost free! Make a deal! To you half price! Two for one! For you free...your husband will pay for it! You tell me how much you want to pay! Only one dollar! " And the beggar kid with the box of gum who says, "Please...please...please for my school," as you watch his mother sit on the steps close by with three other children and one at the breast.

The mornings are calm with just enough wind to ruffle the palms. In the afternoon the inland breeze comes up and blows hot air across the desert and through the city, ending its land rush by powering hot blasts through the open lobbies and halls of the resorts. Taking advantage of the wind, most arches were bordered with long drapes that blow freely through the passageways and out into the sunshine. I loved standing in the main lobby feeling my hair blow away from my face and around my sunglasses.

Michael Jackson died today. I saw the news in a gift shop on a little TV stuck in the corner of the ceiling. The owner switched the channel to CNN so we could understand what was being said.

Thursday night the loud music started again and we were slow to sleep. The Passion Lounge, which is just three floors below our room and open to the night air, was pulsating with the music. We learned to live with what doesn't sound like music, rather a hard base line in a mix master's machine that is waiting for the rest of the song to be added. The volume was high enough to ripple the pool water and young people waved their arms in the air and serpentined their bodies to the endless and never changing beat.

Friday morning dolphins came into the harbor and entertained us. They didn't stay long, but their early morning splashing in our busy bay was a great invitation to us to join them in the Sea of Cortez.

Suzanne and I ate breakfast on our patio while Jordan and Erica returned to one of the beach restaurants. We felt a need to eat up the City Club granola and as much of the milk as possible, while the kids needed just one more great breakfast on the beach. Part of our day was spent around the pool where Jordan and I read wizard books written by Jim Butcher, and the Erica and Suzanne read "Lolita in Tehran" and "The Name Sake."

In the late morning we caught a taxi to the marina where we found a catamaran, which held thirty people, and took a great sail and snorkel dive. Our boat was white and light blue with lots of canvas stretched between the pontoons. The small cabin held two bathrooms that were just big enough to do the job poorly, and had the classic smell of unsuccessfully projected urine.

The folks aboard were an interesting mix of English and Spanish speaking people with golden tans on all of them but our family, who held up our tubes of SPF 80 and smiled. The sail was raised and we pushed off over choppy water towards Santa Maria Bay in the Sea of Cortez where we were promised excellent snorkeling. Lots of beer, tequila and a variety of soft drinks were passed about as 1980's rock and roll pounded out of the speakers. We sailed by Pelican Rock, and then turned north and up the coast to the bay.

I was anxious about being in the water. Jordan and I believe that sharks want to eat us. The word is out around the water world that we are the tastiest of the tasty.

Despite this knowing we both, with our wives, jumped into the watery frying pan and swam about. We gave them their chance, then, when the poor visibility and cold water became more than uncomfortable, we returned to our boat and lived for one more day.

Everyone on the boat was disappointed with the snorkeling and surprised when the wind blew a tuna sandwich off one of the guest's plate. It landed on the surface of the water and, before our eyes; it was devoured by hundreds of hungry fish. It looked like a cow's bad day in a South American river filled with piranha. Where were they when we were in the water?

It was a very choppy sail back to the marina. We all laid back and cooked ourselves in the hot sunshine and drank. Young women stretched themselves out over the arched cabin of the boat, while the bulk of us leaned back against the benches and enjoyed the pounding sound of the hull against the white-capped sea.

I loved my trip to Mexico with my son, and was happy when I return to my life of living with my loving wife, disobedient and disturbed dog, arrogant and aloof cats, noisy and disruptive parrot, and our insane Beta fish, who loves having his back licked by the cats when they drink from his bowl.

Our next trip will be in October. We will spend a week in Hawaii with my sister and her husband Mag.

TRIPPLE DIGITS 2009

I am in the middle of a hot summer much like the boyhood days I had in Yakima, Washington. It's a Tuesday morning and the cats are curled up beside each other on a richly striped Mexican blanket. The blanket is pulled across an old door, which is propped up on a pair of TV stands and against the sliding glass doors that don't open well. I placed the table there because I wanted a place to write and love the view of the backyard and the greenhouse. Today the rain bird sprinkler is watering the garden and the patch of grass that is developing brown spots under the heat of the sun.

The potted plants we inherited from our friends, Bill and Barbara Hall, are thriving in the Portland weather. A few months ago we packed them into the back seat of our Jaguar after they nearly died following a year of no attention at the hand of our Florence home renter. Strange how recently he and both of the Halls died in the middle of their lives.

This morning we harvested a bowl of peas and string beans along with one yellow squash, a handful of garlic, three onions and a half dozen red potatoes. Last year, around this time, we had just moved into the Caretaker House and were in the early stages of planting the garden.

We have already eaten the strawberries, a few too-hot radishes, lots of lettuce, and are delighting in the massive and wild vines that are producing pumpkins, watermelons, and a variety of squash and cucumbers. Some of the prickly leaves are larger than Zulu war shields.

Yesterday we enjoyed temps in the high nineties and are promised triple digits before the week is over. I'm pleased that I squeezed the little air conditioner Jordan didn't want into the window of the media room. Last year it was the second hottest room in the house next our bedroom, which was the hottest.

The exterior fan and ducting that I hooked into our windowless and stuffy bedroom has helped during the evening hours when it pulls fresh Portland air into the room and keeps it cooler.

A soft breeze pushes the trees and shrubs about, while a flawless egg-blue sky serves as their background. The tiger lilies we planted in the early spring are blooming beside the white climbing rose, and the gladiolas are pushing the purple edges of their blooms past their green husks.

I started my morning mowing the grass and pulling weeds from the garden. We them took our Mercedes to the DEQ to have it checked for safe emission levels, then, upon passing, purchased tags for the next two years. We then drove over to the Kaiser Permanente Hospital for blood tests, then on to Bi-Mart for Suzanne's bonus priced work pants. We kept the top down and loved the hot morning sun on our necks while the car's air conditioning kept us cool. At Bi-Mart an old couple enjoyed watching us pull up in the roadster and said, "Look at you two…alive and in love after all your years." It was one of those double-edged compliments.

Once home, we had turkey sandwiches and fell asleep watching Perry Mason. We are both aware that some days our energy levels are low and naps seem like a good idea.

Between my errands, naps, little projects, house-keeping, caretaking job and cooking meals, I often find myself behind my laptop writing about the endless energy and playfulness I enjoyed as a boy in Yakima when triple digits were common and we loved it.

END OF SUMMER 2009

In one week I will be standing on the Outback patio, with a clipboard in my hand, checking off the names of students that have ridden the bus to school. They will be starting their first day of school, and I will be ending my summer.

When school ends for the summer, the campus at Catlin Gabel falls into the hands of the maintenance crews. Paint is applied, carpets cleaned, windows washed, floors scrubbed, repairs and improvements completed, and trees are planted while the grass keeps growing and is expertly mowed.

My days are easier with fewer buildings to open and less to lock. Often while making my security drives through campus I find myself alone, enjoying the tranquility and solitude.

Early this morning, while making my disarm and unlock rounds, I found some teachers at their desks. They claim to be refreshed and ready for another school year. I could use another month of this easy pace.

This summer we grew gardens around the Caretaker's house and watched squash and pumpkin vines rise above tomatoes, carrots, beans, cucumbers and beets. Our lettuce lost its sunlight below mitt-sized leaves, which made harvesting prickly and eventually hopeless.

The vegetable garden was for fun and the three pounds of red potatoes, twenty green salads, single basket of red tomatoes, eight ears of corn, three yellow squash and one small bowl of strawberries were well worth the watering on hot summer days and the price of seeds.

Suzanne and I had many summer projects in mind and few were completed. We both were committed to thinning down our closets of old clothes and rarely used shoes. Our new pup, that destroyed every shoe left on the floor and occasionally those being used, handsomely assisted us in reaching part of our goal. We both shared many words of praise with him every time we discovered his relentless tooth work.

We turned old gardens into grass and claimed ivy covered hills for new ones. Old roses with new trellises, assorted Home Depoe bulbs and flower seeds cast here and there delighted us with blossoms and added to the pleasure of ice tea on our patio.

We had planned many campus B-B-Qs, but didn't have one. It seemed that facility and staff couldn't agree upon good times to get together…so we didn't.

There was an old birdbath in the front yard that found its way into the vegetable garden under the miniature maple tree. Birds spent the summer bouncing between the bath and the wooden feeders we kept full and hung from the Holly tree.

Our greenhouse produced lots of herbs, and attempted to capture our lawnmower with the same pumpkin vines that own the outside garden. When time came to mow, I would unwind vines from the handles and push them back over the beds.

Last year I washed dishes. It took two hours out of the middle of my day and made doing anything else difficult. It was strenuous work, which was probably good for me, but I didn't want to do it this year with Jordan and Erica's baby on the way. When we moved to Portland we had wanted to help out with childcare and I needed my days free to do it. I asked Kitty, my boss, to help me out and she did by setting up the AM bus job. It pleased me immensely to resign from washing dishes and to accept my new post as AM Bus Person. It also was enjoyable to have staff go out of their way to make my life good.

I'm looking forward to greeting the students on their first day of school and tucking the little ones under my care while I deliver them to their classroom. Year number two is about to start.

WALKING 2009

It was wrong and he knew it. He could feel the fall breeze finger the long hairs on his ears and the skin on the back of his neck prickle. On other walks he has seen many leafs dance across the surface of the parking lot next to the path he was walking. But this was different and the longer he watched the more uncomfortable he became. He locked his eyes on the spectacle in front of him and slowly lowered his body.

Sam had walked this trail many times and loved the fresh odors that accompanied the changing seasons. The bite of fall had plucked a few leaves from the old maple and ash trees and dropped them on the ground. A midmorning breeze was lifting many of the leaves and dancing them across the parking lot like gymnasts cart-wheeling across hardwood floors. These leaves were entertaining and not at all like the one swinging in front of him. This curled and golden leaf was floating inches above the dirt and would leap several feet into the air and spin like the windsock hung on the patio roof. It would then return to its spot inches above the ground and continue the gentle swinging.

Sam's young, and very involved in exploring the world. He captures the attention of many who meet him, and has been described as a mini Sheppard. He only weighs twenty-four pounds and is introduced to those interested in patting his adorable head as "not nice." We don't know why Sam has made it clear that the only humans who can touch him are Suzanne and myself… but he has.

Seven or eight feet above Sam and me, a fat and hardworking spider watches us and feels the wind shake the strand of web he has spun between the branch above him and the ground. One of the leaves skipping across the asphalt tangled itself in his web and was acting like a menacing puppet on a string.

It was this spider and leaf that had upset the order in Sam's life. Wanting to relieve his anxiety I swung my hand through the strand dropping the leaf to the ground where Sam scooped it up, mauled it for a few minutes and then proudly carried it home.

Later today my dog and I will have another adventure as we enjoy our time together seeking the perfect place to poop.

BIRTHDAY 2009

He said they wouldn't be calling. They may even wait a day or two before they let any of us know. "Oh…oh…oh," I sadly moaned as I processed his words. Parker, his unborn son and my second grandson, is due in November sometime between my father's birthday and mine. I am anxious to meet him and the thought of being out of the birth loop is painful.

My son and I talked as we completed our third lap on the running track, and I told him I understood but felt a great loss. He wants the birth to be special and private for them and if they make one call the family floodgates would open and they wouldn't have the time they want reserved just for them.

"I'm a private guy, Dad, and if the family was around I would have to tone down my emotions and I don't want to do that, and you know Erica. She would worry and be concerned that she was taking too long or making too big of a fuss. That's not how we want to do it … so we won't be calling. Sorry!"

Jordan and Erica plan everything out. Little happens in their lives that are unplanned and it appears the birth of my grandson, Parker Griffin, will not be an exception. I do know that seeing Parker for the first time will be wonderful, even if it's a day or two after his birth.

Eggs 2009

The eggs were sliding from side to side in the olive oiled skillet and after years of wanting the skill and lacking the courage to give it a try I flipped the eggs. I erupted into laughter as one of the eggs missed the catch and splayed its yoke on the iron grill of the gas burner. It seems being tickled with myself is becoming more common as I enter the last fifth or less of my life.

This Saturday morning the Catlin Gabel School is having a rummage processing party and the campus is almost as active as the school days. After sixty-five years, the same as my age, the historic rummage sale is coming to an end. They report the costs of the function eat up most of the profits, so they have chosen to redirect the volunteer labor into more profitable areas. It's sad to see an established and enjoyable event end, particularly when I find myself thinking more about the end of my life.

I have responded to three building alarms today and it's only mid-morning.

My halftime work assignments this school year are much easier than last, when I had the lunch dishwashing job. This year I am continuing the Caretaker job, which requires me to lock and alarm the campus buildings in the evening and disarm and unlock them in the morning. I replaced the dishwashing with the a.m. bus duty. The new job is easy and Suzanne helps me. We made up a magnet board with the names of all the students who ride the four buses. Suzanne, in her old teacher mode, made a big colorful animal bag, which holds the board, a couple of pencils and a notepad for the names of new riders. We attach the bag to the back of our golf cart when driving across campus and down to the Outback building where the bus's drop off the students. Suzanne sits under the building's patio cover on a folding metal chair, and holds the board on her lap, while I stand beside her with a plastic bowl and catch the name tags the students pick off the board. We have fun remembering names and kibitzing with the kids as they unload with too many stuffed backpacks and book bags.

We, in their eyes, are probably the quaint old couple that lack much cool and are a bit on the goofy side. I wonder how many of them will wait until their sixty-fifth year before they try flipping eggs.

I'M A TEST 2009

It's a test loving me. I have lost most of my flex, although I feel fixed in a fairly open position. I'm amiable to new ideas, and protective of the ones I have accepted. Changing the givens in my life is the source of angst for those that love me, and myself, as they try.

I didn't feel well when I woke at three this morning. My world was spinning and I didn't know why. In an attempt to resolve my problem, I ate half a protein bar and returned to bed. Sometimes my blood sugar is off, causing me to feel weird.

When the alarm sounded at six, I was up and I felt a little better. I snapped my night lamp onto my cap, and thought the cool morning air would clear the rest of dizzy out of my mind.

Jordan called me during the hour I unlock and disarm the campus buildings. A few minutes after we began our talk, I bent over to plug in the cord to the lava lamps he has in his classroom. When I stood I felt unstable and braced myself. "Wow!" I reported, "I'm a little dizzy this morning. I don't think I could walk in a straight line even if I wanted to."

He loves me and was immediately concerned. "Go home Dad! Don't take a chance on it being something serious." I wanted to walk it out, so I told him I was OK. His concern escalated, as did his insistence that I do as he said and go home. The next few minutes were filled with his telling me why he didn't and I shouldn't trust my judgment. His words had a cutting edge, and my feelings were hurt. I was quiet for a moment, and then I explained to him the part of myself that doesn't flex. I get to make the decisions about my life. I am not open to having my past behaviors turned into weapons for beating me into submission, and I don't have to accept counsel. He didn't like it; I didn't like telling him.

I remember giving my parents advice. I don't remember them taking it.

TYPHOON 2009

Typhoon…is that what they called it? Suzanne and I looked out the window and then back to CNN and the weather forecast. The weatherman was pointing to the magic screen and the West Coast, where swirling white arrows were spinning from San Diego to Seattle.

I pulled my chair up to my computer and watched the storm rip across the backyard and across the campus. Beside the window, the potted lavender, that grew well during the summer and is trying to produce its second blooms, vibrated under the push of the wind, then quickly returned to its stiff position with the passing of each gust. The pruned maple, whose rich green leaves are newly edged with autumn brown, imitated the lavender's rigid dance, and refused to give up a single leaf. Beside the greenhouse the massive lilacs, whose long and slender branches granted it the freedom it to swing, performed a storm dance and pranced from one end of the utility building's roof to the other. In the winter, when the leaves have fallen away, the dance will be simple and lack the drama of falls full-leafed branches.

The gladiolas, with their summer blooms dissolving at their base, laid down with the first gusts, while their sister lilies stoutly stood their ground looking like defiant fists being shook in Italian traffic.

Between the maple and the lilacs, the decorative grass we planted in the clay pot, wields its long wine-colored blades like a fallen Roman warrior taking his last swings at his enemy.

The larger fir and poplars created a more graceful dance and held their bend under the huge winds, pushing across the sky that had lost its blue innocence to gray swirling clouds which were difficult to read.

The Blue Jays and smaller yard birds seem pressed to beak up all they could. Again and again they return to the feeders, hanging under the branches of our holly tree and dashing away to the places they consider safe. Soon they would stay there to ride out the storm.

The sun has set and the darkness of night has closed the spectacle of the storm. The sound of the wind gusts and the sight of passing debris continued as the storm built and punched itself into the night.

I was anxious to watch the nightly news and learn about the storm, about what others saw outside their windows, and maybe learn a little more about typhoons.

MAUI 2009

For seven days Suzanne, Judy, Mag and I enjoyed the warmth and beauty of Maui. Sam, our puppy, couldn't come and that was a frustration. We drove him down to Eugene, where he had a weeklong sleep-over with his sister, Coco.

Judy and Mag rose early and flew from Sacramento to Portland where we tied up with them at the airport and shared a flight. The air travel took too long; we had the hassle of getting the rental car, then the drive to our accommodations. We didn't settle down and begin our week of bliss until we entered our room at Kahana Falls and put on our summer wear and sandals.

The Falls had several gas barbecues, a child pool, fitness center, laundry facility, free form swimming pool, three waterfalls, tropical landscaping and two sandy-bottomed whirlpools.

On other trips to Hawaii we have spent lots of money on entertainment and eating out. This year we didn't, and still had a fabulous time. We opted out of the luau shows and saw some great free hula at the Safeway shopping center performed by kids and adults who were surprisingly talented.

We had one meal out and that was lunch at Bubba Gump's. The view from Bubbas is great and the food was good. We did eat several cones of fancy Hawaiian ice cream while we wandered the streets of Lahaina. Lahaina is an old whaler's village and has lots of shops and restaurants. In the center of the town an old Banyan tree covers a full city block and is the town's gathering point.

Before lunch we rode the Atlantis submarine one hundred feet below the surface of the Lahaina Bay. It was a forty-five minute dive during which we saw the Carthaginian shipwreck and a reef teaming with fish. The sub is a real submarine that carries forty-eight passengers, but didn't carry my sister, who was happy sitting on the bank and watching us sail away.

Most of our meals were cooked on one of the gas BBQs Kahana Falls has on their beautiful patio beside the koi pond. Mag is an excellent cook. The Mahi Mahi and short ribs he cooked couldn't have been better. I was the breakfast cook, with eggs and lots of fresh tropical fruits.

Much of our time was spent on our beach, which was across the street and perfect. It was a long beach that wound itself between the blue green ocean water and the hotels standing tall on the landside. The sand was light and firm enough for easy walks. Judy and I share a deep pleasure in wandering the water edge. We did it in the mornings, some afternoons, and most evenings. We set four beach chairs under the only Kukui Nut tree on the beach, and there, with books in hand, we passed many pleasant hours. Every forty minutes or so, we would set our bookmarks and wander to the water's edge where we would wade up to our necks, and bob up and down as the tide moved us in and out.

One day we piled into our red rental convertible, whose top was always down, and assailed the six hundred hairpin turns and over fifty single lane bridges that make up the famous "Road to Hana." It was our only all day adventure, and it was impressive. We enjoyed the smell mangos and the organic fragrance of the rainforest. The road took us over plunging seaside cliffs and deep into bamboo groves. Along the way we passed fresh fruit stands and parked where there were dramatic ocean vistas that took our breaths away. Judy and I are prone to carsickness, yet I was the only one to take on the green cast of the dead.

Another day we drove to the Maui Tropical Plantation. It's a sixty-acre working plantation that has papaya, guava, mango, macadamia nuts, coffee, avocado, bananas, sugar cane and star fruit. We wanted to lunch there, but discovered the restaurant was booked with parties, so we settled for another cone of tropical ice cream.

Once we found it, we spent several hours in Hilo Hattie's and purchased gifts for those we love who didn't get to vacation with us.

Getting home was better than our arrival. God blessed both Judy and Mag and Suzanne and I with an empty seat in our airplane rows. They were the only open seats in the plane, and left us feeling a lot like we were flying first class.

Now that we are home, we have already found ourselves looking for our next vacation location. I am interested in the big island and the others want to do Maui one more time.

Suzanne picked Sam up on Saturday morning. It took him a few minutes to forgive her for the abandonment, and then they were, as they always are, inseparable.

LEAVES AND KIDS 2009

Today the upper school students are raking and filling orange wheelbarrows with leaves, which are packed into yellow barrels, dragged to trailers, then transported, to the northeast corner of the campus where they are pitch-forked onto compost piles. The grounds keepers: Mike, Katharine, Jesse & Elise are keeping an eye on them and supplying them with all the rakes, shovels and barrels they need. It's a great sight to see every corner of the campus filled with kids in old clothes working away.

Some of the students are good workers and are skillful using their bodies. Others seemed to be clueless as to what to do or how to do it, and there are a few who have no interest in working and are looking for every opportunity to play.

The weather has cooperated with blue sky and no rain. Many days this fall have been rain filled, so fixing a day for the annual grounds project was risky.

My fall has been busy with tree trimming, pruning, cleaning rain gutters, blowing off roof debris, washing summer grime off of the house, and hauling it all down to the campus compost and debris area.

The school has some powerful electric John Deere Gators and one 6X4 utility vehicle with a three cylinder, 18hp water-cooled diesel engine. The diesel is the strong one and the one I use when I hitch up the high-sided trash trailer. I've packed the trailer several times this year with lilac branches, trimmings, and the branches I cut off the exotic tree that smells like peanut butter in the front of the house.

The view from my writing desk dramatically improved when I pruned back the small maple tree and the huge lilac branches which kept our yard private and secluded. Now I can watch fall spread its colors across the hillsides until all the leaves have dropped and only the evergreens and bare branches are left.

Suzanne and I are happy this fall. We are comfortable in our Caretaker House and enjoy the jobs we do for the school. Jordan is close by. I knock on his classroom windows with my keys after I finish my morning rounds and check in the students who ride the busses. Sometimes we team up at lunchtime and walk a few laps around the running track.

Jamie and I talk on the phone often and love solving problems together and appreciating the similar ways we deal with life.

Parker is still taking full advantage of his mother and will enter this world within the next couple of weeks. Erica has been pregnant long enough and will welcome his birthday sooner than later.

Jordan has been fighting problems with his back and gut muscles for months and has been frustrated with the relapses and slow healing process. He initially hurt himself two years ago and has had some better days and lots that were less than wonderful. He's hoping that he will feel strong enough to hold his son and actively participate in all the new baby activities he and Erica will share with Parker.

Our first grandson, Skylar, continues to be bright and wonderful. He does well in school and loves music. He's eight had has been studying drum and voice for several years. Yeah rock and roll!!!!

Suzanne is very involved in the Baha'i children classes and has been successful in helping to develop several new programs. Her son, Jason, continues his education in Arizona and reports being anxious to have college behind him. He and Suzanne enjoy lots of phone time and try to catch a Blazer game or two during the season. We continue to hope he will make the Northwest his home following school.

I'm sixty-five the end of this month and Suzanne is a few years younger. Our bodies are doing OK with plenty of room for improvement. My Caretaker job keeps me walking a lot and has helped to trim me up. Although it's hard to get up for my 6:00 am rounds, I always feel better for having done it.

After the first of the year, Suzanne and I are planning on taking care of Parker during the workdays. We have high hopes that we are up to the challenge and look forward to meeting him.

A MOMENT IN TIME 2009

Like a painting on the wall…the moment has frozen.
Birds are perched motionless on branches.
One cloud has settled around the top of the hills and covers the valley.
The pointed branches of the evergreens fade and disappear as they push themselves deep into the haze.
Holding the last of its flickerless leaves a nearly bare and unpruned cherry tree braces itself high in the opaque sky.
Clear honey water drops hang below the red maple twigs and the hooves of the garden horses with no intentions of dropping.
The black rounded water in the stone fountain solidly reflects the glass pane of the garden house window.
Holly berries with abandoned green skins are rich orange clusters well protected by the tree's sharp leaves.
Strawberry plants hold their color while their outer leaves expire under the press of the cold.
Wet garden stones darken while moss climbs the sides and creep into the planting dirt.
Yellowed leaves lay wet and pressed against the hard path surface.
And then…it all stirs as a Fall Spirit drags the hem of his cape across my view.
A cluster of crows abandon their hiding place and fill the sky.
They sweep with bowed wings across its lowest edge and swoop into the nearby trees.
Sparrows land and peck in the harvested garden a lunch I cannot see.

A squirrel pokes his head through a dry rotted hole and dashes across the path.
The leaves rustle and a ribbon of blue sky opens and reflects itself in the ripples of the bird's bath.
The moment has passed and moved us closer to the cold and quiet days of winter.

A DAD JUST LIKE ME 2009

"Dad, I've only had him five days and I don't think I can live without him." Before the birth of his son, Jordan and I talked a lot about the feelings I had for him as a little one. He would smile at me and would respond with, "You've the emotional one Dad, and I don't think it will be that way for me."

I love watching him with his new son. Handling him like a precious toy, he straps him in a belly pack and prances about the house delighting in Parker's coos.

Mom's handle babies carefully and worry about discomforts and disturbances. Dad's like Jordan are more cavalier and share their exuberance with big moves, joyful swoops, and the sounds they made as little boys playing with toy cars and airplanes.

When they gaze upon their children, the doe eyes of mothers look different than Maserati gleams displayed by dads. Jordan has that gleam. I had that gleam. It's a wonderful sight for a father to see in his son, and I knew he would, love being a dad.

FREEZING 2009

Another morning of frost...another day below freezing.
Leaves have wilted and drooped on their branches.
Black bleeds into their color ending their hope of a mild winter and months on the branch.
The bird feeders are full and often visited while the hummingbird's is frozen.

We thaw it several times a day, and feel kind-hearted when the birds arrive and quickly drink their fill.
The birdbath is a mini-rink with dry leaves resting on the ice's surface.
The faucet is wrapped and under a plastic bucket with a brick on it's top.
Thermometers report seventeen and will move little during the day.
Winds are calm but will return tonight bringing with them the promised snow.
It's winter and we are warmly tucked in our home with cats and dog.
The shed is filled with firewood, candles are easy to find, and the blankets are close at hand.

SAM 2009

He eats everything. Last night it was my wonderful helicopter gloves, and yesterday afternoon my new remote mouse. The gloves are stitched back together with a leather inset from a pillow he destroyed several weeks ago, and the mouse is operational only because a wood screw holds the battery end and connection together.

The yet-to-be-repaired family room sofa has several holes chewed in the brown plush fabric that are too big to conceal with color from the brown felt tip pen.

Several pairs of Suzanne's shoes are gone and her red leather sandals were interesting when they were deposited in Sam's favorite pooping spot. For a while we thought he was sick and needed a trip to the Vet, then realized it was Israeli leather, not blood.

He got my favorite hiking boots and a pair of ankle-high dress shoes. They were both brown and more difficult to spot in his stool.

I lost my twenty-year-old Tiva sandals that have accompanied me on all our trips to the tropics. The top edges of my rubber boots are gone as well as the tongues of my fleece lined Sorels.

The wood corners on the oak footstool I made are rounded just like the end of Grandma's rocker. The cross brace on the Persian coffee table is well gnawed, as is the door on the wood school bus I bought for Parker.

The yoke on the Costa Rican ox cart has been reshaped, and the leather cushions on the Stickley sofa and chair, which we had repaired by the upholstery shop after the first attack, have been attacked a second and third time. The rungs on the antique oak chairs and the table my father bought and refinished when I was a boy have been rounded and are beyond repair.

There are several holes nibbled in the wall-to-wall carpet as well at the Persian rugs. He has chewed the plastic base off several of the office chairs and reduced my wireless earpiece for my cell phone to a handful of small electrical pieces.

My eyeglasses, in a matter of moments, were so badly pocked I had to replace them.

He destroyed a bathroom door, cabinet and part of the sheetrock wall when we locked him in while attending a movie.

The door to the garage and Suzanne's sewing room has lost much of its finish. He wants to be by her side when she sews and doesn't know how to knock.

Most of Sam's leashes are shredded in several places. I had to replace the end of his retractable leash with a steel cable.

He has unwound all wicker baskets within reach, and isn't beyond using a chair to reach higher spots and other unprotected items. Sometimes he collaborates with the cats, who bat items off shelves and dressers and counters for his chewing delight.

Sam is only ten months old and we have high hopes that this difficult time will pass and that we won't lose everything we value before he grows old and loses his teeth.

SANTAS 2009

It was only days before Christmas and we had just ended a great visit with our grandson, Parker. He was almost three weeks old and I had talked with him about Santa Claus and was comfortable telling him that I was sure there was only one.

On our way home, we turned west off of Sandy Boulevard and crossed the Burnside Bridge. Close to the Portland Skidmore/Old Town Historic District my belief in Santa was forever changed.

It started shortly after we crossed First Avenue and I noticed dozens of people wearing red suits trimmed in white with long beards. They were walking, skipping, dancing and appeared to be having a wonderful time. "Look Honey, there are Santas on the sidewalk," I said. She looked up from her book and said, "More than a few, Baby. Look up Third Avenue." I glanced to my left and saw dozens of Santas clumped together visiting with women who were wearing similar outfits but wearing short skirts and high heeled white boots rather than long pants and black boots.

I was sure that we were seeing an anomaly, or maybe the coffee I drank at Jordan's house had been laced with a Holiday potion. I rubbed my eyes and as we passed Fourth and then Fifth Avenues I tried to make sense of it all. They were everywhere...and I feared brain damage.

Some were dressed like old European Santas with wide-brimmed hats and long flowing coats. Others wore nothing but red long johns and, God only knows why...they were clean-shaven. There were red-cheeked women with holly and ribbons in their hair dancing with the Santas in a Christmas style square dance I had never seen before.

Their dance moved them from sidewalks out into the streets. I was shocked beyond belief when I saw an amazing display of Santa's athletic abilities...considering the bulk around his belly. They had climbed up on the massive elephant statues displayed in the Park Blocks. There were so many Santa's dancing on the backs of the elephants and hanging from their trunks that, from our distance, the statues appeared red. "What's going on," I squealed as I watched Santas in cheap flannel outfits dance with Santas who were gloriously draped in golden bells and elaborate ribbons.

When we crossed the intersection of Burnside and Twenty-Third Avenue, it all stopped. The Santas disappeared. My sanity returned and sidewalks were filled with holiday shoppers.

We has seen hundreds maybe a thousands of Santas, and as many helpers. We wondered as we drove the rest of our way home how we were going to explain it all to Parker...how we could understand it ourselves.

PEACOCK LANE 2009

It's easy to get stuck on campus and not enjoy all the wonders of Portland, especially during the Holidays. This time of year the school closes for a couple of weeks and the staff takes off to celebrate and refresh. The campus becomes our responsibility making our escapes even less likely.

Months ago when we set up our scheduled weekends off we picked the days before Christmas and found ourselves spending most of our time at on campus. Sunday night I said, "Let's check out the Portland Christmas Lights." Suzanne was up for it, and we were off with addresses from the web and our trusty Garman to guide the way.

In the 1920's a southeast neighborhood on Peacock Lane began decorating their Tudor homes with lights, and have kept up the tradition for ninety years. We weren't surprised when we arrived in the area and found police, street flairs, and cars packed for blocks around like a snake coiled around its kill. We were directed to the end of the tail where we parked in line and began searching the radio for a station playing Christmas music. We thought it would add to the spirit of the event and reduce our frustration of being several coils away from our turn to drive down the lane. Our radio must have been made in India or Israel because we couldn't find a single station playing holiday music. We turned it off and sang a couple of carols. Suzanne knows all the words and I do the background do-da-dos.

We were surprised when twenty minutes passed and we had our turn to drive down Peacock Lane. Respectfully drivers lowered their lights to park as one coil slipped up one side of the street and the other down the other side. The sidewalks were packed with pedestrians singing carols and pushing baby carriages.

The homes weren't mansions but cozy residential Tudors framed in lights. Most all the yards had a Santa sled, manger, or maybe a cut out of the Grinch. None of the displays were ostentatious and they did capture a spirit of a "days gone by" Christmas I experience as a boy in Yakima, Washington. What sealed the deal and made our drive down Peacock Lane exceptional were the BIG old fashion lights many of the home used rather that the little twinkles most folks drape their homes and shrubs with today.

We were close to Jordan and Erica's house and didn't pass up on the opportunity to hold our new grandson, Parker. We visited with the kids, fed Parker, and changed a diaper or two before we left and returned to the campus. It was time to transfer our Caretaker phone back to our number, reducing the likelihood that we would again escape. We did, however, promised ourselves that we would escape again before the Holidays were over.

IS THERE A RUSH?

I worry about my mind.
Do I need to rush?
Do I need to finish my words and lock them to paper?
Is it days or months or years before I follow Mom's lead?
Will I be lucky like Dad?
He didn't need to close a book on his life…he just wanted his papers in order.
Mom waited too long and couldn't close it. It was lost.
It's not much…my book about living.
Like me…it's simple and appreciative.
I like living.
I like being human.
I like sharing my humanness.
That's it!
I want to celebrate being human…with you.
Do I need to rush?

PARKER 2010

Two months have passed since the birth of my son's son. They call him Parker. His skin is fair, eyes are blue, and his hair is light. Suzanne and I think he is a good baby and easy to please. His needs are simple … dry diapers, milk, or sleep.

We started taking care of him last week and enjoyed ourselves. Jordan and Erica, Parkers parents, tell us stories of his wanting to visit all night long. They claim that a good night's sleep is impossible. We get to play with him during the day. If he cries, we fill him up with a bottle of mother's milk, and asleep he goes. They tell us that sometimes at night he cries and won't be consoled. During the day we walk him around a little, pat him on his popo, and he's happy. We figure Parker is good during the day because he likes his grandma and grandpa soooo much. Jordan isn't sure.

We enjoy our drive across Portland after the morning rush has passed. Erica lets the dogs, Buffy and Kona, out to greet us, then once inside, she passes the little guy over and retreats to her office.

He is always dressed like a fashion plate and smiles once cuddled in our arms. The kids tell us that Parker loves swaying in his power swing. That may be true but we don't know. It's difficult for us to give him up, and the swing doesn't care one way or the other.

A couple of years ago Jordan talked about having a baby and asked us to move close. "We both need to work, Dad, and don't want to turn our baby over to some stranger." We were hesitant to leave Florence but when the real estate market dried up and the Caretaker job at Catlin Gabel opened we made the move.

Parker is having one of his rare moments in the swing. We just got back from a walk in the park with the dogs and Suzanne is whipping up some lunch. Soon our half day job will be done and while the traffic is slow we will drive across town to our little puppy, who doesn't like our leaving him home alone.

LOST 2010

They said I should have done this or that.
I didn't!
I paid eighty bucks to fix it last time.
He didn't!
I had two months editing and several new ditties.
Lost!
This time I fixed it myself.
Failed!
I'm low tech.

Sad!
They say it's easy…I can learn.
I'm confused!
I saved what I could.
Not enough!
I boxed it up and sold it to Costco.
Good riddance!
I ordered a new ipad notebook.
I hope it's easy.
We'll see!

GARDEN 2010

We thought Parker would visit our home during the week, but Erica didn't want to be apart from her son. They asked us if we would mind taking care of him in their home so she could peek in on him during the day and nurse him when he was tired or hungry. It's hard for Moms to leave their new babies. The change in plans wasn't a problem for Suzanne, so we agreed and have found the drive across Portland at 10:00am easy.

Erica works out of her home, keeping her office on the main floor of the house and close to the front room where they keep a dressing table, glider chair, and lots of games. Suzanne loves her time with the baby, and I watch him when she needs a bathroom break or time to fix herself a snack. I enjoy the writing time I have, and then find that I need more physical activity and go looking for something to do.

Erica and Jordan complain about their house being perfect except for the very small back yard. On a visit to one of the local nurseries, they arranged to have a landscaper visit their home and draft a plan that would make the most of their little yard.

The yard had a large nicely-poured slab that covered about a third of the area. The balance was packed with massively overgrown lilacs, rhododendrons, and lots of extra dirt. The design called for everything that was growing to go away, as well as the excess dirt.

Most of March was gentle with little rain and an abnormal amount of sunshine. I took full advantage of the weather and hacked, whacked, and dug the yard into a flat field. The gardens were framed with Durawood 2x6's and a triangular deck was built in the corner. The garden paths were filled with fine gravel and spaced with the flagstones I dug up with the dirt removal project.

Beside the house I placed three large garden boxes which were filled with back yard dirt. We have plans to extend the gravel path between the boxes and the house, in addition to adding several sections of lattice fencing and a couple of gates. We have also talked about tilling up the narrow strip of grass by the driveway and setting the 12" pavers we rescued from the back yard on a bed of fine gravel. It's hard to avoid driving on the grass with their narrow 1920's driveway.

It's a big project, I've loved it all, and it has made their home almost perfect.

UNDER THE KNIFE AGAIN 2010

"Man…I can't catch my breath. It feels like it did twenty-one years ago when I tried mowing my lawn and needed by-pass surgery." I just walked out of my doctor's office with a referral to a cardiologist. Lots of thoughts are rushing through my mind as I contemplate having my chest opened again. I promised myself that I wouldn't do it, and here I go making plans.

It scares me when I think about it. I haven't felt well for months and being diagnosed with a bad heart murmur explained why. A few years ago it was just a little murmur, and now it's not. I guess I could live, for a while, feeling exhausted and listless, but I don't want to.

I need to frame this differently. A year from now when my energy is high and my chest is healed, I will be glad I did it. Now…I need to set aside the fears and plan for better days. If it ends up being the end of my life…it's OK. My relationship with God is good, and my work here is mostly completed. It's the gravy time of my life with a wonderful wife, grown and successful children who love God, grandchildren who fill my broken heart with joy, tropical vacations, and leisure time to record my thoughts and walk our dog.

Humm…maybe I should put a rush on finishing this book.

LUNCH WITH PARKER 2010

He's sitting beside me in his highchair banging his hands on its table. Grandma is fixing his lunch and he's watching me write. He looks great in his green safari shirt, opened to expose just the right amount of six month old manly chest.

I told him that in twenty years he'll be sitting under a tree somewhere reading the words I'm writing. My hope is that he will find it interesting and maybe have a better understanding of his Dad and Grandpa. The nut doesn't fall far from the tree, even though he may think so.